THE RELIGIOUS NATURE
and
BIBLICAL NURTURE
of GOD'S CHILDREN

THE RELIGIOUS   NATURE
and
BIBLICAL   NURTURE

of

GOD'S CHILDREN

A Guide for Parents and Teachers

Jack Fennema

Dordt College Press

Unless otherwise noted quotations from Scripture are taken from the NIV.
Scripture taken from the HOLY BIBLE, NEW INTERNATIONAL VERSION®. NIV®. Copyright ©
1973, 1978, 1984 by International Bible Society. Used by permission of Zondervan Publish-
ing House. All rights reserved.

Printed in the United States of America.

Dordt College Press   www.dordt.edu/dordt_press
498 Fourth Avenue NE
Sioux Center, Iowa 51250
United States of America

ISBN: 978-0-932914-57-6

The Library of Congress Cataloging-in-Publication Data
is on file with the Library of Congress, Washington, D.C.

Library of Congress Control Number: 2005927860

Cover design: Jamin Ver Velde

Dedicated to my grandchildren:
Scott
Abigail
Gabriel
Samuel
Michael
Annalyse
—the "next generation."
Grandpa Fennema

****

I will open my mouth in parables,
I will utter hidden things, things from of old—
what we have heard and known,
what our fathers have told us.
We will not hide them from their children;
we will tell the next generation
the praiseworthy deeds of the LORD,
his power, and the wonders he has done.
He decreed statutes for Jacob
and established the law in Israel,
which he commanded our forefathers
to teach their children,
so the next generation would know them,
even the children yet to be born,
and they in turn would tell their children.
Then they would put their trust in God
and would not forget his deeds
but would keep his commands.
Psalm 78:2–7

TABLE OF CONTENTS

PREFACE

I will never forget the birth of my first child. The event really began the evening before, when my wife and I drove to a nearby scenic overlook to reminisce and think about the life-changing event that would be taking place the next day. The day of his birth was more predictable than most, for he was overdue and the doctor had decided to help things along by inducing labor. The big event was scheduled for the next morning, so we had this last evening with just the two of us. We knew that life with a child would alter everything forever, so we decided to spend some time contemplating how life would soon be changing as we moved from being a couple to becoming a family. I was feeling both excited and scared at the same time.

Twenty-four hours later, as I gazed down on my newborn son, a sense of awe overwhelmed me. I saw a perfectly formed, very tiny, and very real person—a gift from God, yet my very own son. He was flesh of my flesh. The awesomeness of it all flooded over me, for I was responsible, at least in part, for the very existence of this little one. I thought about the two of us growing up together and what that would be like. I wondered what life would hold for him. Would it be fulfilling? Would it be painful? And I pondered over the nurture of one of God's children. Would I be up to the task? Could I be a good example? Yes, it was an awesome moment, in so many different ways.

The years have passed, and the small baby has become a grown man. Yet the sense of awe over tiny babies, small children, budding adolescents, and maturing young people has remained with me. What a blessing! And what a responsibility! Who, indeed, feels prepared and adequate to nurture children in a manner that is pleasing to God? Who are these children? What makes them tick? And what about their created nature should I be aware of so that I can parent and teach them in the way God intended? Those are the questions that I want to address in this book, first, by focusing on the *nature* of the children whom God has given to us, and second, by focusing on the *nurture* that God has entrusted us to provide his kingdom kids.

Jack Fennema

SECTION ONE

THE CONTEXT

FOR

NATURE AND NURTURE

* * *

KINGDOM AND COVENANT

Chapter 1

Born into an Eternal Kingdom and a Covenantal Relationship

Introduction

In the beginning—*God.* This is the proper place to begin a study of the nature and nurture of children, for to focus first on the children would be misleading from the start. The only way to truly understand children and our responsibilities toward them is to begin with God. Thus, a divine context or setting needs to be developed. For this, a story can be told.

Long ago in a land before time, a king ruled over a kingdom. There never was and never again would be a king like this king. He governed his kingdom with great power and great sensitivity. He was just and righteous yet loving and merciful. His wisdom and wealth were unmatched anywhere.

Now this king had a son whom he loved very much and who was very pleasing to him. In fact, the king had such great love for his son that, as was the custom, he decided to present his son with a gift that would demonstrate this love. He searched his mind for the perfect gift, one that would truly represent the honor he wished to bestow. Finally, it came to him! He would find a bride for his son—an untouched virgin. This bride would be very much like his son, cut from the same cloth, so to speak. She could respond to his love with a love of her own that would bring great joy to his heart. An inseparable and faithful union could be formed.

But there was more. Before the royal marriage could be consummated, a home, a place of residence, would have to be provided. Both the king and his son began creating such a place for the bride-to-be. Just as his current kingdom reflected the king's wealth and creativity, this newly created habitat had to be a place of great beauty, diversity, and enjoyment as well. It also had to be a place in which the bride and bride-groom could busy themselves with activities that would be personally meaningful and fulfilling yet pleasing and honoring to the king, who was providing all of this for them.

So the king and his son created such a dwelling, and when they had finished, they saw that it was very good.[1]

A fairytale, you say. Yes and no. You no doubt can recognize truths from the Bible enfolded within this story, but perhaps you never saw the pieces put together quite like this. Yet, to understand the nature of children, we must go all the way back to the beginning and look at the big picture. That big picture begins with God, and then it unfolds into a story that has yet to be completed. God, indeed, created a place, a kingdom on earth *in which* to dwell, and a people, a covenant people on earth *with whom* to dwell. To understand the purpose and place of children, a godly context must be provided. That context centers around two key themes of Scripture: an eternal kingdom and a covenantal relationship.[2]

God's Children Have Been Born into an Eternal Kingdom

Ask yourself this question: What is it that I want most for my children? In other words, what is your life's goal for your children? That is a pivotal question for parents and teachers to ask, for on it rests the nature of the nurture that will be provided to your children during their formative years. The answer to that question will tend to direct decisions concerning the children, from the purchase of their Christmas gifts to the type of formal education they receive.

As I answer this question for my one child still living at home, my desire for her is that she profess with her total being that Jesus Christ is Lord. Let me try to unpack that a bit.

No doubt many of you may have answered that you want your children to accept Jesus as their Savior, so that you and they can enjoy eternal life together. I desire that for my daughter as well, but I want more. And I think God does, too, for salvation was never intended to be an end in itself; rather, it is meant to be a *means* to an end. As the Westminster Shorter Catechism states, "Man's chief end is to glorify God, and to enjoy him forever." The focus, then, is not on the self or on personal salvation; it is on God and our response to him. I know that for my daughter to acknowledge Jesus as Lord, she must first accept him personally as her Savior, but the emphasis remains on the ultimate goal of lordship. Let me illustrate.

Several years ago, when I was principal of a Christian high school, a sixteen-year-old girl came to my office to inquire how she could determine whether she was a Christian. After some thought, I replied that if she were a Christian, she would want to be pleasing to God in her attitude, words, and actions. Her instant response was: "Oh, that wouldn't be any fun at all!" Her words spoke for themselves, and they reflected a popular notion that one simply needs to accept Jesus as Savior from sin and that's all there is to it. Now who wouldn't want such a deal! It's an offer too good to pass up, requiring very little from the individual. But such "cheap grace" or "easy believism" misses the central point of salvation. While it is true that we have been saved *from,* the ultimate purpose is to be saved *for.* In fact, this theme permeated every aspect of the earthly ministry of Christ.

To rightly understand Christ's ministry and how it relates to the "chief end" of humans, we must return to the creation story. God desired to create a people who would be the bride of his Son, Jesus. But first, he, jointly with his Son and Spirit, had to create an earthly home for this bride. This home was to be an extension of his kingdom, a kingdom that had already been fully established in the heavenly realms. As sovereign King, he would rule over the newly created territory, with "every square inch of it" being his. This home would, however, be a work in progress. It would not be created in its fully developed form; thus, it would not initially be "sanctified" as a completed praise offering to the King. That task would be left to the bride. She was mandated both to care for that which had been given her and to unfold and to develop its potential. While whole and very wonderful, her creation home would not be complete. That would take place over many years.[3] Then, at a time only the Father knew, the Son as bridegroom would come to consummate the marriage. The heavenly kingdom would merge with the fully sanctified earthly kingdom, and a great marriage feast would take place.[4]

That was the plan. And the plan had a good beginning. Although impossible for us to understand, the Father actually spoke his Son—the Word—and the creation was formed. The Son was also spoken *into* creation, thus providing it with unity, lawfulness, and purpose. The structure was solid, and things were heading in the right direction.

But as the account in Genesis 3 tells us, it was not long before the plan took a bad turn. The fallen archangel Lucifer and what had been, perhaps, one-third of the heavenly host of angels executed a coup, a takeover, of God's earthly kingdom.[5] This coup was accomplished through deceit, without firing a shot. The bride was sullied; she no longer was "radiant, without stain or wrinkle or any other blemish" (Ephesians 5:27). The relationship was broken. Her intended marriage to the Son could no longer take place. The creation home, while still "good" in its structure,[6] became a place that brought dishonor to the King. While his creation still belonged to him, the people who occupied it claimed it as their own, to do with as they pleased. Lucifer, also called Satan, appointed himself as prince of the earth, and many people followed his evil, God-defying ways.

For many centuries, things were dark and appeared to be hopeless. The bride was both tarnished and very weak. The forces of the evil one occupied the creation. Yet, at just the right time, God the Father sent his Son, Jesus, the bridegroom, to earth on a divine rescue mission to redeem both his bride and their creation home. To redeem his bride, the Son had to pay the ransom price, sacrificing himself to save her. The chains that held the creation in the grip of the evil one also had to be broken, so that the bride, in the role of a militant church, could take up the sword of reclamation herself. The occupied territory had to be reclaimed for its rightful owner. The original mandate, to care for and develop creation, had to be resumed. The anticipated *shalom* of the consummated marriage and kingdom had to be reestablished as an achievable goal.

This account of the Creation-Fall-Redemption story makes clear that the purpose of Christ's earthly ministry was to reassert God's sovereignty over every part of his creation. It was a kingdom venture. To accomplish this purpose, Christ had to redeem his bride, the church, by personally meeting God's standard of perfect obedience and by paying the penalty for his bride's sin. His victorious resurrection broke the stranglehold of death, thus assuring his bride that the marriage would indeed be consummated and that she would become a part of his eternal kingdom. The resurrection also broke the chains of bondage for creation. The reclamation of society and culture "for Christ's crown and covenant"[7] could begin.

Perhaps it is becoming clear why God's children can rightly be called "kids of the kingdom," for they have been born into kingdom citizenship. As citizens of God's kingdom, they are called to pledge allegiance to Jesus Christ as Lord of their lives and of their world. They are to be equipped to assume the task of kingdom citizenship: reclaiming and developing this world's arenas—from business to politics to the arts—for God's glory. Christ began the *re*-establishment of God's kingdom on earth. He then commissioned his bride—his body, the church—to continue the process until he returns to consummate their relationship and to establish his kingdom in its fullness. This is the life task for God's children, but it begins with their personal acknowledgement that Jesus is Lord.

God's Children
Have Been Born into a Covenantal Relationship

No one really knows the reason God created Adam and Eve and, subsequently, the entire human race. That mystery remains in the mind of God. We do know, however, that even before the creation of the world, God had already chosen a people to be his special possession (Ephesians 1:4–6). These people are the church—the bride of Christ. During the Old Testament era, the church was centered in the Hebrew nation of Israel. The Jews were God's specially chosen people. With the dawn of the New Testament era, the church was expanded to include non-Jews— those people called Gentiles, who come from every tribe and nation.

In the first chapter of Genesis, God is referred to by the Hebrew noun *Elohim,* which means "the one true God." He is sovereign King; he is Lord of all, for he is the creator of it all. In the second chapter of Genesis, God is referred to as LORD God. LORD (Hebrew YHWH, "Yahweh") is the personal and covenant name of God. The use of both names together makes reference to the same one and only God. God is both the King of a kingdom and a personal God of covenantal relationships.

From the beginning, God chose to relate to his people through arrangements called covenants. A covenant is a binding agreement between two parties. In this case, God initiated the covenants, which contained both promises by God and obligations by his people. The first covenant made by God with Adam was called the Covenant of Works.[8] God's promise was his faithful presence and blessings; Adam's obligation was his obedience. The test of Adam's obedience was whether he would eat the forbidden fruit of the tree of the knowledge of good and evil. The concept of obedience has been a central theme of the relationship between God and humankind from the beginning, and, consequently, it is a concept that must be central within the parent- or teacher-child relationship as well. Adam, who had been created with the ability to make choices, freely chose to eat the fruit of the tree and disobey God. The primary consequence of that choice was a broken relationship between God and Adam, a penalty passed down to every one of Adam's descendants through all subsequent generations.

That one sin could have signaled the end for the bride of Christ. She could have been "quietly divorced" in much the same manner that, years later, Joseph would consider about Mary. But God is gracious, and he chose to intervene in the moral free fall of humankind. He instituted a second covenant, one called the Covenant of Grace.[9] Evidences of this newly established covenant were present already in the Garden of Eden, when God came to Adam and Eve, who were hiding in shame, and clothed them. Shortly thereafter, he promised them a Savior who would someday crush the head of the serpent Satan (Genesis 3:15). This Savior would be Jesus, the bridegroom, through whom God would establish this new covenant. The penalty of sin, eternal separation from God, would be canceled through Jesus' atoning death on the cross, and the humanly impossible standard of perfect obedience would be met vicariously through Jesus' sinless life. Living in the awesome presence of God could become a reality once again. This time, however, it would not come through personal obedience or by good works, but through grace, the freely bestowed gift of God. To claim this gift of grace, one had to believe that Jesus, the Son of God, did indeed both live and die for the purpose of restoring humankind to fellowship with God—an exercise of one's faith. The beauty of this sacrificial act of Jesus for his bride is captured in the words of Paul in his letter to the Ephesians:

> Husbands, love your wives, just as Christ loved the church and gave himself up for her to make her holy, cleansing her by the washing with water through the word, and to present her to himself as a radiant church, without stain or wrinkle or any other blemish, but holy and blameless. In this same way, husbands ought to love their wives as their own bodies. He who loves his wife loves himself. After all, no one ever hated his own body, but he feeds and cares for it, just as Christ does the church—for we are members of his body. "For this reason a man will leave his father and mother and be united to his wife, and the two will become one flesh." This is a profound mystery—but I am talking about Christ and the church. (Ephesians 5:25–32)

The Covenant of Grace has been established with the bride through Jesus, the bridegroom, both individually and corporately. A person comes to Jesus as an individual, but one is then immediately ushered into the broader fellowship of believers called the church. There is a critical link between the two, however, and that is the family.[10] The family has been instituted by God as the primary agency through which he assures the continuity of the church throughout all ages to the end of time.

Jesus gave us our marching orders when he said, ". . . you will receive power when the Holy Spirit comes on you; and you will be my witnesses in Jerusalem, and in all Judea and Samaria, and to the ends of the earth" (Acts 1:8).

Most church-growth specialists agree that the key to church growth is for church members to invite their friends to church. I do not want to minimize the importance of church members inviting unchurched friends to church. Reaching the lost with the Gospel is surely part of the Great Commission given to us by our Savior, and it is our privilege and responsibility to obey with zeal. What I do think is that this should not be the front line of offense in a church-growth strategy.

The biblical model for church growth begins with covenant families. The seed of Christian parents should be our primary target group. The first question that should be asked when communicating a strategy for church growth is: How many adult members have a "Timothy testimony" (2 Timothy 3:15) and have known the holy Scriptures "from infancy"? It is in answer to this question that we should see the most enthusiastic show of hands. It is affirmative answers to this question that will energize the church for the second wave of church growth, the unchurched.[11]

Families are vital for the growth and well-being of the church, and they are a key to the unfolding and advancing of the kingdom of God on earth. The children of believers are very special to God. Our Covenant God, in a manner reminiscent of many earthly grandparents, states his reason for desiring the faithfulness of a husband and wife as being the seeking of "godly offspring" (Malachi 2:15). God wants believers to reproduce, literally! And these godly offspring are to serve as critical links to the next generation of believers. The psalmist wrote:

> [God] decreed statutes for Jacob and established the law in Israel,
> which he commanded our forefathers to teach their children,
> so the next generation would know them, even the children yet to be born,
>   and they in turn would tell their children.
> Then they would put their trust in God . . . . (Psalm 78:5–7a)

Jesus also spoke of and demonstrated the importance of children in the coming of his kingdom when the disciples came to Jesus and asked, "Who is the greatest in the kingdom of heaven?"

> He called a little child and had him stand among them. And he said: "I tell you the truth, unless you change and become like little children, you will never enter the kingdom of heaven. Therefore, whoever humbles himself like this little child is the greatest in the kingdom of heaven. And whoever welcomes a little child like this in my name welcomes me.
> "But if anyone causes one of these little ones who believe in me to sin, it would be better for him to have a large millstone hung around his neck and to be drowned in the depths of the sea." (Matthew 18:1–6)

> Then little children were brought to Jesus for him to place his hands on them and pray for them. But the disciples rebuked those who brought them.

> Jesus said, "Let the little children come to me, and do not hinder them, for the kingdom of heaven belongs to such as these." (Matthew 19:13–14)

More will be written in Section Three on the special status of the children of believers, but let it be sufficient to say at this point that these children and their believing parents are inseparably entwined with the church as the body and bride of Christ. God has covenanted with his chosen people *and their children* to be "the God who is there" for them. Indeed, God's children have been born into covenantal relationship— with families, with the church, and with their Covenant God.

Chapter Conclusions

Who are God's children? What is God's purpose for their lives? These are two essential questions for any study of the nature and nurture of children. To answer these questions from God's perspective, one must understand the creational context for the universe, the people created to occupy that universe, and the task that draws the universe and people together. That setting or backdrop is found in two themes central to Scripture: kingdom and covenant.

Many years ago, two college students and I sat around a snack-bar table interviewing a candidate for a teaching position in the college at which I was a professor. I can't remember much about that interview, even the name of the candidate. But I do remember a question asked of the candidate by one of the students: "Where are you coming from?" The student wanted to know the worldview, the framework of reference, the foundational thinking of this person who could easily be teaching him during the next few years. What a wonderful question for a student to ask! It showed genuine insight into a very important issue, that of context or contextualization. The framework or, as psychologists refer to it, the field, which provides the setting or background for any issue being discussed, makes all the difference in the world as to how the issue will be perceived. For instance, the concept of "family" will likely be defined quite differently by a person coming from a biblical perspective than by one who comes from a humanistic or secular perspective, for they are "coming from" two different views of the world.

This chapter provided a context for the remainder of this book, painting the background so that the concepts of nature and nurture can make sense within a biblical framework. Two primary contact points between God and children were presented: kingdom citizenship and covenantal relationship. This explanation of "where we're coming from" colors the meaning of everything that follows.

But it's not enough for one to be *coming from* somewhere; one also has to be *heading toward* somewhere. There must be a target or goal. That, too, was dealt with in this chapter. Both God-given nature and God-directed nurture need to be heading somewhere; there has to be a purpose to it all. The terms *lordship* and *kingdom* fill in these blanks quite nicely. Without becoming too philosophical, parents and teachers need to spend some reflective time on the ultimate question: What is the purpose of life? Toward what end have we and our children been created? When we arrive at an answer to that question, we will be able to proceed in the nurturing process, for the goals for our children will have been determined.

One final thought. Christian parents typically believe that God has a plan for their children. He may want them to be a homemaker, an attorney, a doctor, a teacher, a carpenter. But what if God's plan for your children is to image God in such a countercultural way that they suffer greatly—even to the point of death—for unashamedly proclaiming in the marketplace that Jesus is Lord? That is a very serious question. But it is within this "seriousness of life's purpose" that this book has been written. There are many books on child-rearing that are quick-fix and feel-good. This book is not one, for our task as nurturers of God's kingdom kids requires focus, commitment, and courage. The nurture of God's children is a serious, life-and-death matter. Eternally.

Chapter 1: Further Thoughts to Consider

1. Why is it important to begin with God in the discussion of the nature and nurture of God's children? What difficulties might emerge with beginning the discussion elsewhere?

2. What possible reasons for God to create the universe are provided by Scripture? How do they relate to the nature and nurture of children?

3. How does the role of Jesus as Savior relate to the role of Jesus as Lord? Can there be salvation without lordship? Why or why not?

4. Describe what you believe to be the kingdom of God. What does it look like? What does it have to do with children?

5. Do you agree with the statement that "the purpose of Christ's earthly ministry was to reassert God's sovereignty over every part of creation"? Why or why not?

6. Compare and contrast the Covenant of Works with the Covenant of Grace. What other covenants described in the Old Testament might be considered subsets of the Covenant of Grace?

7. In which ways is the concept of obedience a central theme in Scripture? What does this concept have to do with the nurture of children?

8. Francis Schaeffer once said that to ignore the first three chapters of the Bible would be to remove essential parts of his worldview. What do you think he meant?

9. What does Susan Hunt mean by the statement that "the biblical model for church growth begins with covenant families?" Do you agree with her? Why or why not?

10. Are the themes of kingdom and covenant a proper context for understanding the nature and nurture of God's children? Why or why not?

Chapter 1: Notes and References

1. This scenario is not original with me. During a course in systematic theology, Knox Chamblain, a professor at the Reformed Theological Seminary, suggested that this approach to the question about the creation of humankind may have some merit. I agree.
2. I once asked Rev. B. J. Haan, the founding president of Dordt College, to summarize the essence of Christian education as he understood it. Without hesitation, he answered with two words: "covenant kingdom."
3. In Genesis 1, the creation was declared by God to be "good" and "very good," but it was not declared holy. In the creation account, only the seventh day was declared holy (Genesis 2:3), because it represented completion, or full sanctification, as will be the case for all of creation with the advent of the eternal Sabbath Rest (Hebrews 4:1–13).
4. Revelation 19:6–9; 21:1–5.
5. Isaiah 14:12–15; 2 Peter 2:4; Jude 6; Revelation 12:4.
6. Romans 8:19–22; Colossians 1:17; 1 Timothy 4:4.
7. This was the rallying cry of the Scottish Covenanters of the 1600s who rejected the divine rights of kings in favor of humankind's duty to God.
8. The Covenant of Works is recorded in Genesis 2:15–17. It was established with Adam, the federal head for all humankind.
9. The Covenant of Grace is first made explicit with Abraham, recorded in Genesis 15 and 17. A "new" covenant is specifically referred to in Jeremiah 31:31ff, Hebrews 8, and Hebrews 12:24.
10. Susan Hunt, in *Heirs of the Covenant,* provided a succinct summary of the right relationship between family and church: "Each Christian family should be a snapshot of God's kingdom values, but the church is the mural. The church, the covenant community, is to be the compelling panorama of grace. The home and church must work together to teach the covenant way of life" (Wheaton, IL: Crossway Books, 1998, 91).
11. Hunt, 115–16.

SECTION TWO

THE RELIGIOUS NATURE

OF

GOD'S CHILDREN

Chapter 2

CREATED BY GOD
WITH RELIGIOUS NATURES

Introduction

I once heard a convocation speech by the president of a Christian college that sought to promote the value of Christian higher education from a unique perspective. Typically, such a convocation speech would have welcomed the student body to a new academic year by citing the distinctives found within their particular Christian college that would presumably be absent from the secular institution down the road, thus seeking to reinforce the students' excellent choice of a college. This particular speech, however, took a reverse position and began with the question: What would education look like if God did not exist? The president proceeded to list several consequences of such a phenomenon. One was the absence of purpose of education, for without God the purpose for life and education would be nonexistent. Another was the absence of predictability, for who could guarantee that the equation $2 + 2 = 4$ would be true each and every time if a lawful and providential God were not present. He proceeded to list several other negative features of such an education, ending up with a rather frightening picture. It was an effective presentation. I believe such "out-of-the-box" approaches often can help us to gain a new appreciation for things that we sometimes take for granted and, consequently, accept without much thought.

Now I have a related task for you. Read the title of this chapter. What effect do the words *created by God* have on you? My guess is that if you are honest about it, you may have a bit of a ho-hum response, perhaps followed by "So what?" or "What else is new?" Yet that statement has profound implications for how we understand the nature of children and how we seek their nurture. This chapter explores the full range of meaning contained in that phrase. It begins by citing the implications of children having been created. Next, it explores the implications of children having been created by God. Finally, it expands on the meaning of the phrase *with religious natures*.

God's Children Have Been Created

One of the greatest fears of humankind is to be a free-floating speck in a mass of nothingness. Picture the scenario. There are no connections with things, for there is nothing else; nor are there relationships with other people, for no one else exists. One is utterly alone. That nihilistic vision immediately engulfs one with a heart-wrenching sense of extreme loneliness.

As horrific as this scenario may be, people often choose to view life in such existential isolation, and many children are nurtured and educated in this manner. Yet, without a reference point outside of oneself, a person cannot formulate a sense of reality or identity. For outside of relationship, there is no meaning. The following story from the life of Archimedes illustrates the human need for such a reference point.

> Archimedes in 250 B.C. made levers with which he could do extraordinary things. He had such confidence in the stupendous strength of these tools, that, so the story goes, he even declared he could raise the earth from its foundation if he were supplied with a fixed point of support. It goes without saying that this fixed point of support would have to be located outside of the earth.[1]

To move the earth, Archimedes had to locate the fulcrum point *outside* of the earth. To understand the meaning of life on earth, the same principle is true. In this context, God can be cited as the divine Archimedean point—the Ultimate Reference Point for humankind. Francis Schaeffer wrote that "unless there is a universal over the particulars, there is no meaning." He continued, "Jean-Paul Sartre (states that): 'If you have a finite point and it has no infinite reference point, then that finite point is absurd.'"[2] Only by acknowledging an Ultimate Other outside of themselves can children gain a sense of personal identity and find meaning in life. Only by locking-in on the Divine North Star can children plot a truthful course through life. And the journey begins with the fact that they have been created.

Created, not evolved

The concept of having been created is really a no-brainer for most Christian parents and teachers. Since we believe the Genesis account of creation and reject the theory that humankind evolved from lower forms, we have no trouble accepting our children as creations of God. Eve acknowledged this already when she gave birth to the first child of the human race: "With the help of the LORD I have brought forth a man" (Genesis 4:1). David captured the awesomeness of this creative act of God:

> . . . you created my inmost being;
>> you knit me together in my mother's womb.
> I praise you because I am fearfully and wonderfully made;
>> your works are wonderful, I know that full well.
> My frame was not hidden from you
>> when I was made in the secret place.
> When I was woven together in the depths of the earth,
>> your eyes saw my unformed body.
> All the days ordained for me were written in your book
>> before one of them came to be. (Psalm 139:13–16)

Children are not simply highly developed members of the animal kingdom; in fact, they have been appointed by God to be *rulers of* the animal kingdom. Satan's lie regarding the "origin of the species" seeks to undermine the dignity that accompanies the task given by God to his children in the beginning—that of being rulers over "the fish of the sea and the birds of the air, over the livestock, over all the earth, and over all the creatures that move along the ground" (Genesis 1:26).

But the lies continue. Today's lie about children is that they are highly developed machines, complex computer-like beings. Behavioral psychologists developed this mechanistic view of humankind during the first half of the last century. The result is learning theories based on operant conditioning and approaches to discipline based on behavior modification. A more current learning theory called information processing takes this view one step further as children are likened to humanoid computers. While there may be kernels of truth in these theories, their proponents tend to absolutize the kernels into the whole truth, leaving no room for God's involvement.

The greatest danger of an evolutionary or mechanistic view of children is not found in the overt references made in life science books produced by Carl Sagan and others of like mind or in K-12 textbooks. These can be countered quite easily by Christian parents and teachers, and even used as object lessons. The greater danger is the more covert integration of these theories into television programming and films that children watch and the developmental and educational psychology textbooks studied by future teachers. Such desensitization to the absence of a godly context or perspective can subtly neutralize kids of the kingdom *and* their teachers.

Creaturely dependence

Children were not created to be autonomous, self-sufficient, or independent centers of their universe. They were created to be dependent, for they are creatures of their Creator. Children are not to look inward for the ultimate answers to life, nor are they to look outward on a horizontal plane. They are to look upward to God in a dependent and creaturely way.

Within the school setting, the creaturely dependence of children means that students, while being central to the purpose of a school, are not the ultimate center of their experience or of their classroom. They do not function for their own purposes. They are called to acknowledge that there is a sovereign God, an Ultimate Being outside of themselves, to whom they must bend their knees.

Dependency on God can be a difficult concept to teach children, because most of us in the Western world haven't experienced much stark dependency. The "give us this day our daily bread" petition of the Lord's Prayer can easily have a hollow ring to it. The paycheck is usually on time, and we often have room in the budget for "wants" as well as needs. An illustration of the dependency and trust that is most pleasing to God was provided by Jesus when he sent his disciples to the Jews to preach, heal, and drive out demons. He told them, "Do not take along any gold or silver or copper in your belts; take no bag for the journey, or extra tunic, or sandals or a staff; for the worker is worth his keep" (Matthew 10:9–10). When Jesus wanted to teach dependency, he didn't fool around! How many of us have stepped out in faith, leaving all security and support behind, and walked into the unknown, trusting that God's hands of provision would be there? Somehow, we need to build into the lives of our children at least a taste of such dependent trust. For the promise is there: If we "seek first the kingdom of God" (Matthew 6:33)—seek to do that which is pleasing to him no matter what the risk—God tells us that all of our needs will be met.

God is the heavenly Father of his children; thus he wants their love and day-by-day dependence on him. He wants them to trust him, to have faith in him and his Word—both savingly and daily. God delights in giving good things to his children. They are to be encouraged by word and example to ask, seek, and knock,[3] for dependency is a vital part of the Christian life. Yes, we are to nurture our children toward independence but always within the context of dependence on their Creator, Lord, and King.

With God-given identity

The identity of children does not come from within them, whether it is based on their DNA code, their talents and gifts, or their physical appearance. Nor does it come from elsewhere—the pedigree of their parents, the side of town on which they were born, or their ethnic or racial makeup.

Identity for children is found in relationship, in their being known by others. The "who they are" is based on "whose they are." The primary identity of children emerges from their relationship with God, the One who calls his sheep by their names. Identity in a secondary sense is gained through one's family and through the broader body of believers—here, again, through relationship.

The issue of identity is one in which the gurus of political correctness have actually made a contribution. They point out that people often place descriptors *before* the word that refers to another person. For instance, one might say "a female attorney," "an African-American teenager," "a blind man," or "a Jewish author." This word order takes the focus off of the person (or the personhood of the person) and places it on the descriptor—how someone is different from rather than similar to. A more politically correct way, and in this case, a more biblical way, would be the following: "an attorney who is female," "a teenager who is African-American," "a man who is blind," "an author who is Jewish." In each instance, the focus begins with the individual as a person. Each person is first and foremost a creation of God, not a gender, racial, disability, or ethnic descriptor.

The issue of identity is an interesting one within our society. For instance, I remember sitting next to strangers at Rotary Club luncheons, and, in an attempt to find out who these people were (i.e., to determine their identity), I would ask, "And what do you do?" With many men, the identity issue is work related. That is the reason men who have lost their jobs may experience an identity crisis. Women, on the other hand, often find their identity through relationships, such as those found within their families.

Teachers may remember reading about the psychosocial development theories of Erik Erikson during teacher training. Erikson believed that adolescence was the time period during which the search for identity took place. The following is a definition of identity as viewed from Erikson's developmental perspective:

> The central issue for adolescents is the development of an identity that will provide a firm basis for adulthood. The individual has been developing a sense of self since infancy. But adolescence marks the first time that a conscious effort is made to answer the now pressing question, "Who am I?" The conflict defining this stage is *identity versus role confusion.*
>
> Identity refers to the organization of the individual's drives, abilities, beliefs, and history into a consistent image of self. It involves deliberate choices and decisions, particularly about work, values, ideology, and commitments to people and ideas. If adolescents fail to integrate all these aspects and choices, or if they feel unable to choose at all, role confusion threatens.[4]

Note the focus on self, a primary source of identity according to Erikson. The other focus is on role or vocation—not too dissimilar from Rotary Club conversations! Lacking, obviously, is any reference to God or to the foundational questions of life: "Where did I come from?" "Why am I here?" and "Where am I going?" For a Christian view of identity to be developed, those questions need to precede Erikson's "Who am I?" question.

God's Children Have Been Created by God

Children have been created. That means that they must look beyond themselves for their origin. The first words of the Bible identify that source: "In the beginning *God.* . . ." In these few words, humanistic self-sufficiency is destroyed and is replaced by a thought too large to comprehend: Children have been formed by the sovereign God of the universe!

God's children

Sometimes parents and even teachers can believe that the children in their charge belong to them. While it is true that life begins with a mother and a father, it is God who ignites the actual spark of life. God's children belong to him. They are, however, entrusted to parents as God's representatives who have been commissioned to care for and nurture his children in his Name.

The dedication of infants in churches can sometimes reinforce the notion that children belong to parents rather than to God. More appropriate would be a ceremony that acknowledges that the children of believers already belong to God, because from the moment of conception they were consecrated by him to himself and his purposes (1 Corinthians 7:14). To the best of their ability and in God's strength, however, parents should promise to nurture his children toward lives of commitment to him through Jesus Christ. The children should also be presented to and accepted into the church community, which, in response, should pledge its support for the parents in their nurturing task.

Biblical nurture recognizes that children have been created in the image of God. Parents have *not* been instructed to re-create their children in their own image or likeness. Yet that is precisely what often happens. Parents create their own agenda for the children who have been entrusted to them, and they seek to impose parental values and parental expectations rather than the values and expectations of God. Scripture responds by warning that children must be nurtured and admonished *in the Lord* or they will become "exasperated" and "discouraged" (Ephesians 6:4; Colossians 3:21).

Under authority

The person who creates or forms a product normally owns that product and can do with it as he or she pleases. Most people accept that as being true. It is especially true that God, as sovereign Lord of all, has authority over his creation and over his creatures. He has that right, first, because he is God and, secondly, because he is the Creator. Obedient submission to the authority of God is a central theme of Scripture from the very beginning. God gave Adam and Eve all sorts of freedoms and blessings, but he also provided one very simple test of their willingness to allow him to be in authority: They were not to eat of the tree of the knowledge of good and evil. Eating the fruit of the tree was not the central issue; obedience was, and the fruit was simply a way of measuring compliance to a command.

Submission to authority was an issue before the Fall, and it certainly has been an issue since the Fall, for a sure sign of our rebellion is that we don't like restraints and we don't like people telling us what to do, whether they are parents, teachers, bosses, or God himself. Because of this, God continues to have a word for us regarding submission:

> The Lord says:
> "These people come near to me with their mouth
>   and honor me with their lips, but their hearts are far from me.
> Their worship of me is made up only of rules taught by men.
> Therefore once more I will astound these people with wonder upon wonder;
> the wisdom of the wise will perish,
>   the intelligence of the intelligent will vanish."

> Woe to those who go to great depths to hide their plans from the LORD,
> who do their work in darkness and think, "Who sees us? Who will know?"
> You turn things upside down,
>   as if the potter were thought to be like the clay!
> Shall what is formed say to him who has formed it,
>   "He did not make me"?
> Can the pot say of the potter,
>   "He knows nothing"? (Isaiah 29:13–16)

God is telling us, "What makes you think you are smarter than I am? Simply obey me, and trust me, for I am God." Some of these words sound rather familiar to those of us who work with adolescents. Teens and preteens love to challenge authority, because they tend not to believe that their parents and, at times, their teachers are tuned in to the way things really are. As irritating as that is for us, we are inclined to turn right around and do the same thing to God. Kids today call this "dissing," which can be loosely translated as "Dismissing a person by using words or, preferably, a look of superiority or arrogant disgust and then turning away in a gesture of tuning the person out of existence."

Children are under God's direct authority. They are to obey his mandates, his commands, and his commissions. Such obedience is an act of love directed toward God. God has also placed children under delegated authority. They are to obey their parents and anyone to whom the parents have, in turn, delegated authority, including teachers and babysitters, "for there is no authority except that which God has established. The authorities that exist have been established by God" (Romans 13:1). God says, "Children, obey your parents in the Lord, for this is right" (Ephesians 6:1). That exhortation does not say that "parents are right"; it says that *obedience* is right. Children are to obey their parents even if their parents are wrong, for the issue is obedience, not the particular request. Children may disobey their parents only when obedience would cause them to break God's (higher) law. There may be times when each of us needs to "obey God rather than men" (Exodus 1:17; Acts 5:29). Ordinarily, however, children should obey their parents because obedience "pleases the Lord" (Colossians 3:20). God likes it.

It is sad to observe parents and teachers who don't take the obedience of their children very seriously. We have all observed noncompliance by children in supermarkets and restaurants. Both as a school principal and a college supervisor of student teachers, I have observed similar disobedience in classrooms. Students are told to be quiet, get into their seats, or get on task, and they simply ignore the teacher and continue doing what they have been doing. Teachers fail to realize that their unwillingness to insist on compliance teaches a very *un-godly* lesson, quite the opposite from the mandate of the school. Just as children have been placed under authority, so parents and teachers have been given mandates to nurture children in a manner that pleases the Lord. Failure to teach children the important lessons of authority and obedience is displeasing to God (1 Samuel 3:11–14; 8:1–3).

Accountable

With authority comes accountability. Children can and must be held accountable for their choices, for they have been given the ability to choose as part of their natures. It would have been easy for God to have placed himself in authority over his human creations and then controlled their actions as one might with puppets on a string. All of their activities could have been programmed in advance and thus have been quite predictable. If God had so chosen, he could have created humankind, including children, in this manner, and sin would never have entered the world. But God chose to provide humankind with the ability to obey or to disobey, to walk in his ways or in their own ways. He gave Adam and Eve the freedom to choose to sin or to not sin. Obedience or disobedience was *their* choice, not his. God coveted a freely chosen response of obedience by those he had crafted in his own image. He desired to be loved by them, not because they had to, but because they wanted to.

This ability to choose means that children can be held personally accountable for their actions, for all actions result from personal choices. Blaming others doesn't work. It didn't in the Garden of Eden; it doesn't today. "The devil made me do it" doesn't cut it as an excuse, because the devil doesn't *make* us do anything. For that matter, no one outside of ourselves makes us do anything. The complaints that "He hit me first," or "He called me a name," or "He made me mad" simply don't fly, for all children have the ability to choose whether to retaliate or to walk away. This is a vital lesson to teach our children. They are personally accountable for their choices; they can blame no one else.

Children have been created with the ability to choose so that they may freely respond in acts of obedient worship to the Creator. Their actions are purposive and goalistic, not causistic or deterministic. Sigmund Freud said that the behavior of children is caused by the actions of their parents, especially during the first few years of the children's lives. The father of behavioristic psychology, B. F. Skinner, said that the behavior of children is determined by their environment, which is outside of their control. Yes, it is true that parents and the environment influence children's behavior, but to say that they cause or determine behavior denies personal accountability. Rather, children choose actions because of personally purposeful goals that they have freely established for themselves. They are not victims of their past nor of their present-day circumstances. Their actions are primarily future oriented, focused with purpose of intent on personally meaningful goals.

Before concluding this topic, a warning should be provided regarding the accountability of children. Adding the words "to the degree of their understanding" may be appropriate, for one cannot be held accountable for that which one cannot understand. Children move through various stages of development, each providing its own level of understanding. Small children think as small children, not as miniature adults. So be careful not to require of children that for which they are not yet capable. Accountability does have some limitations.

Finite

We live in a day and an age when children aren't supposed to experience failure or limitations, for there is a fear that failure can negatively affect children's self-esteem. Consequently, grade inflation and social promotion are rampant; concern with how children feel competes with how much children know; and parents complain to the coach, the principal, and the school board president when their child is cut from the basketball team. Part of the legacy of the baby boomers is their intense focus on achievement, competition, and the need to be good at everything. Many boomer parents seek to infuse these values into their children through the acquisition of life experiences. These "nurturing" experiences are purchased rather than provided by the parents for several reasons: one, parents today often have only one or two children on whom to spend; two, when both parents earn salaries, such life experiences are easily affordable; three, parents have little time to spend personally with their children; and four, parents either fear or experience guilt that, as busy as they are, they are not being good parents. The theory is that if enough life experiences are purchased, one's children will be successful in whatever they attempt to do, and that success will, in turn, produce positive self-esteem. In response to the statement that all children are finite and have limitations, one can almost hear the boomer response, "Not *my* kid!"

The Bible counters this theory in several ways. First, it reveals a God who is infinite—one who is beyond measure and has no limitations.

Next, it tells us that God's human creations are finite; they indeed do have limitations and shortcomings. The "body passages" of Romans 12 and 1 Corinthians 12 provide evidence that not every kid can be the pitcher, and, even if he or she is the pitcher, not every pitcher throws a no-hitter. Every person has been created with abilities that differ from those given to others, for how could a body function if every part were the same? Diversity has an important place within God's scheme of things. Finally, the Bible provides many examples of people falling flat on their faces in failure and how, in God's strength, they were able to pick themselves up, dust themselves off, and try again. The Christian religion is a religion of fresh beginnings through forgiveness and grace.

As previously mentioned, much is made today about the need for positive self-esteem. The Bible says, however, that knowing the truth will set one free (John 8:32). Truth can, of course, refer to Jesus, but for the sake of this conversation, truth will be applied to children. A truthful image or mental picture of oneself is a healthy self-image. And the truth is that each child has certain pluses and minuses, each has positive and negative qualities, and each has strengths and limitations. That's just the way it is! Children need to be encouraged to be true to the person who God has created them to be. For some, that means "acing" math without breaking a sweat; for others, it means receiving a D in math after trying their very hardest. For some, that means playing in the band, while for others, that means making the basketball team, and for still others, that means taking first place in an art competition.

Finally, a few things need to be said about failure. First, failure is part of the human experience and does not cause one to *become* a failure. Everyone fails sometime in some thing. Second, failing at something has at least two benefits. One is that failing to achieve a goal is an excellent source of motivation. After having failed to do something correctly, how many of us became upset and twice as determined to succeed the next time? In fact, the Bible tells us that "perseverance produces character" (Romans 5:4). For that reason, parents and teachers need to allow their children to fail at times. A second benefit of failing is that it can create a need for assistance from others. The kingdom of God has no room for Lone Rangers, but at times that lesson must be learned the hard way—though failure to be able to accomplish something by oneself. Failure can force people to their knees before God in dependency. In fact, failure may be the only way to get a proud, self-sufficient individual to that humble position. We all need to be reminded that "the Lord's power is made perfect in weakness" (2 Corinthians 12:9).

God's Children
Have Been Created by God with Religious Natures

Children have been created, *and* they have been created by God. But there is more truth to consider. God's created children are *religious* in their very nature. In this regard, they differ from every other part of creation. The religious nature of children is evidenced in a number of ways.

Formed by God's hands

God chose to create the first human being in a manner that was quite different from the way he created the rest of creation. All other parts were formed as a result of God's Word; they were spoken into existence. But Genesis records that "the LORD God formed the man from the dust of the ground and breathed into his nostrils the breath of life, and the man became a living being" (Genesis 2:7). The Divine Potter gently and intricately molded a ball of clay into a human form. Isaiah wrote,

> . . . O LORD, you are our Father.
> We are the clay, you are the potter;
> we are all the work of your hand. (Isaiah 64:8)

Children, too, have been created by design and not by random chance. Each has been crafted in a unique manner. Each is an original, distinct from all others. Each is very special to God, formed by his hands to be an instrument for use in those same hands.

Possessing God-breathed life

Children are God's workmanship, molded by his hands. But their very life's breath comes from God as well. In the beginning, God breathed into the nostrils of humankind the breath of life. That cannot be said of any other living creature. God continues to be the breath of life for all of his image bearers, and this includes children.

God, therefore, not humankind, gives life. And the sanctity of that God-given life dictates that only God has the right to take the breath of life away from one of his human creatures, whether they are the unborn, the disabled, or the elderly.

Immortal souls

Plants die. Birds die. Animals die. But children will continue to live past time and into eternity. Unless Christ returns beforehand, of course, all children eventually will die physical deaths. But as immortal souls, they will continue to live for all eternity. The children in every home and in every school are souls who, at some future point, will move from time into eternity. This profound reality, sadly, receives little attention by many parents and teachers. It is imperative that believing adults, those who understand the truths about life after death, share these truths with their children. The religious souls who live in our homes and study in our classrooms need to know where they have come from, but they must also know where they are going.

Souls with spirits

Just as the Godhead includes a Spirit, so a soul or a person possesses a spirit. The spirit of humankind tends to "represent man in his God-ward side."[5] When reference is made in Scripture to humankind in relationship to God, the word *spirit* is most likely used. One's spirit serves as an inner compass. It is the spiritual "principle of life and action that controls the body."[6] Thus, one's spirit can both provide direction and serve as a source of one's will.

All people, including children, possess spirits from conception. It is an aspect of God's image within them. But at the time of regeneration or the new birth, one's spirit, in fellowship with the Spirit of Christ, takes on a new character,[7] and, from that moment forward, "the Spirit himself testifies with our spirit that we are God's children" (Romans 8:16).

With direction-giving hearts

The heart is the moral direction-giver for a person. Whoever or whatever is on the throne of a person's heart dictates the moral direction taken by that individual. And there are only two directions to be facing and walking in this world, either toward God in obedience or away from him in rebellion.

The Bible contains over 800 references to the heart as one's spiritual center and moral compass, for it is the wellspring of the inner person from which "flow the issues of life" (Proverbs 4:23). As the heart is, so is the person. Christ spoke about how the heart is the source of that which can be observed outwardly about a person: ". . . out of the overflow of the heart the mouth speaks. The good man brings good things out of the good stored up in him, and the evil man brings evil things out of the evil stored up in him" (Matthew 12:34–35). One's heart determines the direction of every thought generated, every word spoken, and every action carried out.

God wants the hearts of his children to be directed toward him in to-tal love and commitment. He says, "My son [my daughter], give me your heart" (Proverbs 23:26a). For when he has their hearts, he has their all.

Created to worship

All children possess an intrinsic desire to worship, because they have been created for the purpose of worshiping God. Anthropologists have long said that people within all cultures worship; they either worship a part of creation, another human being, or the true God. No one told them to; they possessed the felt need to worship because it is a part of their human nature. They were born with that desire, and they are to act on that desire in a God-honoring way.

Worship is a total life experience, not just one hour of formal worship on Sunday mornings. The Bible instructs: ". . . whatever you do, do it all for the glory of God" (1 Corinthians 10:31). There are to be no secular portions of life, either at home or at school. At home, all chores, all forms of entertainment, and all relationships are to bring glory to God. The same is true at school. Assignments, athletics, and friendships are to be holy unto the Lord (Zechariah 14:20). Totally religious children are called to totally surrender their all to their Lord and King. That is their reason for living.

Image bearers of God

A scenario with which I have challenged college students is to role-play a job interview with the principal of a Christian school. I ask the students to answer the following question, posed to them as a teacher candidate by the principal: "Since you are a Christian teacher and you are being interviewed for a teaching position in a Christian school, how would you view your students in a distinctively Christian manner? In other words, how might your view of children differ from that of your counterpart in the secular school down the road?" (I always add that second question for the students who want to answer the first question with "I would love them," since most teachers in secular schools love their students, too.) About 99.9% of their answers include some reference to children being created in the image of God. "Good answer!" I say. But then I ask two follow-up questions: "What does it mean to be created in the image of God?" and "What tangible difference does it make in the teaching/learning process?" Unhappily, about 99.9% of the students cannot answer those two questions. That is sad, for image bearing has much to say about who the student is and the student's place in the world. It is a concept that probably does more than any other in defining the God-given nature of children.

We immediately face a dilemma, however, when we begin a study of children as image bearers of God, for the question is posed: Of which image are we speaking? Let me explain. If we were to focus on image bearing at the time of creation, we would be studying the original image. If we focused on image bearing following the Fall, we would have to study the profaned image. And the atonement of Christ provides the opportunity for a renewed image. Finally, with the second coming of Christ, there will be the perfected image. Image bearing will be the focus of the remainder of this section on the nature of God's children.

Chapter Conclusions

God's children are totally religious beings for a number of reasons. They are souls with spirits. They are immortal; their existence will continue from time into all eternity. They have heart centers that both unify them and provide direction. They have hearts designed to be responsive to their Creator, and God indeed desires to have their hearts. And they have been created in the image of God.

The view that children are totally religious beings is not readily accepted within secular schools. At best, children are acknowledged as being partly religious, having only a portion of their lives function in a spiritual manner. The logical implication of this theory is that certain times of the day or week are devoted to spiritual things and the remainder of the time is free for secular pursuits. This sacred-secular dichotomy fragments the wholeness of life and produces token Christianity. Children are *totally* religious. Each of their thoughts, words, and actions contains religious significance. They are either responding in thankfulness and obedience to their Creator, or they, in essence, are worshiping another.

This chapter dealt with the relevance of God to children by answering the question of what difference it makes that children have been created by God with religious natures. Children are not alone; there is a Creator with whom to relate. Their Creator is holy, righteous, and just. Their Creator also loves them—as a Father. Because God's children know where they came from, they know whose they are. That sense of identity is further enhanced as they uncover what it means to image God.

The next three chapters deal with image bearing. Chapter 3 describes the original image, Chapter 4 the profaned image, and Chapter 5 the renewed image.

Chapter 2: Further Thoughts to Consider

1. Biblical Christianity acknowledges a transcendent reference point—God. Secular humanism cites an immanent reference point—humankind. How do these two differing viewpoints affect understanding the nature of children?

2. In which ways does evolutionary theory affect our society and culture?

3. Why is one's identity defined by reference points that are external to oneself? Illustrate your response.

4. How does failure fit within a biblical perspective on life?

5. Explain why the actions of children are purposive and goalistic rather than causistic or deterministic. What difference might this make in the nurturing process?

6. According to 1 Corinthians 7:14, the children of a believing parent are holy. What does this mean? What difference might this make in the lives of these children?

7. Seven descriptors of a religious nature have been listed in this chapter. Try to cite one implication of each for the lives of children at home and/or at school.

8. Define the term *worship* as it is used in the statement "All children possess an intrinsic desire to worship."

9. How might you answer the two follow-up questions on image bearing: What does it mean to be created in the image of God? and What tangible difference does it make in the (nurturing or) teaching-learning process?

10. Do you agree or disagree with the author's reason for opposition to secular education stated in the Chapter Conclusions? Explain your viewpoint.

Chapter 2: Notes and References

1. L. Kalsbeek, *Contours of a Christian Philosophy* (Toronto: Wedge, 1975), 56.
2. F. A. Schaeffer, *Pollution and the Death of Man: The Christian View of Ecology* (Wheaton, IL: Tyndale, 1970), 89.
3. Matthew 7:11 and 7, respectively.
4. A. Woolfolk, *Educational Psychology,* 8th ed. (Boston: Allyn and Bacon, 2001), 68.
5. A. A. Hoekema, *Created in God's Image* (Grand Rapids, MI: Eerdmans, 1986), 214.
6. L. Berkhof, *Systematic Theology,* (Grand Rapids, MI: Eerdmans, 1941), 194.
7. Romans 8:10.

Chapter 3

IMAGE BEARING AT CREATION: THE ORIGINAL IMAGE

Introduction

Children have been created to reflect the very likeness of the God of the universe. Each one of them bears his image. What an awesome reality!

The Bible explicitly speaks of image bearing in four passages, two of which are from the pre-Fall era and two from the post-Fall time period.[1] We first read about the original image in the Genesis account of creation.

> Then God said, "Let us make man in our image, in our likeness, and let them rule over the fish of the sea and the birds of the air, over the livestock, over all the earth, and over all the creatures that move along the ground."
>
> So God created man in his own image, in the image of God he created him; male and female he created them. (Genesis 1:26–27)
>
> When God created man, he made him in the likeness of God. He created them male and female; at the time they were created, he blessed them and called them "man." (Genesis 5:1b–2)

Yes, the Bible clearly states that humankind was originally created in the image or likeness of God. But to glean from these two references what image bearing looked like at the dawn of creation is not easy to determine.

Historically, *image* has been viewed as a (predicate) noun— humankind is an *image* of God. Here, image bearing is seen as a matter of being. Thus, humankind *looks like* God in certain finite ways. The attributes of rationality, creativity, and sociability often have been cited as God-like in nature. Because the verses cited above lack such evidence, however, these conclusions are derived more from general revelation than from Scripture. John Calvin stated in his *Institutes:* "Without knowledge of self there is no knowledge of God."[2] Indeed, we can learn something about God-likeness by looking at God's human creations.

More recently, however, the view of "image" as an action verb—humankind *images* God—has gained credence. In this case, humankind acts like or acts for God, again, in a finite manner. Here, image bearing is a matter of *doing.* The Scripture passages cited above do, in fact, provide a few hints about the nature of this activity. Humankind is told to "rule over" the other parts of creation as God's representatives, or vice regents. This is supported by the Creation Mandate that immediately follows the Genesis 1 image-bearing passage. Image bearing, then, is seen as having a responsive, or functional, dimension.

The truth about the nature of the image of God actually appears to lie with *both* positions. Humankind *is* the image of God in his and her ontological being or essence. This aspect of image bearing can be referred to as imaging God in structure.[3] Humankind also actively'[mages God in responsive discipleship, in doing or in function. Both human structure and function are affected by moral direction, which is set by one's heart.

The following illustration may help in understanding these three concepts. A newspaper story reported that the houses built by Habitat for Humanity, a volunteer organization that builds homes for the poor, tend to withstand hurricanes better than those built by typical contractors. The reason for this is that the volunteers, who don't always know much about building houses, pound several nails in where only one is normally needed—just to make certain! This practice results in buildings that are very structurally sound. The houses are well built. They have integrity of structure. Function, on the other hand, is the intended purpose or usage of the structure. In this case, the structures being built are houses and, consequently, they are intended to function as houses. Finally, direction reflects whether or not this structure and its actual function are God-honoring, whether they are holy or profane. Houses built by Habitat for Humanity ordinarily are pleasing to God, for he has instructed those with resources, position, and power to show concern for the disenfranchised in society. So, in this case, the structure, function, and direction of the house are good. The same is true for the original image of God at the time of creation. It was declared by God to be "very good" in all three aspects.

Each of these three aspects of being created in the image of God will be developed further in this chapter, as well as in the two that follow.

The Original Image—in Direction

God is sovereign Lord of all. That is the proper starting point for a discussion of "direction." The psalmist wrote, "The earth is the LORD's, and everything in it, the world, and all who live in it . . ." (Psalm 24:1). The "*all* who live in it" refers to those who have been created in the image of God. They belong to God, for he is their Creator, Sustainer, and Possessor, and, therefore, worthy of worship and honor as "the King of glory" (Psalm 24:7–10). Because they belong to God, they are sacred or holy, consecrated or set apart for the worship and honor of God. Their sole purpose in life is to bring glory to God. God's people (and the original two images *were* God's people) are called his "treasured possession," a "people belonging to God," a "kingdom of priests," a "holy nation" consecrated to do the will of God (Deuteronomy 19:5–6; 1 Peter 2:9).

Human beings were created physically upright, and they were created to be morally upright as well. God created his image bearers to stand vertically, upright, to be able to oversee quite naturally the creation over which they were to have dominion and to gaze upwardly to their Creator in awe, obedience, and worship. God also called his image bearers to be "upright in heart" (Psalm 7:10; 64:10; 119:7). They are to be honorable and just, doing what is right. God's people have been instructed "to love the LORD [their] God and to serve him with all [their] heart and all [their] soul . . . to walk in all his ways and to hold fast to him" (Deuteronomy 11:13, 22). This "walk in the ways of God" is to be toward God, in his direction, gazing upwardly with faces that reflect his glory. An upright walk is directed by the heart, the spiritual and moral compass that points image bearers in the way that they should go.

In the beginning, the image bearers of God were guided toward God by holy and upright hearts. They faced God, and they walked toward God in adoration and service.

The Original Image—in Structure

God created Adam and Eve in his image. They were created as *persons* who, in a finite manner, "looked like" God. Their very essence or being reflected the very essence or being of God. In structure, humankind was (and continues to be) God's image.

(It is interesting at this point to consider the second commandment, which prohibits creating idols or "graven images." Only God has the right to create God-images. And, according to the first commandment, only the original, not the image, is to be worshiped.)

The word that best describes the image-bearing structure of humankind is integrity. Integrity can mean soundness—being complete or undivided. A structure that has integrity possesses integrality: wholeness, or a lacking of nothing essential. Integrity can also mean righteousness, goodness, or unimpeachableness. Both definitions reflect the source of humankind's integrity of structure: Jesus Christ.

Paul's letter to the Colossians describes Christ as the One in whom "all things hold together" (Colossians 1:17). The book of Hebrews describes Christ as the One who is "sustaining all things by his powerful word" (Hebrews 1:3). The Gospel of John describes Christ as the Word, or *Logos* (John 1:1), the One who brings order and harmony to all things. The essence or structure of humankind possesses integrity because of Jesus Christ.

This integral unity was evidenced as the Godhead—the three in one of the Trinity—formed creation. The first verse of Scripture reads: "In the beginning *Elohim* [plural noun] created [singular verb] the heavens and the earth" (Genesis 1:1). As the Spirit hovered over the waters, the Father spoke the Word—the Son—and creation was formed. Then the Trinitarian God created humankind with the words "Let *us* make man in *our* image" (Genesis 1:26, emphasis mine). Images of God possess, in a finite way, certain characteristics of the unified Trinity.

Humankind, then, reflects a unified God of integrity. One cannot pull apart the personhood of God. All his traits exist at the same time: his justice, love, holiness, righteousness, faithfulness, grace, mercy, patience, wisdom, goodness, and sovereignty.

Christ, the very image of God, reflects this integrity of being through his body, the Church. While the Romans 12 and 1 Corinthians 12 descriptions of the body of Christ may appear to focus on the diversity of its parts, each part has been designed to be knit into the unified whole. God desires that the beautiful array of persons he has created be viewed as parts of a mosaic or tapestry—as a unified whole.

Children, as images of God, are integrally unified persons, reflecting their Creator. This integrity of structure is evidenced in several ways. First, children are integral souls. Second, children are directed by integral hearts. Third, children possess integral personalities. And fourth, children possess integral modes of expression.

Children are integral souls

In the beginning, "the LORD God formed man from the dust of the ground and breathed into his nostrils the breath of life, and the man became a living being" (Genesis 2:7). This being or person can also be referred to as a soul. Persons, then, do not have or possess souls; persons *are* souls. The children we nurture at home and instruct at school are organic souls (or beings or persons) with multifaceted personalities.

This concept of wholeness has always been an important part of the God-human relationship. Christ desires wholeness—*shalom,* God's perfect peace, for his bride. Within this peace, the body functions with balance, harmony, congruence, and cohesion, rather than in a fragmented and competing manner. Hebrew thought has focused on the wholeness of life, whereas Greek thought has focused on the parts, often resulting in split thinking or dichotomies that never were intended. Many modern views of humankind reflect the fragmented and split views of Greek thinking rather than the holistic, integral view of Hebrew thinking and of the Bible.

A question must be raised at this point, however. At times, the Bible describes humankind as body, soul, and spirit. This is commonly known as a trichotomy. The Bible also describes humankind with two terms, body and soul. This is called a dichotomy, which is even more commonly accepted. The third option, one that we believe to be true, is that humankind is not split into parts at all but is, rather, a whole, a unity. Yet, what is one to do with the three terms *body, soul,* and *spirit?* They are in the Bible, so we can't simply dismiss them. The following chart places each of these words next to the other in an attempt to identify their similarities and their differences.

word in English	soul	spirit	body
word in Hebrew	*nephesh*	*ruach*	*basar* (flesh)
word in Greek	*Psyche*	*pneuma*	*soma* (body) *sarx* (flesh)
common definition	whole person	whole person, breath, interchangeable with soul	whole person, when combined with soul
unique definition	self, person; one's inner aspect; seat of person-to-person relationships	life-giving, direction-giving center; self-conscious center of all experience; seat of God-human relationships	one's physical, external aspect

The Greek perspective of soul, spirit, and body states that they are three separate parts. Within Greek thought, the "unique" definitions stated in the chart above would be adopted as the primary definitions. A Hebrew perspective, however, would side with the "common" definition that views humankind as an organic unity, with the soul, spirit, and body simply being three dimensions that are distinguishable, but not separable. Rather than being different and separable dimensions of humankind, soul, spirit, and body are primarily terms that provide different ways of viewing the whole person. Secondarily, however, each term also embodies a meaning that is unique, one that can help one better understand the various ways of viewing a person.

Children, as image bearers, are meant to be unified wholes. Their wholeness has been designed to be greater than the sum of their parts.

Children are directed by integral hearts

Just as the physical heart is the center of one's biological functioning, the spiritual heart is the center of one's soul or self. It is the point from which all of the soul's life-issues originate. It is the core of a person; it is the unifying center of one's personality.

To understand the role of the heart in the lives of children, it may be helpful to define the term in much the same way as the terms *soul, spirit,* and *body* were previously defined. The word for heart in Old Testament Hebrew is *lebh,* and in New Testament Greek, *kardia.* The word *heart,* too, has two definitions.

The primary meaning for heart is "the mini-me," for the heart of the person represents the whole person to the world outside of itself. It depicts unity of person. In fact, more than any other term in the Old Testament, the word *heart* stands for "person," and the New Testament usage is very similar. "Heart" represents one's whole, unified self.

First, then, the heart is the microcosm of the soul or person. It is "the pivotal point" around which all life for humankind revolves, "the hub where all the spokes which hold the wheel of life together converge."[4] Just as the central characteristic of the soul is its integral wholeness, so the heart reflects and represents persons with structural integrity. This integrity can be viewed from many different perspectives, as *lebh,* the Hebrew word for heart, is represented through several different facets of one's person or personality. The whole, then, is viewed through multifaceted lenses. To illustrate, *lebh* is used in the following different ways within the Old Testament:

a. Physical or figurative—29 times
b. Personality, inner life, or character in general—257 times
c. Emotional states of consciousness, found in the widest range—166 times
d. Intellectual activities—204 times
e. Volition or purpose—195 times[5]

The second definition of heart focuses more narrowly, as the heart is seen as the governing, direction-giving center for the various dimensions of personality. In addition to representing the unity and integrity of the soul, the heart also serves as the soul's direction-giver. It is the governing core, the "mission control center" of a person. The heart is at the center, with various other facets of personality circled around it. Note the two sets of arrows in this diagram. One set emerges from the heart, indicating that the heart gives direction to a person through one's personality. The other set of arrows, pointing in from the environment, reflects the input one can gain through social and cultural interaction. These arrows also reflect the interrelatedness of the dimensions of personality. The fact that they stop at the heart illustrates certain truths. First, the heart, rather than the environment or any part of one's personality structure, is the sole source of direction for a person. Second, only the Holy Spirit can penetrate and change the direction of one's heart. Heart-change does not originate with the environment or within oneself; it comes from God.

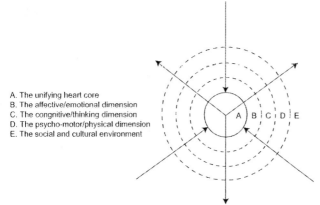

A. The unifying heart core
B. The affective/emotional dimension
C. The congnitive/thinking dimension
D. The psycho-motor/physical dimension
E. The social and cultural environment

Children possess integral personalities

The unifying center of the soul is the heart. The other primary facets or dimensions of personality, illustrated in the diagram above, include the affective or emotional dimension, the cognitive or thinking dimension, and the psychomotor or physical dimension. This latter dimension is the same as the flesh or body described in the chart on the soul.

It should be noted that the psychomotor dimension is placed closest to the social and cultural environment because it is the dimension that can be accessed most easily from forces outside of the person, as behaviorists would attest. On the other hand, the affective dimension is the most difficult to access from the outside; thus, it is placed closest to the heart.

Even though the diagram illustrates each dimension separately, they in fact function in interrelational and interdependent unity. Each dimension of personality continually relates to and depends on the others. Thus, the personalities of children possess integrity.

The physical dimension is the most difficult to accept as a seamless part of an integral whole, because the body appears to be a separate part of a person. This is most apparent at the time of death, when the physical body remains behind as the spirit or soul is ushered to its eternal reward. Once again, we need to return to the chart above to note that the primary definition for body is "the whole person." Rather than possessing a body, a person *is* a body, just as a person *is* a soul. Persons are embodied souls or spirits who cannot be separated into several parts. At the time of death, a dimension of the soul, rather than an outer shell, is left behind. During that intermediate state of existence, the person experiences a temporary lack of wholeness that will be remedied at the second coming of Christ. At that time, persons will become whole once again as their bodies rise from physical death and rejoin their souls.

Children possess integral modes of expression

God created children as images of himself, with unity and integrity of structure. There is a wholeness, a completeness, about them. In Scripture, unity always trumps diversity. (The world, on the other hand, places diversity above unity, the parts over the whole. Fragmentation and individualism reign.)

The creation that God made, however, is complex, diverse, and multifaceted. The kids of the kingdom whom God has created are complex, diverse, and multifaceted as well. That is necessary, for each was created with the other in mind.

Herman Dooyeweerd, a Christian philosopher, developed an approach to viewing the multifaceted ways in which children can respond to creation. These "modes of expression" are a part of the image-bearing structure.

Modes of Expression

Faith
Love
Morality
Creativity
Values
Social interaction
Language
Culture formation
Rationality

Each of the modes or ways of expression reflects something about the nature of God that is found in no other part of creation. It is special for humankind. These modes of expression are listed below in order from the least complex to the most complex. According to Dooyeweerd, these modes of expression form a hierarchy, with each including and building on the previous ones. Each is integral to the next and to the whole. Faith expression, then, incorporates all of the previously listed modes of expression. This hierarchy illustrates, once again, the integrality of structure that exists within image bearers of God. Each of these modes of expression can be developed to show the God-child connection and how parents and teachers can make use of these insights in the nurture of their children.

A rational mode of expression

For something to appear rational, it must make sense. For something to make sense, it needs to be connected. The connection could be to a context or backdrop, or it could be a connection to another part of the whole. In fact, insight or learning takes place only when two or more things are seen in meaningful relationship for the first time. Thus, we exclaim, "Eureka! I've got it!" It's the "aha" moment—something suddenly makes sense. And it makes sense because it has been seen in relationship. This simple but profound concept is the foundation for all learning theory. Show children how things connect, and learning will take place. It is the formula for acquiring new insights. That is one reason an organized, sequential lesson is more effective than one that is disorganized and random.

Rationality is one of God's attributes. Only in him does life make sense. He is a God of relationships and connections, and without relationship there is no meaning. God not only exists in relationships himself, he has formed a creation that is unified and connected. Creation was designed to make sense, to be logical and rational.

As mentioned before, a connection exists between creation and children. For creation to be cared for and developed by God's children, it has to make sense to them. They, in fact, have been created with rational minds that are able to comprehend a rational creation designed by a rational God. They are able to see how it all fits together.

The possession of rational minds is further evidenced by the desire within each person to make sense out of something that doesn't, to bring order out of confusion, if you will. All people have a built-in desire—even a need—to make sense out of their world. If they walk into a chaotic situation, they immediately try to bring some cognitive order out of disorder so that it can make sense to them. Too much confusion can produce a sense of disorientation, a feeling that one may be going crazy. This need for order in our lives, in fact, can be a great motivating tool in the learning process. Lessons can be presented as problems to resolve. Cognitive dissonance, something that doesn't make sense within our minds, can be strategically created by the teacher. The natural human response is to try to solve the problem and to bring order out of dissonance.

God created an organized, unified world, one that is held together relationally by Jesus Christ (Colossians 1:17). God also created image bearers of himself with organized, unified minds, persons who can meaningfully interact with their creation home. Rationality is part of imaging God.

A culture-forming mode of expression

In the beginning of time, God placed humankind in a creation that was full of potential, and he mandated his image bearers to develop the raw material of creation into a culture that would bring honor to his name. In essence, he said, "I am Lord over all things. Develop an earthly civilization that reflects my sovereignty."

To have this Cultural Mandate carried out, God had to equip his image-bearing culture formers with special tools. These tools include a sense of time, a need for a place, and the dignity of a task.

a. A sense of time. Knowing what time it is on "God's redemptive timeline" is important for kingdom advancement on earth. We are told that "when the time had fully come, God sent his Son . . . to redeem those under the law . . ." (Galatians 4:4). New Testament writers often refer to living in the end times, with Christ's second coming being imminent. But even as Christ himself warns that no one except the Father knows the time of his return (Mark 13:32–33), we are also told that "now is the time of God's favor, now is the day of salvation" (2 Corinthians 6:2). And we are admonished elsewhere in Scripture to "number our days" (Psalm 90:12) and to "redeem the time" (Ephesians 5:16, KJV). Time is an important tool in culture-forming kingdom advancement.

The concept of time is important for God's children. They need to understand where they stand on the historical-redemptive timeline. What has taken place? What needs yet to take place? What does it mean to live in two ages, in the "already" and in the "not yet" of the kingdom? They must possess a sense of time if they are to feel the urgency of their kingdom responsibilities.

b. A need for a place. Everyone needs a place. A sense of place provides a sense of belonging and security. Having a place within which to live and from which to work is a human need. We all need a "base of operations." Being homeless or stateless is not a natural state of affairs. Even when the people of Israel were exiled from their homeland, they were told: "Build houses and settle down; plant gardens and eat what they produce. . . . Also, seek the peace and prosperity of the city to which I have carried you into exile. Pray to the LORD for it, because if it prospers, you too will prosper" (Jeremiah 29:5, 7). Each of us has been placed by God in a neighborhood, a community, and a nation, and he tells us to bloom where we have been planted. Until God calls us to move to a different place, as he did with Abraham, the place where we live is the place in which and from which God wants us to advance his kingdom.

Children need to experience a sense of place within the community of believers. The body of Christ should be home to them. They must learn what it means to live in community—with both its joys and sorrows. The Christian home, church, and school are proper nurturing places within which to learn communal living.

c. The dignity of a task. Our God-given task serves as the capstone for cultural formation. The dignity of a task provides us with a reason for living. There is purpose to life. Our contribution makes a difference. It counts for something. God does not need us in the establishment of his kingdom on earth, but God graciously calls us to be the instruments through whom he accomplishes his purposes. Each of us is a necessary part of the body; each of us has a unique portion of the task to fulfill.

The task of kingdom advancement calls for cultural engagement rather than cultural avoidance. The good creation is to be normed and developed by God's image bearers. We are to work toward its sanctification, acknowledging Christ's lordship over all things. Such cultural engagement often calls for countercultural activity, for there is warfare in this world between the kingdom of light and the kingdom of darkness. The battles continue even though Christ has already won the war.

Children must be able to understand their life task within an historical-redemptive context. They should have no doubt about the end toward which they are being nurtured. As culture formers in training, children must have a clear mental picture of the kingdom goals that they are to be busy seeking. The Cultural Mandate, recorded in Genesis 1:26–28 and 2:15, serves as this foundational statement. It gives directions—rule and subdue creation, a creation over which the kids of the kingdom are to function as vice regents in the service of their King.

A lingual mode of expression

Language is a special gift from God to his image bearers, for through it they can communicate and establish meaningful relationships. The two basic relationships of life—those between God and humankind and between humans and other humans—function primarily through lingual communication. God has revealed himself to us through his Word—the creation Word, the inscripturated Word, and the Incarnate Word. We respond to God through words of petition and words of praise, through prayer and song. Language was used to disperse the peoples of the world so that they could become culture formers throughout God's entire creation (Genesis 11:1–9). Language was also used at Pentecost to rejoin the disparate peoples of the world under one kingdom vision (Acts 2:1–13).

Language is a culture-forming tool. Children learn to speak the words they hear. They are spoken to and nurtured through language. They are told that they are loved, and they are corrected and guided—all through language. Children respond through language in both spoken and written form. Children delight in reading language written by others, and they learn through the written word about that which transpired before they were born. Language competency is an important tool for active participation in the kingdom of God.

All schools teach language arts. Kingdom schools, however, should think through their language programs more thoroughly than most, for language is the means by which God's children can communicate their prophetic message. For example, consideration might be given to teaching Hebrew and Greek so that the Bible could be read in its original languages. Modern foreign languages also serve several kingdom purposes: sharing the good news of the kingdom, transforming global culture, ministering to the marginalized and disenfranchised, and simply enjoying exotic places within God's good creation. Other language skills required for kingdom activity include learning how to present the gospel effectively and to listen to others empathically. Kingdom kids also need to know how to respond extemporaneously, to debate the issues of life, and to defend their faith. The list could go on, but the point is that language is a tool that needs to be developed within both the home and school so that God's children can be fully equipped to assume their kingdom responsibilities.

A social mode of expression

Perhaps John Donne said it best: "No man is an island." The reason this statement is so true is that God considered it important that humankind be socially interactive. Once again we can state the truism that "outside of relationship there is no meaning." Our relationship with other people is a vital part of our being fully human.

God's children have been created to be interactive rather than simply active or reactive. The active position, one that emerges from self-centered humanism, views children as being their own gods, morally good and autonomous beings who act on their world. Children are seen as having built-in drives toward self-actualization. They are like flowers; place them in a nurturing environment and watch them bloom—all by themselves. In contrast, the reactive position, one that emerges from behaviorism, states that children have no ability to initiate actions whatsoever; rather, all actions are merely responses to their environment—people or things outside of themselves. Behaviorism doesn't really care about the inner self of children, whatever that may involve. Only the physical or outer self that can respond to environmental stimuli is of any concern. Children, then, are manipulated much like puppets on a string, whose actions are considered emotionless and mindless. In contrast to these extremes, the biblical position is that children are interactive; they can both initiate and respond within their relationships.

The Bible supports the idea that people are meant to be in social relationships. We are told that from the beginning God recognized that it was not good for humankind to be alone. Companions, helpers, and friends were needed. Later, we are told that the second most important thing for us to do, next to loving God, is to love other people. They need our love, and we need their love. Emphasis is also placed on the importance of the church as a community and how it must remain unified. The parts of Christ's body are to mesh in harmonious relationship. Finally, we are told of a banquet in the consummated kingdom that will be a social event that no one will want to miss. Life in both the present and the future has been designed to be very social!

Our "horizontal" relationships are secondary, however, to the "vertical" relationship we have with God. Yes, we worship God as our Creator, Redeemer, and Sustainer. But we also are meant to have a relationship of friendship and fellowship with him. The Westminster Catechism tells us that we are to "enjoy God." Social interactivity with God means that we are to spend time focused on God, speaking to him and allowing him to speak to us. God desires to be included in family activities—birthday parties and anniversary celebrations. He wants to be a part of our recreational activities and our vacations. He enjoys being with us, and he wants us to enjoy being with him. His presence in our daily activities should be as natural and necessary as breathing.

Children need to experience the merits of Christian community from their earliest years. What does "loving others" look like? Who are our neighbors? What responsibilities do we have toward them? How should we deal with people who are different from us? What are proper roles for husbands, wives, parents, and children? What is biblical discipline? What are proper parameters for authority? How can people resolve conflicts in a healthy and respectful manner? Where do individuality and competition fit in this equation? Parents are the ones ultimately accountable to God for providing their children with answers to these questions, but the church and school need to share these responsibilities as well.

Sports, whether they are community- or school-sponsored, often get rapped for their unbridled competitiveness, and, in many cases, justifiably so. But, on the positive side, team sports can teach kingdom-type skills like few other activities. From self-discipline to coordination to cooperation, being a member of a team offers great preparation for working with others. On a team, there are strategies and rules, leaders and followers, others to listen and submit to. Teams experience success and failure, both of which call for godly responses. Involvement in team sports can, indeed, teach children a lot about how the body of Christ functions in harmony as it seeks the prize for which God has called it.

Finally, two learning theory issues that relate to social interaction should be mentioned. First, children learn from each other, sometimes more effectively than from adults. Second, learning is not a spectator sport; it requires interactivity. This includes both initiating action and responding to the actions of others or to the environment. Children have been created with a social mode of expression; consequently, they need to be interactive, both in their learning and in their lives.

A values mode of expression

How we spend our time and money reflects what we value. What we value reflects our belief system. And what we *say* we believe is really of little consequence. Our children understand this quite well. They live in a day and age of rhetoric and image. Words, of which there are many, mean very little to them. For instance, parents may decry the dangers of drugs and yet be personally dependent on alcohol or tobacco. Parents may teach their children that sex outside of marriage is wrong and yet watch television programs and movies, often with their children present, that promote open sex as the norm. Parents may talk about stewardship and the needs of the poor and homeless, but the extra household money goes toward sport utility vehicles, boats, cottages, and other expensive toys. And on it goes. That is truly scary, for most children by age thirty have adopted the value systems of their parents. And the value systems that ultimately are adopted by children are not necessarily the ones that were taught formally; rather, they usually are the ones that were lived-out in front of them.

Christian parents need to be careful in the establishment of their value systems, for the children who have been entrusted to them really belong to

God. It is God's value system, therefore, that must be the plumb line against which to evaluate time used, money spent, and decisions made. Because God's values are not esteemed by much of society, Christian parents have their work cut out for them. Just as the people of Israel wanted a king so that they could be like the surrounding nations, our children tend to see the values of the world as norms for life. The ways of the world are attractive to our children, and they want very much to be like other kids.

Christian teachers also have their work cut out for them, for all education is value-laden. The curriculum, for instance, contains three dimensions: content, skills, *and* values. Every textbook has an author or team of authors with their own value-laden agenda. That agenda may be a very good one from a biblical perspective, or it may reflect a set of values that runs contrary to Scripture. Both teachers and students need to exercise the skill of discernment as they use curriculum materials in their classrooms. Teaching discernment, in fact, is a key facet of kingdom education.

The ultimate answer to the values issue within our homes and schools is commitment by parents, teachers, and children to Jesus Christ and his lordship. It is dying to self and to one's subjective system of values; it is rejecting the values of the world, no matter what the cost. It takes more than self-resolve to do this; it takes the supernatural power of the Holy Spirit. Until our children commit their hearts and lives to Christ and, thus, can personally appropriate the power of his Spirit, parents and teachers must act on their behalf, making many value-laden decisions for them.

A creative mode of expression

Only God truly creates, for he alone forms something from nothing—*ex nihilo*. When image bearers of God create, they really *synthesize,* forming a new product from things that already exist. Most of us freely admit that our ideas are not truly original; rather, they are triggered or stimulated by ideas that we heard somewhere else. We then combine these with other ideas that already exist in our minds and form or synthesize something new. In that process, we are creators who image God.

We are told that God created all kinds of trees that were "pleasing to the eye" (Genesis 2:9). Our eyes attest that the entire creation was designed by a gifted Architect and color-coordinated by an Artist of great skill. Any casual observation or detailed study of the cosmos arrives at the same conclusion, that a Being with great imagination, creativity, and aesthetic sensitivity was responsible. Children, too, in a limited, finite sense, are creators.

Image-bearing children can form unique and "original" products, and they can do that with an aesthetic flair that reflects the ultimate Creator.

Products are formed that are "pleasing to the eye." Children are capable of recognizing, appreciating, and forming products of beauty that express unity and harmony, whether they are in music, movement, literature, art, architecture, or other such fields. Just as rational humankind seeks relationship and order in the world, aesthetic humankind is drawn toward harmony, congruence, and consonance. We are called to give expression to the beauty of God's holiness and his holy array evident within the world and within ourselves.

Parents and teachers need to help children develop their abilities to create. Parents, for example, could replace the gift of a model train that runs mindlessly in a circle or an equally mindless video game with a set of materials that can be creatively formed into new products. Historically, these have been Tinker Toys, Erector Sets, and Legos. Today they may be electronic and include computer chips, but you get the idea. Teachers, too, can, at least on occasion, replace pencil-and-paper tests with the formation of products by students. Science fair projects are a good example. Products could be anything that uses the higher-level thinking skills of application and synthesis. Teaching strategies that use problem-solving and discovery approaches can stimulate the creative juices of children, as well. As image bearers mandated to uncover and develop creation potential for God's glory, children need to be encouraged to develop their creative abilities.

Children also need to have their aesthetic sensibilities cultivated. They are exposed to huge amounts of sheer garbage on the radio, on television, and through videos, and, as the saying goes, "Garbage in, garbage out." Children need to be introduced to that which is noble, right, pure, lovely, admirable, excellent, and praiseworthy (Philippians 4:8). That includes the best in the performing and visual arts, music, and literature. To cultivate children's aesthetic sensibilities, three things must occur. First, parents and teachers need to have strong convictions on this issue. Being countercultural with today's children is not for the faint-hearted. Second, the word *no* must be voiced regarding certain music, posters, magazines, books, television programs, and videos. The garbage must go. Finally, children need to become familiar with the good stuff of God's good creation. There are a zillion ways to do this, but one example comes to mind. In one city where I served as the teaching principal of a small secondary school, the opera company, for a very small ticket price, invited students to dress rehearsals on the evenings before opening nights. The performances were intentionally interrupted at times by the director, who would use those opportunities to explain to the students what was going on. The kids loved attending those performances, and it wouldn't surprise me if some of them became hooked on opera for life. Providing creative and aesthetic opportunities for children takes effort, but it is part of being godly parents and teachers.

A moral mode of expression

Adam and Eve were created as morally responsible agents. Up until the first sin, however, they did not experientially "know" both good and evil and the difference between the two. But they did understand obedience and disobedience, for God had provided them with instructions and the ability to understand. They also had been given the ability to choose, and they freely chose to succumb to temptation and to respond to God in a disobedient and sinful manner. That one act changed everything for all time. Scripture states:

> And the LORD God said, "The man has now become like one of us, knowing good and evil. He must not be allowed to reach out his hand and take from the tree of life and eat, and live forever." (Genesis 3:22)

Generally speaking, all people possess some sense of right and wrong. There is a universal presence of moral standards within the image bearing structure of humankind. Even the unredeemed have "the requirements of the law . . . written on their hearts, their consciences also bearing witness . . ." (Romans 2:15). This is part of God's providential restraint of sin within the world. But, having declared the presence of conscience to be universal, a number of qualifications need to be noted. The conscience can, in fact, be developing, redeemed, underdeveloped, or desensitized. Let's briefly explore each.

a. The *developing conscience* is found in most children during the early years of life before they reach the age of personal understanding. Older persons in their lives, usually parents and teachers, are shaping their consciences. Young children typically respond more to the (anticipated) consequences of their actions than to an internal moral code, called a conscience. But as their mentors teach them right from wrong, both verbally and through imposed consequences, the consciences of children begin to develop. The "rights and wrongs" learned during their formative years often serve as their moral compass during adulthood.

b. The *redeemed conscience* is found within people who have experienced regeneration. Renewed hearts have the laws of God written upon them so that born-again believers can have consciences that are spiritually sensitive and trustworthy. God says. "I will put my law in their minds and write it on their hearts. I will be their God, and they will be my people" (Jeremiah

31:33; Hebrews 8:10). Followers of Christ "know" right from wrong, because it has been branded on their hearts. As they grow in sanctification, the "rightness" (or righteousness) of God is clarified even further.

c. The *undeveloped conscience* is seen in children and adults who failed to bond with another human being, usually their mother, during the first years of their lives.[6] Their emotional and social "umbilical cords" were never connected to the rest of the human race. They experience the ultimate terror of "not being." They do not have a sense of their own existence; there is deadness within them. Persons who experience this attachment disorder can hurt and sometimes kill others without remorse, and they are habitual liars. As the family has fragmented over recent decades, children and young people who for all practical purposes have never developed consciences are becoming increasingly visible within society. After age seven, little hope is given these people. Only the blood of Jesus is able to break these chains of bondage.

d. The *desensitized conscience* develops when people experience the sordid side of life to such a constant and high degree that the tragedies of sin no longer bother them.[7] Police officers, prison guards, and sometimes social workers can fall prey to this. Children and young people who experience or watch sinful conduct also tend to incorporate that conduct into their own lives as something that begins to feel quite natural—they become desensitized to sin. The further people move from the presence and holiness of God, the more easily they can be led by their natural sinful desires. The stark contrast between God's holy light and Satan's sordid darkness becomes dimmed. The Bible explains that their "consciences have been seared as with a hot iron" (1 Timothy 4:2). Hearts can become hardened as with Pharaoh of old (Exodus 8:15, 32; 9:34).

Yet even among thieves there is honor. They may not follow the law of God as they administer their own forms of justice, but they develop their own code of acceptable conduct nonetheless. Jesus alluded to this when he warned: "Do not judge, or you too will be judged. For in the same way you judge others, you will be judged, and with the measure you use, it will be measured to you" (Matthew 7:1–2; Romans 2:1). There is no escape from standards of justice. And there is, indeed, a universal presence of moral standards. All persons are born with an innate sense of right and wrong.

A loving mode of expression

The most important thing that God wants from his children is their total love. The second most important thing he desires is that his children sacrificially love the people with whom they have contact. But for children to be able to express love, they must first experience love. Children are not the source or originators of love. God is. The Bible tells us that God is love (1 John 4:16). The Bible also says that "we love because [God] first loved us" (1 John 4:19). Consequently, for children to be able to develop their potential to love, they must experience the love of God personally. Parents in particular are God's love-surrogates for their children. God's love for children is meant to flow through parents. Parental love, then, is the way in which children begin to experience and understand the love of God. And it is the primary way through which children learn how to love others.

The next question to ask, then, is: What does parental love look like? There are, in fact, a number of things parents (and teachers) can and should do to demonstrate love toward their children.

a. Touch children in a warm, secure, and appropriate manner. The need to be touched is a human need at all age levels, and it begins at the moment of birth. Children need to be held, cuddled, hugged—touched lots. This helps to keep their emotional tanks full, which in turn helps create good feelings about themselves ("I'm loveable!") and good feelings toward others. On the other hand, absence of physical contact or the presence of inappropriate physical contact can damage children.

b. Make eye contact during positive talk. The eyes are called the "avenue to the soul," and having their eyes looked into during "sweet talk" is balm to the inner reaches of children, no matter what their age. Interestingly, the eyes of persons being disciplined usually look downward in shame, and we need not insist on eye contact during those times.

c. Provide times, even moments, of focused one-on-one attention. Essentially, these times tell children that they exist, are noticed, and are important in their own right. They communicate that children are neither numbers nor important solely because they are part of a family or a classroom. Children are most vulnerable in one-on-one relationships (versus triangular or group situations), thus they are most open to receiving love during those times.

d. Address children by their names. Barriers can be overcome and connections established by using children's names when addressing them. This practice establishes a sense of intimacy that comes from the feeling that "This person knows me." An *I-thou* relationship can be established rather than one that is *I-it* in nature.

e. Work and play together. Doing things together tells children that they are important. This is especially appropriate for adolescents, because the focus of the relationship is not on them directly, which they might have difficulty handling, but rather on the activity being shared. Adults who have their acts together can, in this way, provide inner strength to younger people who are in the process of getting their acts together. Call it an "ego transfusion"!

f. Tell children what they are doing right. Parents can tend to function like mechanics with their children—trying to fix them by telling them what they are doing wrong. It is vastly more productive to compliment or commend children when they do something right. A "Good job!" or "I really like that!" goes a long way in helping children feel centered and more self-confident. Such reinforcing statements also motivate children to repeat and expand upon the behavior.

g. Listen to children when they desire to share. Listening includes focused attention and, for the most part, remaining silent ourselves. It's *their* time; let them talk. As children get older, their willingness to share their innermost thoughts tends to lessen; thus, it is even more important with adolescents to "be there" when *they* feel like talking. Anticipate "teachable moments." Riding together in a car at night, for some reason, often produces such moments.

In a newspaper survey of what makes parents cool, teens stated as number one: "They are willing to listen first, and then offer their opinions."[8] This points out the need to hear out our teenagers when we think they have messed up, before we let loose. Speak *with* children in those times of crisis, not *at* them. That involves listening. Also, teens hate to be yelled at. It turns them off and shuts them up. And it's impossible to hear them if they aren't speaking.

h. Discipline in love. Punishment, which is often done in anger, must be replaced with biblical chastening or correction. If our children experience fear when they are being disciplined, our approach to discipline need to be examined. The Bible states: "There is no fear in love. But perfect love drives out fear, because fear has to do with punishment. The one who fears is not made perfect in love" (1 John 4:18). This approach to discipline will be explored more completely in Section Three.

i. Love children unconditionally. Love them for who they are, not for what they do or don't do. This is, perhaps, the most difficult thing for parents to do. Many children feel the love of their parents only when they are well behaved or perform well. When children either fall short or overreach, they too often feel a withholding of love by their parents, whether intended or not. As we have heard many times, we need to hate the sin but love the sinner. This needs to be communicated to our children, perhaps more nonverbally than verbally. They need to know that there is nothing they could do or not do that is so bad that the important people in their lives will ever stop loving them. As God's love-surrogates, parents are able to teach their children a profound object lesson in God's love and grace.

Biblical love is sacrificial action, not a warm feeling. It is also the embodiment of the fruit of the Spirit. Only the Spirit of Christ flowing through children allows them to love in the way that Christ loves. As image bearers of God, children have been created with the potential to love, but they must be nurtured in love and redeemed from above for this love to find full fruition.

A faithful mode of expression

Young children tend to express faith blindly. Such blind faith fits the biblical definition of faith: ". . . being sure of what we hope for and certain of what we do not see" (Hebrews 11:1). Children can exercise faith because they have been created as worshipful beings. They have been designed to place their trust in—to depend on—their Creator. It's part of their structure, their very essence. Faith can be expressed savingly or as an everyday part of life.

Saving faith has three stages, much like the Hebrew concept of knowing: cognitive understanding, heart commitment, and responsible action. Faith must have a knowledge base. Blind faith is not based on ignorance but on that which is not yet tangible or visible. God's children are to be instructed in God's threefold revelation of himself—Jesus Christ, the Bible, and creation. And faith must be exercised. Children, upon reaching their age of understanding, must let go of the personal crutches and support systems on which they typically depend and place their faith in the saving power of Jesus Christ.

God's children are also to exercise day-by-day living faith. Stepping out in faith, testing the promises of God, responding in faith during a crisis or calamity, and walking in faith during lean times are all very real ways through which to teach children how to place themselves into the hands of their Heavenly Father. Within limits, our children should not be sheltered from the problems that we adults face at home or school. Such difficult issues are wonderful on-the-job training for them to learn how the community of faith deals with hard times and scary opportunities. Don't squander these ready-made object lessons. In this way, the faith experience can become very real to children of all ages.

The Original Image—in Responsibilities and Function

God created children as souls with direction-giving hearts, personalities, and various modes of expression. In this way, children reflect or image God ontologically, in being or in essence. They *are* God's images. In some limited way, they look like him.

But there is more to the original image. There is the verblike *doing* dimension. What on earth is humankind to be busy doing with this integral, ontological structure? What is the purpose of life? The Westminster Larger Catechism, in its first question and answer, provides a wonderfully succinct and accurate answer:

> *Question:* What is the chief and highest end of man?
> *Answer:* Man's chief and highest end is to glorify God, and fully to enjoy him forever.[9]

Scripture provides credence to this answer:

> For from him and through him and to him are all things.
> To him be the glory forever! Amen. (Romans 11:36)

> So whether you eat or drink or whatever you do, do it all for the glory of God. (1 Corinthians 10:31)

Humankind was created to glorify God and to enjoy him. These can be done by actively imaging God through *responsibilities* and *by function*.

The responsibilities of an image bearer

Image bearers of God function within three basic relationships—with God, others, and creation. God has provided a responsibility for each of those relationships; both God and others are to be loved, and creation is to be cared for.

Love God

The very best way to bring glory to God and to find enjoyment in him is to obey the first and greatest of all commandments: "Love the Lord your God with all your heart and with all your soul and with all your mind" (Matthew 22:37). God *is* love. Image bearers are to reflect God and love him back. This love is to be holistic, total. God wants all of us, for he is the sovereign Lord. This love is expressed through obedience and fellowship.

As mentioned before, a central theme of Scripture is obedience, for it is the primary mode through which we can demonstrate to God our love for him. Jesus explained the connection between love and obedience:

"If anyone loves me, he will obey my teaching. My father will love him, and we will come to him and make our home with him. He who does not love me will not obey my teaching. These words you hear from me are not my own; they belong to the Father who sent me." (John 14:23–24)

The Apostle John virtually repeats these words of Jesus later in one of his letters: "This is love for God: to obey his commands" (1 John 5:3). Obedience is more than outward conformity, however; it must come from a submitted heart. The words of Samuel to Saul tell us this:

"Does the LORD delight in burnt offerings and sacrifices
  as much as in obeying the voice of the LORD?
To obey is better than sacrifice,
  and to heed is better than the fat of rams." (1 Samuel 15:22)

A teacher of the law, while in conversation with Jesus over which of the commandments is most important, said virtually the same thing:

"To love [God] with all your heart, with all your understanding and with all your strength, and to love your neighbor as yourself is more important than all burnt offerings and sacrifices." (Mark 12:33).

Following the "spirit" of the law is always more important than simply following the "letter" of the law. A broken and contrite heart is always more acceptable to God than outward religious ritual. Obedience that comes from the heart is our way of telling God that we love him.

One of the first things God did with Adam was to introduce the concept of obedience to him:

And the LORD God commanded the man, "You are free to eat from any tree in the garden; but you must not eat from the tree of the knowledge of good and evil, for when you eat of it you will surely die." (Genesis 2:16–17)

From the very beginning, Adam was commanded to obey God, for that was the primary way for him to demonstrate that he loved God with his entire being.

The second part of the Westminster Catechism answer speaks of "enjoying" God. That, too, is an act of love. As is true in any relationship, enjoyment comes through spending time with, fellowshipping with, getting to know, and communicating with another person. The same is true for our relationship with God. It appears that Adam and Eve enjoyed this kind of fellowship with God when they lived in the Garden of Eden. They could recognize "the sound of the LORD God as he was walking in the garden in the cool of the day . . ." (Genesis 3:8). Relationship carries with it these types of responsibilities. Communing with our Heavenly Father through prayer, Bible reading, meditation, quiet times, worship, and walks in the woods enhances the enjoyment and depth of the relationship. Parents and teachers need to help children discover this enjoyment of the relationship with the personal and covenanting God.

Love others

The primary responsibility for image bearers in their relationship with others is to love, for the second greatest commandment is to "Love your neighbor as yourself" (Matthew 22:39). The Greek word for love that is used here, *agapao,* calls more for an action than for an expression of emotion or affection, which would be *phileo.* Agape love is sacrificial and unconditional in nature. It is doing righteousness—what is right—for another. It is relational obedience, whether one feels like it or not. In answer to the "Who is my neighbor?" question, Jesus told the Parable of the Good Samaritan (Luke 10:25–37). It is obvious from this parable that neighbors are any persons of need with whom we have contact.

The importance to God of loving relationships can be seen already in the first chapter of Genesis. As mentioned, this is first evidenced in the cooperative work of the Trinity in the creation act: As the Spirit of God hovered, God the Father spoke Jesus the Word and creation was. Then God said, "Let *us* make man in *our* image" (Genesis 1:26, emphasis mine). The Godhead itself is relational.

The second chapter of Genesis begins using the covenantal name for God—the LORD God, or *Yahweh.* From the beginning, God has been a God of covenantal relationship with his chosen people.

As the creation saga unfolded, God saw something that was "not good." He said, "It is not good for the man to be alone" (Genesis 2:18). From Adam's rib, God created a complementary partner, one who was whole in her own right, yet Adam's other half. The Covenant of Relationship was established by God as an antidote to aloneness: "*For this reason* a man will leave his father and mother and be united to his wife, and they will become one flesh" (Genesis 2:24, emphasis mine). Loving relationships have always been a part of God's way of doing things.

One of the first questions asked of God at the dawn of history was, "Am I my brother's keeper?" (Genesis 4:9). Throughout the pages of Scripture, God responds with an emphatic "Yes!" He tells his children to love other images bearers with sacrificial actions.

Since "God is love" (1 John 4:16), children are to image God's love to their neighbors—people who need that love. Next to loving God totally, the most important thing children can do is love other people as much as they love themselves. The Bible mandates love for family members, for church members, and even for one's enemies. The Bible is so full of the love message that it is impossible to isolate the key references, for the entire Bible is a book about love and relationship.

Exercise dominion

The third basic relationship that image bearers have is with the rest of creation. God provided the responsibility within that relationship to Adam and Eve:

> Then God said, "Let us make man in our image, in our likeness, and let them rule over the fish of the sea and the birds of the air, over the livestock, over all the earth, over the livestock, over all the earth, and over all the creatures that move along the ground."
>
> So God created man in his own image,
>> in the image of God he created him;
>> male and female he created them.
>
> God blessed them and said to them, "Be fruitful and increase in number; fill the earth and subdue it. Rule over the fish of the sea and the birds of the air and over every living creature that moves on the ground."
>
> . . . The LORD God took the man and put him in the Garden of Eden to work it and take care of it. (Genesis 1:26–28; 2:15)

God is the sovereign Creator of and Ruler over the universe. When he had finished forming the skies, the seas, the land, and the life forms that inhabit them, God formed persons who imaged himself who would rule and create in their own right. These human creatures were God's final creative act; they were the crown, or pinnacle, of his creation. The psalmist was awestruck as he contemplated this:

> When I consider your heavens, the work of your fingers,
>> the moon and the stars, which you have set in place,
> what is man that you are mindful of him,
>> the son of man that you care for him?
> You made him a little lower than the heavenly beings
>> and crowned him with glory and honor.
> You made him ruler over the works of your hands;
>> you put everything under his feet:
> all flocks and herds, and the beasts of the field,
>> the birds of the air, and the fish of the sea,
>> all that swim the paths of the seas. (Psalm 8:3–8)

The task assigned to humankind at the dawn of creation has been called the Creation Mandate, but because it really applies to more than just the natural world, it has been expanded into a Cultural Mandate. This mandate addresses God's human creations as his vice regents, those who rule in his name. It deals with two aspects of stewardship: the caring for creation—conserving, protecting, and nurturing it—and the development of creation—uncovering the secrets implanted by God in the beginning.

Today, the two sides of this mandate sometimes produce conflict, as conservationists battle developers. On one extreme, creation can be worshiped in a pantheistic manner, as in some Eastern and animistic religions. On the other extreme, creation can be raped for personal profit and greed. Neither extreme is acceptable, but as we can see in the original mandate, both sides are legitimate. Their differences need to be reconciled in a harmonious, balanced manner. The creation is to be served for the glory of God and the welfare of humankind.

Years ago, Dutch statesman-theologian Abraham Kuyper uttered the now-famous words: "There is not a square inch in the whole domain of our human existence over which Christ, who is Sovereign over *all*, does not cry: 'Mine!'"[10] That statement provides a wonderful framework for the formal education of God's children. In other words, all of creation belongs to God, and God's royal offspring are to be equipped formally to rule over his creation in his name. Education is more than learning how to make a living; it is learning how to bring glory to God through ruling as his imagers over his earthly kingdom.

The concept of *culture*, as in Cultural Mandate, is quite inclusive. Yes, overseeing the physical world of "rocks and stars" and the natural world of plants, birds, and animals is a part of it. Definitely, we are to take care of the physical and natural world and develop its resources. But the original mandate must also be applied today to areas as diverse as business and politics on one hand and the fine and performing arts on the other. In fact, the entire curriculums of schools fall under this mandate, for each discipline possesses its own culture-forming dimension. We must take every thought in every subject "captive . . . to make it obedient to Christ" (2 Corinthians 10:5).

The Cultural Mandate is to be carried out with a certain creative flair. God provided the raw materials and then turned us loose to see what we could produce as image-bearing creators. He wants us to find and uncover the potential that he has implanted within creation. He tells us to "Go for it! See what you can do. Be creative. The sky's the limit!" He tells us to build beautiful buildings that are pleasing to the eye. But he cautions us against building "towers of Babel" for our own purposes. They must bring glory to God and serve humankind in his name. Both parents and teachers should allow creativity in the responses and products of their children, for they have been called to image a creative God.

The functions of an image bearer

Function can be described in two ways. First, it can refer to a position or office. Second, it can describe what one does within that position or office. The Bible lists three image-bearing offices, each with a particular function: prophets who exercise true knowledge, priests who exercise true holiness, and kings who exercise true righteousness.

Prophets, with true knowledge

Today, prophets are often thought of as persons who foretell future events. In the Bible, however, prophets were God's spokespersons. They relayed messages from God to a particular audience, often a king or an entire nation. Sometimes these messages included a forecast of what would be happening, but not always. The emphasis was more on communicating God's revealed truth to others. In doing so, the prophetic function has several characteristics.

First, prophets communicate the message that God has revealed to them, not their own thoughts. Prophetic messages are revelations from God, thus they are true, or truthful knowledge. Scripture relates this form of knowledge to image bearing:

> . . . you have taken off your old self with its practices and have put on the new self, which is being renewed in knowledge in the image of its Creator. (Colossians 3:9–10)

Second, prophets must know the truth personally before they can communicate the truth to others. To know Jesus and to hear the voice of the Holy Spirit, one must be regenerated. To know what God is saying through his Word and his world, one must be literate in both. That speaks powerfully for the need for biblically based education. One cannot possess a prophetic voice unless one personally knows the truth.

Third, prophets are controlled by the truth that they are communicating. They have personally submitted in obedience to the claims of their truthful message. Thus, they exhibit integrity of person.

Fourth, prophets "know" and "speak" the truth with their entire beings. God's truth is not meant to be communicated in solely a cognitive manner. Biblical knowing is more than head knowledge; it is holistic. Persons who image God face him, walk toward him, spend time in his presence, commune and fellowship with him; consequently, they will radiate his likeness no matter where they are or what they are doing. Their presence in the room, in the group, or on the team will be noticed as much for who they are and how they conduct themselves as for what they say.

Priests, with true holiness

The function of the priest within the original image was relational. Adam and Eve "were holy as God was holy," to paraphrase Peter's words,[11] because they were in constant and intimate fellowship with God. There were no barriers, no gulf between them, as would later be the case. They were drawn toward God through his irresistible love, and the closer they got, the more of his holiness they experienced.

The Hebrew word *shalom* describes the product of true holiness: God's perfect peace. This peace is evidenced when relationships are right, when connections are made, when genuine unity exists. It is harmony, consonance, and congruity. This type of language obviously speaks to human relationships, but it also speaks to all other aspects of society and culture. The more that the sovereign God is rightly acknowledged as Lord of every thought, word, action, and product—holiness in action—the greater the sense of *shalom,* of being one with God in his person and purposes. Scripture tells us to "put on the new self, created to be like God in true . . . holiness" (Ephesians 4:24).

Kings, with true righteousness

What did it mean to rule in the pre-Fall Garden of Eden? Adam's first act of dominion was to name the animals (Genesis 2:19–20). In ancient times, to name something or someone implied having dominion or ownership. The kingly function applies to those situations in which one is in charge of something or someone. Being "in charge" means having "the right to act." The person in authority who seeks to image or reflect the way God does things will seek to exercise true righteousness—doing the right thing according to God's standards, for they have been "created to be like God in true righteousness . . ." (Ephesians 4:24).

Ruling with righteousness comes from a "servant's heart." Yes, one must lead and show initiative. But a righteous leader always seeks the welfare of others in the process. Leadership of people always begins with the command to love. Ruling over creation maintains the delicate balance between the stewardly care and assertive development of creation. We are mandated to conserve, protect, and nurture, while at the same time uncovering the secrets God implanted. And all is to be done rightly, for that is what it means to image God as kings.

Chapter Conclusions

In the beginning, God created humankind in his own image, both male and female. And he declared his creations to be very good. The original image, the image before the Fall, was, indeed, very good in every respect.

God's images can rightly be viewed from two perspectives—in their *beings* and in their *doings*. The former has to do with their structure; the latter has to do with their responsibilities and functions.

In structure, the operative word is integrity; there is soundness, wholeness, in their beings, for in Christ there is divine unity. Consequently, the children we parent and teach are integral souls who are provided moral direction by integral hearts. They possess integral personalities that express themselves though a variety of integral modes. All children possess rational, culture-forming, lingual, social, values, creative, moral, loving, and faithful modes of expression that reflect their Creator.

The responsibilities of image bearers are threefold, corresponding to the three relationships within which they exist. They are to love God totally, through obedience and fellowship. They are to love their neighbors as much as they love themselves. And they are to exercise dominion over creation as God's vice regents.

The offices and functions of image bearers are threefold as well: as prophets who exercise true knowledge; as priests who exercise true holiness; and as kings who exercise true righteousness.

The original images of God were very good because their hearts, their moral direction-giving compasses, were committed to loving God by obeying and enjoying him. That was soon to change, however, as Adam and Eve broke faith with the One whom they were created to image.

Chapter 3: Further Thoughts to Consider

1. What biblical evidence can you cite to support the view that image bearing describes how we "look like" God in certain finite ways? That image bearing describes how we "act like" God in certain finite ways?

2. Did the illustration of the house built by Habitat for Humanity help you to understand structure, function, and direction in creation? If not, what in particular do you not understand?

3. In what ways does the integrity of structure in creation reflect the nature of God?

4. Why is it important for humankind to be viewed as a unity rather than as a dichotomy or trichotomy?

5. Why does God want our hearts?

6. Why would it be helpful for a parent or teacher to understand the nine modes of expression that each child possesses?

7. In what ways are values a part of every classroom?

8. What might hinder parents and teachers from carrying out certain of the suggestions listed under the loving mode of expression?

9. Can the responsibilities of an image bearer rightly be reduced to three? Can you think of responsibilities that might not fit under the three listed?

10. List activities that children could do as twenty-first-century prophets, priests, and kings.

Chapter 3: Notes and References

1. One other reference to image bearing is found in 1 Corinthians 11:7, where it reads, " . . . he is the image and glory of God."
2. *Institutes of the Christian Religion.* Book I, chapter 1, section 1. (Philadelphia: Westminster, 1960).
3. A. A. Hoekema wrote about structure and function on pp. 68–73 of his book *Created in God's Image* (Grand Rapids, MI: Eerdmans, 1986), and Albert M. Wolters wrote about structure and direction on pp. 72ff of his book *Creation Regained* (Grand Rapids, MI: Eerdmans, 1985).
4. G. J. Spykman, *Reformational Theology: A New Paradigm for Doing Dogmatics* (Grand Rapids, MI: Eerdmans, 1992), 220.
5. J. D. Douglas, *The New Bible Dictionary* (Grand Rapids, MI: Eerdmans, 1962).
6. For additional information on this topic, read *High Risk: Children Without a Conscience,* by K. Magid and C. McKelvey (New York: Bantam Books, 1987), and *Lost Boys: Why Our Sons Turn Violent and How We Can Save Them,* by J. Garbarino (New York: The Free Press, 1999).
7. Two articles that deal with violent tendencies within children are: D. Grossman, "Trained to Kill," *Christianity Today* (August 10, 1998), 31–39, and James Dobson, "Dr. Dobson's Solid Answers," *Focus on the Family* (September 1998), 5.
8. L. O'Connel, "What Makes Parents Cool," *Des Moines Sunday Register* (July 9, 1995), 3E. Other qualities listed are: respect for their child's friends; personalized rules; involvement in school functions; gender-blind curfews; willingness to apologize; a sense of humor.
9. *The Westminster Larger Catechism:* Question & Answer 1. (Richmond, VA: The Board of Christian Education, The Presbyterian Church in the United States, 1969).
10. Abraham Kuyper, "Sphere Sovereignty," in *Abraham Kuyper: A Centennial Reader,* ed. James D. Bratt (Grand Rapids: Eerdmans, 1998), 488.
11. 1 Peter 1:16.

Chapter 4

IMAGE BEARING AFTER THE FALL: THE PROFANED IMAGE

Introduction

God created Adam and Eve in his image. He looked at the products of his hands and declared them to be "very good." Indeed, God's original image was good in all respects.

God's desire for his image bearers was that they would respond to his love for them with a total love of their own. This love was to be evidenced through obedience and fellowship. It was also to be a product of their own free will, so Adam and Eve were given a choice—a test, if you will.

> And the LORD God made all kinds of trees grow out of the ground—trees that were pleasing to the eye and good for food. In the middle of the garden were the tree of life and the tree of the knowledge of good and evil. . . . And the LORD God commanded the man, "You are free to eat from any tree in the garden; but you must not eat from the tree of the knowledge of good and evil, for when you eat of it you will surely die." (Genesis 2:9, 16–17)

Adam and Eve failed the test. They freely chose to disobey God's command, and, when they did, everything changed.

Death replaced life after the Fall

One result of Adam and Eve's sin was a loss of life, the life that can be found only in God. They had been warned that "when you eat of [the tree] you will surely die" (Genesis 2:17). This spiritual death is an existence that is separate, apart from God, for all eternity. More than physical life or death is at stake here. Life in God is abundant, meaningful, fulfilling. It is living beyond our dreams, in God's perfect peace, or *shalom*. It is *really* living. Death apart from God is quite the opposite.

Moses captured this stark contrast between life and death as he admonished the people of Israel before they entered the land promised to them.

> See, I set before you today life and prosperity, death and destruction. For I command you today to love the LORD your God, to walk in his ways, and to keep his commands, decrees, and laws; then you will live and increase, and the LORD your God will bless you in the land you are entering to possess.
>
> But if your heart turns away and you are not obedient, and if you are drawn away to bow down to other gods and worship them, I declare to you this day that you will certainly be destroyed. You will not live long in the land you are crossing the Jordan to enter and possess.
>
> This day I call heaven and earth as witnesses against you that I have set before you life and death, blessings and curses. Now choose life, so that you and your children may live and that you may love the LORD your God, listen to his voice, and hold fast to him. For the LORD is your life, and he will give you many years in the land he swore to give to your fathers, Abraham, Isaac and Jacob. (Deuteronomy 30:15–20)

The words *for the LORD is your life* really say it all. Years later, Jesus would state, "*I* am . . . the life" (John 11:25). And he said that if we would love God and our neighbor, we will inherit eternal life and "live" (Luke 10:25–28). Without God, without Jesus, there is no life, only death.

Images of God became profaned by sin

A second result of the Fall was that the original "very good" images of God became profaned. Adam and Eve chose to believe the lie of the great deceiver rather than the truth of God, and, in so doing, they turned away from God and began walking in their own ways toward destruction. The moral direction of their hearts reversed itself. No longer did they face God and reflect his glory. They turned their backs on him in rebellion and idolatry. The Fall profoundly affected the images of God.

In Genesis 3 we read about humankind's fall into sin and the original image becoming a profaned image. The sacred, holy original image was desecrated, no longer directed toward service to and worship of God. Two of the four references to image bearing found in Scripture reflect this profaned state. One speaks of murdering an image of God, the other of slandering people made in God's likeness.

> "Whoever sheds the blood of man, by man shall his blood be shed;
> for in the image of God has God made man." (Genesis 9:6)

> With the tongue we praise our Lord and Father, and with it we curse men, who have been made in God's likeness. (James 3:9)

The James passage has particular significance, because it, in effect, states that even after the Fall, humankind continues to bear the image of God. Theology professor Anthony Hoekema, after a thorough analysis of this text in the original Greek, concludes the following:

> This passage does not tell us exactly in what the likeness to God consists. Neither does it tell us what man's fall into sin has done to that likeness or what happens to that likeness when God by his Spirit recreates us in his image. But what the passage does say with the utmost clarity is that, whatever the Fall has done to the image of God in man, it has not totally obliterated that image. The passage would be completely pointless if fallen man were not still, in a very important sense, a being who bears and reflects a likeness to God—a being who is still, in distinction from all other creatures, an image-bearer of God.[1]

Indeed, even after the Fall, the profaned image continued to bear a semblance of its Creator. This chapter deals with both the disastrous effect the Fall had on this image and how the grace of God is evident in its preservation.

The Antithesis and Spiritual Warfare

Before examining the state of image bearing after the Fall, a context needs to be developed, for what took place at the time of the Fall is much larger than image bearers or even the creation itself. Charles Colson wrote a book several years ago titled *Kingdoms in Conflict*.[2] The kingdoms he referred to are God's kingdom of light and Satan's kingdom of darkness. This conflict began in the heavenlies, but it was taken to planet Earth shortly after the creation of our first parents. This spiritual warfare has been referred to by some as the "antithesis." Since the Fall, this antithesis, the struggle between the forces of good and evil, has been a part of every person, of every group of people, and of every institution. It is spiritual warfare in the fullest sense.

Spiritual warfare was brought home to me in a very real way several years ago at a school in which I was serving as principal.

> *The Christian school, operated by a Pentecostal church, was located on the edge of a large city in the midwestern United States. Many of the students were from the city proper and from broken and abusive homes. When the doors opened for the children each morning, I could almost feel spirits of evil entering with them—not because of the kids, but because of the neighborhoods and homes they had left behind earlier that morning.*

I wasn't the only person to feel the presence and threat of evil forces. The board president did, too. He and his wife came to the school early each morning, before teachers and students arrived, and prayed at the door of each classroom. They claimed each room daily for Christ, rebuking the evil one as Pentecostals truly can.

I had never been in a school like this, one in which evil seemed to have such a presence and influence. Sometimes during the school day chaos and mischief would be so prevalent that I would send a note to the teachers to take a moment to pray for God's hedge of protection. There was no doubt in my mind that the students in that school were targets of the evil one. Those who had once been in his grasp were now in the care of Christ followers, and he didn't like it.

Spiritual warfare is real. Not to believe this or not to take it seriously is to play into the hands of the evil one. Many Christians and Christian organizations have been neutralized by the enemy because spiritual warfare was seen as the figment of radical imaginations. Yet, the Bible speaks of a spirit world in which conflict is present. Two illustrations from the Old Testament come to mind. One is the time when the eyes of Elisha's servant were opened so that he could see the armies of heaven protecting them.[3] The other took place in the time of Daniel when an angel appeared to him and apologized for being late, for he had been "resisted" and "detained" by a demon for twenty-one days, and the archangel Michael had to rescue him.[4] In the New Testament, we read many accounts of Jesus confronting demons and even Satan himself. The hosts of darkness seemed to congregate in Palestine during the time of Jesus' ministry, for they knew that they were in for the battle of their lives. The Apostles Peter and Paul both took spiritual warfare seriously as well. Peter warned about the devil who "prowls around like a roaring lion looking for someone to devour" (1 Peter 5:8). And Paul issued a call to arms, recorded in Ephesians:

Finally, be strong in the Lord and in his mighty power. Put on the full armor of God so that you can take your stand against the devil's schemes. For our struggle is not against flesh and blood, but against the rulers, against the authorities, against the powers of this dark world and against the spiritual forces of evil in the heavenly realms. Therefore put on the full armor of God so that when the day of evil comes, you may be able to stand your ground, and after you have done everything, to stand. Stand firm then, with the belt of truth buckled around your waist, with the breastplate of righteousness in place, and with your feet fitted with the readiness that comes from the gospel of peace. In addition to all this, take up the shield of faith, with which you can extinguish all the flaming arrows of the evil one. Take the helmet of salvation and the sword of the Spirit, which is the word of God. And pray in the Spirit on all occasions with all kinds of prayers and requests. With this in mind, be alert and always keep on praying for all the saints. (Ephesians 6: 10–18)

God's children are primary targets of the evil one, for they are the future leaders of Christ's militant church. Christian schools, in particular, if they are rightly seen as "boot camps for kingdom training" rather than as "cities of refuge from the world," are places that should expect spiritual warfare. Not to experience such warfare is a sign that the enemy has yet to be engaged and that there needs to be increased seriousness of purpose exhibited. For the resistance of the evil one is felt most keenly when Christ's redemptive powers are vigorously applied in offensive warfare—attacking Satan's strongholds. The lack of warfare may signal that no threat has been perceived.

Even though we speak of spiritual warfare as something that is ongoing, the war between the kingdom of light and the kingdom of darkness has already been won; it is a *fait accompli*. The perfect life, atoning death, and victorious resurrection of Jesus Christ were decisive in the ultimate defeat of Satan and his kingdom. It is much like the landing on the beaches of Normandy in France on D-Day during World War II. When Allied forces established their beachhead on the European mainland, the war was, in effect, won. It was simply a matter of time and a mopping-up exercise before the Axis forces would surrender on V-E Day, a year later. But just as the battles continued and lives were lost after D-Day, so the spiritual battles continue today with casualties. It is not a time to relax and lay down one's arms.

The Profaned Image—in Direction

With the Fall, sin profaned the images of God and altered their directional stance. To the degree that sin profanes things, it makes them secular, or worldly. God's human creations, the people who were designed to image him, became secularized with their fall into sin. To be profane is to be unholy or unsanctified, no longer consecrated to God's purposes. After the Fall, humankind no longer reflected God directionally in responsive obedience.

For us to understand the ways in which the Fall affected the structure and functions of image bearers, we must begin with the moral direction taken by hearts because of the Fall. The question about the moral nature of humankind is one that has been debated at great length by scholars and one about which there is little agreement.

Are children born morally good, bad, or neutral?

Imagine that you are attending class in a secular university, and the professor poses the question: "Do you believe that children are born morally good, bad, or neutral?" What responses might there be? First, there probably wouldn't be very many responses, for this is an issue that few university students are thinking about, especially in a postmodern world. In fact, the issue of the moral nature of children is virtually non-existent in any of their textbooks. So the classroom may be *very* quiet. But, perhaps, a student who believes that tiny babies are innocent bundles of joy might venture that they are born morally good. After all, they haven't had time to do anything bad yet. Right? This suggestion, however, causes you concern, for you have been taught that children are conceived and born in sin. But does that make them bad? What does *bad* mean? Since you are unsure of your position, you don't say anything. Finally, the professor breaks the silence and explains that, while it is true that there are a few romantic naturalists who believe that children are morally good, most people who think about such things have concluded that children are morally neutral at birth—sort of blank moral slates. The professor quickly adds, however, that there are persons who take exception to this view, such as Calvinists, who believe in total depravity, and fundamentalist Christians, who teach that children enter this world as sinners because of original sin. You want to respond to that last remark, but now you are fearful that you will sound *both* dumb *and* radical. So you say nothing, and this one "religious" discussion in your three years of secular graduate studies comes to a whimpering conclusion.

That scenario actually took place in one of my doctoral classes. Two things about it have bothered me ever since. One was the stark emptiness and bankruptcy of the secular education I received. This, in fact, *was* the only "religious" discussion in my entire program. The very foundation of my belief system was virtually never dealt with. That is both sad and scary. The other was that I didn't have my act together enough to provide a reasonable response to the professor's question. I have, however, spent a great amount of time thinking about such issues ever since! The question at least got me thinking.

I am certain that there must be secular textbooks that deal with the moral nature of children, but so far I have come across only one—*Learning Theories for Teachers,* by Bigge and Shermis. Following are their definitions of *bad, good,* and *neutral.*

If we assume people's moral nature to be innately bad, then we can expect nothing good from them. If left to themselves, their badness will naturally unfold; persons will show no traits other than bad ones. Conversely, if we assume that people are innately good, then unless they are corrupted by some outside force, everything that comes from them will be good. Assumed neutrality in people's basic moral nature simply means that by nature they are neither bad nor good but merely "potential" in a way that has no connection with innate badness or goodness.[5]

After having read these three options, which one would you choose? Are children morally good, bad, or neutral? Personally, I don't care for any of the options. They are too limited in scope. For instance, an argument could be made that children are good—at least in structure. We also know that children are sinners; so, from that vantage point, they could be considered bad. Finally, until children reach their ages of moral understanding and accountability, it might be argued that there are certain aspects of "neutrality" about their moral status. This issue then, in one sense, is very complex. But in the ultimate sense, it is really quite simple: All children are born with sinful natures. Let's explore now what that means.

Children are born with sinful natures

Early in the history of humankind, God mused to himself that "every inclination of [man's] heart is evil from childhood" (Genesis 8:21). Later, David wrote, "Surely I have been a sinner from birth, sinful from the time my mother conceived me" (Psalm 51:5; also see Psalm 58:3). Children do not become sinners because they sin; rather, children sin because they are born sinners. By nature, the hearts of children are inclined toward sin.

The sinful nature of the hearts of children at conception or birth is a matter of direction. Before the Fall, the hearts of humankind were directed *by* God and, consequently, were directed *toward* God. Post-Fall hearts are directed by sinful natures. Sinful hearts, in turn, negatively influence or color the thoughts, words, and actions of all people. Because their heart-direction is inward rather than upward, people tend by nature to be self-centered, rebellious, and disobedient—from earliest childhood.

This sinful nature originated with Adam; thus, we have the term *original sin*. The Bible says, ". . . sin entered the world through one man, and death through sin, and in this way death came to all men. . . . The result of one trespass was condemnation for all men. . . . Through the disobedience of the one man the many were made sinners . . ." (Romans 5:12,

18, 19). Because, many years ago, Adam chose to disobey God's command, every child born today possesses a sinful moral nature—a heart that is directed by sinful inclinations. That may sound harsh, but that's what the Bible says.

The Profaned Image—in Structure

Two seemingly contradictory things can be said about image-bearing structure after the Fall: one, it remains a part of God's "good" creation; and, two, it is comprehensively profaned. To properly understand both of these points, one must understand the nature of sin.

Sin is a parasite

Return for a moment to the description of image-bearing structure provided in the last chapter. Structure refers to one's essence or being. This structure is both sound in its completeness and integral in its wholeness. In Christ, all structure (i.e., reality) is "held together." Within image bearers, this structure consists of an integral soul or person with a personality and a direction-giving heart. Also included are attributes or modes of expression that, in a limited way, reflect the likeness of God. Before the Fall, God declared the creation of his images to be "very good." After the Fall, the same can be said, at least in part, for structurewise the images of God continue to be a part of God's good creation. Every aspect of image-bearing structure listed in the last chapter is as true about persons after the Fall as it was true before the Fall. How can that be? The answer lies in the nature of sin. It is parasitic.

Sin feeds off of the unchanging structure of God's good creation. Sin infects, enslaves, taints, perverts, twists, distorts, warps, misuses, and exploits. As a parasite, sin needs structure, but it remains separate from structure. It is not and cannot become a part of the creation structure itself.

But sin does *affect* structure. It promotes abnormality. Things aren't the way they're supposed to be. They don't function the way they were designed to function. Neal Plantinga wrote, ". . . sin is . . . an uninvited guest that keeps tapping its host for sustenance. Nothing about sin is its own; all its power, persistence, and plausibility are stolen goods. Sin is not really an entity but a spoiler of entities, not an organism but a leech on organisms. Sin does not build shalom; it vandalizes it."[6]

Sin, then, causes creation structure to be directed away from God. Rather than becoming sanctified—developed and used for God's glory—the essence of image bearers has become profaned and per-verted. A Creator-creature disconnect has occurred. Death and decay have become commonplace. People don't function the way they should. Yet sin never *becomes* structure, and structure cannot be destroyed by sin. People remain image bearers with personalities and direction-giving hearts. They remain rational, social, and creative. Image bearers of God are not throwaways. They remain "good"—meaning structurally sound, with integrity—and redeemable.

Sin is comprehensive and all-pervasive

From birth onward, everyone is a sinner and everyone sins. The Bible says that "all have sinned and fall short of the glory of God" (Romans 3:23). As far as sinfulness is concerned, there are no good guys and bad guys, only the bad—the fallen. Everyone deserves eternal death. Sin is comprehensive.

Some would limit the effects of sin to human beings, but when sin entered the world, every part of society, culture, and creation was affected. This was made evident as God cursed the ground that Adam tilled:

> "Cursed is the ground because of you;
>> through painful toil you will eat of it
>> all the days of your life.
> It will produce thorns and thistles for you. . . ." (Genesis 3:17–18)

The Apostle Paul further explains the effect of sin on creation in his letter to the Roman church:

> The creation waits in eager expectation for the sons of God to be revealed. For the creation was subjected to frustration, not by its own choice, but by the will of the one who subjected it, in hope that the creation itself will be liberated from its bondage to decay and brought into the glorious freedom of the children of God.
>
> We know that the whole creation has been groaning as in the pains of childbirth right up to the present time. (Romans 8:19–22)

The effects of sin are comprehensive, and they are all-pervasive as well. There is not one part of our beings (i.e., structures) that is not infected and affected. Every thought, word, and deed contains the taint of sin, for the heart is the source of our wills, and our hearts are "deceitful above all things and beyond cure" (Jeremiah 17:9). Jesus said that "out of the heart come evil thoughts, murder, adultery, sexual immorality, theft, false testimony, slander" (Matthew 15:19). The heart, as the control center of our beings, directs us toward rebellion and idolatry—and, ultimately, to self-destruction.

Not only have the hearts of image bearers been affected by the ravages of sin, other dimensions of our beings have been profaned as well. The Fall has polluted our thinking. It has ravaged our bodies. It has corrupted our emotions. Our very personalities are those of sinners. We misuse language and abuse social relationships. Our values and morals are self-serving. We love things and use people. We have "exchanged the truth of God for a lie, and worshiped and served created things rather than the Creator" (Romans 1:25). Indeed, sin is all-pervasive.

Profaned structure—a summary

Several years ago, a church bus full of children and young people from Louisville, Kentucky, was returning home after a daylong outing at Kings Island, a theme park near Cincinnati, Ohio. While on an interstate highway in Kentucky, a pickup truck, traveling at a high rate of speed on the wrong side of the highway, crashed head-on into the bus, killing many of its occupants. The antinormative aspect of this horrible tragedy had little to do with the structure or essence of the pickup truck. The truck was traveling down the highway in the manner of a pickup truck. It was doing what trucks do. The problem lay with the direction in which it was heading.

In the beginning, God created a world that was declared "very good" by him. The creation was "good" in its structure, its direction, and its functioning. The structure of creation was "top of the line," for its designer and creator was God, and its internal integrity was guaranteed through the presence of Jesus Christ. In essence, creation was good! It was also heading in the right direction. Consequently, it was functioning within the purpose for which it had been formed.

Part of this creation consisted of human beings made in God's image. They, too, were "very good" in their structure and in their direction. The integrity of their structure was evident in their unified souls and in their unifying hearts. They were integral beings. In this way, they were the image or likeness of God, who is the ultimate in integrity. Essentially, humankind, in a finite way, possessed many features that resembled those of God. But these bearers of God's structural image also imaged God in their direction. Because they were facing and reflecting God, they obediently functioned within the roles and relationships for which they had been created.

When sin entered the world, the structure of creation and of humankind remained intact. The creation that God had declared "good," remained God's good creation, even following the Fall. To return to the graphic analogy above, the pickup truck could easily have passed a safety test the morning of the accident. It could have been declared to have been in "good" condition. But the sin of a driver under the influence of alcohol changed everything. The truck was headed in the wrong direction, and it no longer was functioning within its intended purpose. Rather than being used for pleasure or business, the truck became an instrument of death and suffering. Sin has the same corrupting effect on that which God has declared to be good.

Sin is a parasite—alien to the good creation, not a part of it. Sin and its effects are comprehensive and radical, thoroughly affecting every part of humankind, society, culture, and the natural world. But the creation remained "good" in its essence or structure, even after the Fall. Its direction was affected; things no longer functioned in the way intended. Normative use became misuse and abuse. Abnormativity became the norm. What was abnormal in the eyes of God became normal in the eyes of humankind. But God's preserving presence and redemptive power continued to be manifested. Quoting Plantinga once again, ". . . sin is a fearfully powerful spoiler of the good, but it cannot finally overpower either the original or renewed project of God in the world."[7]

The Profaned Image—in Responsibilities and Function

Image-bearing responsibilities after the Fall

Some things changed with humankind's fall into sin, and some things didn't. The structure of God's image bearers remained sound or "good," even though the parasitic appetite of sin comprehensively ravaged it. The responsibilities given to image bearers by God did not change, either. The purpose for humankind's existence was not altered. God's mandate for his image bearers continued to be to bring glory to his name. That would continue to be accomplished through heartfelt obedience to the three primary commands of life: loving God, loving one's neighbor, and having dominion over the earth and its creatures. What *had* changed was the ability to keep these commands. People couldn't. They were no longer able not to sin. In fact, every thought, word, and deed became tainted by sin. People couldn't help it, for that was their new nature. The ability to function in obedience as image bearers of God was lost with the Fall.

Image-bearing functions after the Fall

With the advent of sin in the world, the people who were created to image or reflect God turned their backs on him and began walking away. The glory of God's countenance no longer shone on their faces, for they no longer faced God in love and adoration. No longer did God reign in their hearts; sin reigned. In moral direction, image bearers traded obedience for rebellion and the worship of the one true God for idolatry. It was all a matter of heart direction.

As a consequence of this redirection, the ability to function as image bearers was compromised. Isaiah wrote, "All of us have become like one who is unclean, and all our righteous acts are like filthy rags" (Isaiah 64:6). Not only did people lose their innocence, they lost their true knowledge, holiness, and righteousness as well. Consequently, they could no longer really "know" with a mind that thought God's thoughts after him. They became profaned, no longer consecrated to the things of God. And they were no longer inclined toward or capable of doing "right." As a result of this loss, image bearers ceased bringing honor to the office of prophet, priest, and king. They had neither the capability nor the desire to function as images of God with the responsibilities and roles that accompany that position.

But God is gracious. In his curse of the evil one, he included a promise of hope:

> And I will put enmity
>> between you and the woman,
>> and between your offspring and hers;
> He will crush your head,
>> and you will strike his heel. (Genesis 3:15)

The outcome of the antithesis, the titanic struggle between God and the evil one being played out in the hearts and history of humankind, is not in doubt. Eve's offspring, Jesus, did indeed crush the evil one through his victorious resurrection, when death was conquered once and for all. And he provided life once again, for all who would believe, through his own perfect life and atoning death.

This saving grace was foreshadowed by another kind of "grace" that became evident at the time of the Fall. God's preserving presence has held in abeyance the full impact of the death that resulted from sin. Life has not become death in the fullest sense. Earth has not become hell. Life is still livable; hell has been restrained.

Sinful Children
Continue to Bear God's Image, *albeit* Dimly

Return for a moment to the university classroom discussion of whether children by nature are morally good, bad, or neutral. If, in fact, you were to bravely declare that all children are born with sinful natures because of Adam, what do you think would be the response of your classmates? My guess is, besides thinking that you were somewhat "out to lunch," they might argue that, if your thesis were true, classrooms would be totally chaotic. Sinful kids would tear the place apart. They would be uncontrollable. And that simply is not the case in most classrooms. How would you respond to that argument, which, indeed, has some merit?

The answer is found in the doctrine of common grace, or, as others may prefer to call it, the doctrine of God's preserving presence. This doctrine is typically seen as having three modes of expression. First, God provides certain blessings for all people. He "causes his sun to shine on the evil and the good, and sends rain on the righteous and the unrighteous" (Matthew 5:45; also see Psalm 145:9; Ezekiel 33:11, 18:23; Matthew 5:44; Luke 6:35–36; Acts 14:16–17; Romans 2:4; and 1 Timothy 4:10). Second, God restrains evil and preserves good through *external* means. For instance, governmental authority has been established by God "to do you good" and "to bring punishment on the wrongdoer" (Romans 13:4). Another example of external restraint is the sanctifying presence of believers in the marketplace. Third, God restrains evil and preserves good through *internal* means. The latter two modes or means of God's preserving presence need to be explored more fully, since they speak directly to the nature and nurture of children.

External restraint of evil and promotion of good

One reason that young children are able to behave in a civil manner is that they are susceptible to the influence of older persons in their lives. The reason for this is twofold. First, during their early years, children are motivated primarily by extrinsic (i.e., external) stimuli. They learn chiefly through their fingertips—stimulus-response fashion—and through experimentation, by trial and error. This is the reason that behavioristic theories for learning and discipline work so well with young children. Their five senses are everything to them. If actions are followed by pleasurable results, the actions tend to be repeated. The reverse is also true. Painful results usually mean that actions will not be repeated. Second, on the flip side, with young children not much is happening yet intrinsically (i.e., internally). Their direction-giving hearts have not yet matured or fully developed, nor have their thinking and reasoning abilities.

The diagram below illustrates this moral or spiritual paradox within the lives of young children. It shows how the *nature versus nurture* argument is very relevant to children's behavior. By nature, children are sinful at birth, but, thankfully, that tendency is not well developed at that time. Nurture, however, is very operative at birth and during the early years in particular. Thus, with proper nurture, the conduct of children can be expected to be rather in line with God's norms for living. But as children grow older, two things begin to happen: One, the influence of nature increases—sinful hearts begin to develop and reflect a fallen society and culture; and two, the influence of adult nurture decreases—children rightfully become more independent. This is all well and good *if* the nurture received in early childhood is godly—based on the Word of God. Unhappily, an absence of biblical nurture will likely result in a combination of the worst of two worlds—intrinsic sinful inclinations increasing along with the absence of positive extrinsic adult nurture and control. The diagram shows the change in influence from external forces to internal ones during a child's formative years.

**INFLUENCES ON MORAL BEHAVIOR:
THE NURTURE VS. NATURE JUXTAPOSITION**

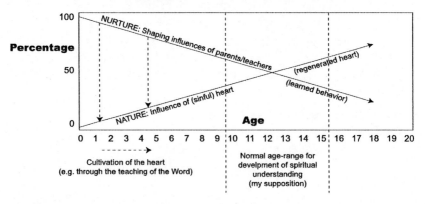

Despite the sinful nature with which children are born, their behavior can be molded or shaped by significant adults in their lives. Simply stated, young children can be taught to behave in a civil manner. But they must be nurtured toward that end. They need to receive consistent instruction and correction in the Lord during their early, most formative years.

Internal restraint of evil and preservation of good

Two internal dimensions of post-Fall image bearers provide evidence that God has not abandoned children to be as bad as they could be. One is *conscience,* the other is *structure.*

The requirements of the law are written on all hearts

Paul writes in his letter to the Romans:

> Indeed, when Gentiles, who do not have the law, do by nature things required by the law, they are a law for themselves, even though they do not have the law, since they show that the requirements of the law are written on their hearts, their consciences also bearing witness, and their thoughts now accusing, now even defending them. (Romans 2:14–15)

All people have consciences. (See the discussion of the moral mode of expression on pp. 49–50.)

All people have some sense of right and wrong. For God has placed the requirements of the law on the hearts of all people. The law serves as a governor, or restraint, for the evil that is present in every heart. This is true for all children, no matter what the religious orientation of the family.

The structure of all children remains "good"

As has been discussed previously, the image-bearing structure of children remained intact even after their moral nature became fallen. Humankind continues, even after the Fall, to bear the image of God, although this is done in a limited and dimmed manner. Even though the rebellion of God's human creatures has directed their hearts away from God and tarnished the beauty of his image within them, they did not suddenly become nonhuman. Their images may have become distorted, blurred, and misdirected because of the ravages of sin, but children continue to bear a semblance of the image of God through the "goodness" their structure.

The truth is that children in their fallen state are not as bad as they could be. Things could be worse. Because of the preserving grace of God, sin and its effects are being restrained. God has not abandoned his creation or his creatures. If he were to have done so, the chaos of hell itself would prevail in homes, schools, and society in general. But just as God graciously promised Adam's race a guilt-covering Savior, and just as he provided Adam and Eve with shame-covering clothing,[8] God continues to intervene and preserve and, someday, will fully redeem the structure of his good creation.

This preserving presence is the rationale for Christ's mandate to be salt in the world.[9] Salt's primary purpose in Jesus' day was not flavoring, but preserving. Just as salt can preserve meat from decay, so the presence of both the Spirit and body of Christ in the world preserves the goodness, or integrity, of its structure. Even with the havoc that sin wreaks on creation, sin will never destroy the integrity of the creation structure, which is preserved and maintained by the Logos himself.[10]

This truth is especially encouraging for Christian teachers working with children who have unbelieving parents and who have not personally professed Christ as their Savior. These children have much in common with students who come from Christian homes and/or have experienced the new birth, for they, too, bear the image of God in their structure. Structural good can be found in every child, for each is included in God's "good" creation.

At least three evidences exist of God's restraint of evil and the preservation of good in his image-bearing children: One, children are totally rather than absolutely depraved; two, children have the ability to do natural, civil, and moral good; and three, the antithesis runs through children, not around them.

Evidences of God's restraint of evil and preservation of good

Children are totally rather than absolutely depraved

Several years ago, Lake Erie was so polluted that most marine life died as a result. The water was full of industrial waste and contaminants. There were no fish to be caught; swimming was deemed to be unhealthy. Yet at no time did the water of Lake Erie disappear, only to be replaced by the pollutants. The pollution never became Lake Erie; the pollution only contaminated Lake Erie. This distinction illustrates the difference between total depravity and absolute depravity. Children are depraved *totally* in the sense that every part of their beings has been affected and infected. Were children to be depraved *absolutely*—which is impossible—they would be replaced by sin and, consequently, cease to exist. They would *become* sin, rather than simply *be affected by* sin.

As a parasite, sin can attach itself to structure and even can mess up structure rather well, but, because of Christ's preserving presence, sin can never destroy structure. Neither can sin become a part of or replace structure. Created structure maintains its essence and integrity. It remains "good" in that sense. It can be redeemed from the effects of sin and need not ultimately be destroyed.

Children are not as depraved as they could be. Each of their thoughts, words, and actions is tinted and tainted by the dye of sin, but children never become sin incarnate. Sin is always an additive, something that can be removed or destroyed by God. It is an alien in God's good creation.

Children can do natural, civil, and moral good

If we were to tell teachers that our children were born with totally depraved, sinful natures, the message might easily create some apprehension within them. Such a message sounds rather grim. Would there be any hope for such children? Would they be able to do anything right? Thankfully, the answer to both questions is "Yes." As a result of their being totally rather than absolutely depraved and of "training our children in the way they should go" from an early age, children are able to do "good" on a human level. This includes natural good, such as eating; civil good, such as buying and selling; and moral good, such as feeding the hungry and providing shelter for the homeless. People perform natural, civil, and moral forms of good every day. They are evidence that humankind continues to bear God's image, even in a limited fashion. They are also evidence of God's conserving presence in the restraint of sin in the world.

But these types of good actions are conducted only on a horizontal, human plane. They do nothing whatsoever to satisfy the requirement of God that human beings live a perfectly holy and righteous life to be able to enter his eternal kingdom. That would require doing only spiritual good, which is something people cannot do in their own power, for their best efforts remain on the horizontal plane, tainted with sin. Only people redeemed through Jesus Christ can think, speak, and act obediently on the vertical plane. But this is not because of their personal merit; it is purely through God's grace, his unmerited gift, that this is possible. For activities to be called spiritually good, they must be presented to God the Father as perfect and God honoring. That, too, is humanly impossible, even for the believer. But through the mediation and advocacy of Jesus Christ at God's right hand,[11] the spiritual good that emerges from a redeemed and renewed heart is presented perfect and acceptable to God.

The antithesis runs through all children, not around them

Sin invades and pervades every aspect of children. There is no getting away from it. They have no neutral or sin-free zones. But all children also have moral consciences that help them determine right from wrong, and all children are structurally sound or good in their very beings. All people—redeemed and unredeemed alike—are a mixed bag. The antithesis between good and evil—between the Spirit of God and the spirits of darkness—doesn't affect some people and avoid others. The battle line of the antithesis cuts right through all people. Redeemed individuals, who are directed by the Spirit of Christ in their hearts, continue to struggle with their old nature within them. The battle of the antithesis rages within everyone. Paul wrote:

> So I find this law at work: When I want to do good, evil is right there with me. For in my inner being I delight in God's law; but I see another law at work in the members of my body, waging war against the law of my mind and making me a prisoner of the law of sin at work within my members. What a wretched man I am! Who will rescue me from this body of death? Thanks be to God—through Jesus Christ our Lord! (Romans 7:21–25)

Both sin and the restraint of sin, if you will, leave no room for a distinction between good guys and bad guys. Both preachers and politicians have destructive and redemptive qualities. Too often, however, we draw the line of antithesis *around* people rather than *through* them. Consequently, we distinguish between good people and bad people. This type of thinking negates humility that is based on the attitude that "there but for the grace of God go I." A "we have arrived" paternalistic attitude is demonstrated, rather than one that reflects a beggar sharing a piece of bread. And we tend to establish a defensive posture of us versus them toward a world with which we are to be engaged for Jesus Christ, a world with which we share a great deal of bondage and brokenness. Acknowledgment of an antithesis that cuts through people rather than around them is a sure antidote to Christian elitism. It allows us to view all children in a light that shows both the good and the evil in them.

The conclusion can be drawn, then, that even though all children are sinners, all is not lost. Even in their sinful state, glimmers of image bearing and God's grace shine through. Ultimately, however, the answer for the sin and the sinful natures of children must be found in the atoning sacrifice of Jesus. For only then can sinful natures be transformed and actual sins be covered.

Chapter Conclusions

A number of years ago when I was a struggling student in seminary, my brother-in-law gave me a thirteen-year-old Pontiac junker. The car had been well cared for mechanically, but the body was rusting out in many places. In fact, I placed a sticker on the trunk that read: "Rust is my favorite color!" Except for problems with the radiator overheating and a muffler that kept coming loose, the car served me well. Upon graduation I bequeathed it to another struggling seminarian. Who knows, the old Pontiac may still be transporting students today.

I thought of that car as I was writing this chapter. The ever-present and ever-consuming rust reminded me of sin as a parasite that lives off of God's created reality. Without the car, there would have been no rust. Rust has no life in itself. The rust and gaping holes it created made the car look really ugly. It ate away at the body of the car, but it did not destroy the car. It also did not become the car. I did not ride around in rust; I rode around in a car. The car functioned as a car; it did not become a noncar. It continued to be of value to me. It was no throwaway. Rather than consigning it to a junkyard and the fate of being crushed into a heap of scrap metal, I took such redemptive measures as tune-ups, oil changes, and the provision of new parts.

When sin entered the world, it attached itself to both human and creation structure. The image-bearing essence of humankind was affected and infected by parasitic sin, but it was not destroyed or replaced by sin. God's human creatures remain the capstone of his redeemable good creation.

Children born today have sinful natures. No part of their beings is free from the taint of sin. But the integral essence of their beings continues to reflect a similarity to God, although in a finite and dimmed way. God's preserving presence is evident in them as he restrains their tendency toward evil and allows them to behave in a civil and moral manner.

It is obvious, though, that the status quo is not acceptable. Sin must be dealt with, and the image of God needs to be restored. The opportunity to image Christ in both direction and function must be provided for God's children. Only then can the marriage of Christ and his bride take place as originally planned.

Chapter 4: Further Thoughts to Consider

1. What is meant by "death" in the statement that if "you eat of [the tree of the knowledge of good and evil] you will surely die"? Describe the "life" Adam and Eve enjoyed before sin entered the world.

2. Compare and contrast the original image of God with the profaned image.

3. What biblical proof is there that humankind continues to bear God's image even after the Fall?

4. Do you agree with the statement about Christian schools: "Not to experience spiritual warfare is a sign that the enemy has yet to be engaged and that there needs to be increased seriousness of purpose exhibited"? Explain your response.

5. Do you believe children are born morally good, bad, or neutral? Can you defend your position from Scripture? What difference does this issue make for parents and teachers?

6. What does it mean that sin is a parasite?

7. What does it mean that sin is comprehensive and all-pervasive?

8. Why are people redeemable and not throwaways? How does your answer relate to the question of creation being or not being a throwaway?

9. If children are born with sinful natures, why are all children not hellions in the classroom?

10. Why is it important to acknowledge that the antithesis runs through people and institutions rather than around them? What would be the result if this were not true?

Chapter 4: Notes and References

1. A. A. Hoekema, *Created in God's Image* (Grand Rapids, MI: Eerdmans, 1986), 20.
2. C. Coison, *Kingdoms in Conflict* (Grand Rapids, MI: William Morrow and Zondervan, 1987).
3. 2 Kings 6:17.
4. Daniel 10:10–14.
5. M. L. Bigge & S. S. Shermis, *Learning Theories for Teachers,* 5th ed. (New York: HarperCollins, 1992), 15.
6. C. Plantinga, *Not the Way It's Supposed to Be: A Breviary of Sin* (Grand Rapids, MI: Eerdmans, 1995), 89.
7. Plantinga, 88.
8. Genesis 3:15, 21–22.
9. Matthew 5:13.
10. John 1:1–3; Colossians 1:16–17; Hebrews 1:1–3.
11. Romans 8:34.

Chapter 5

IMAGE BEARING IN CHRIST: THE RENEWED IMAGE

Introduction

Their village was under attack, and, as they fled, the refugee children become separated from their parents and older brother. They took up residence at a camp in a neighboring country and tried to eke out a meager existence from the squalor in which they found themselves. They felt lonely and afraid. But, over a period of years, the children's memory of their parents and brother began to dim.

That changed rather suddenly, however, when one day the older brother walked into the camp. He had been sent by the father to find his siblings. The children recognized their brother, and, because he was so much like their father, the father's memory soon began to take shape once again. Others commented on how much the older brother and the children looked alike. They could see that they were from the same family. But that is where the similarity ceased, for their poverty had led the children into lives of begging and stealing. The older brother was horrified with this, and he soon began to re-instill within them the values of the father. This continued for some time, for it was still too dangerous for the children to return home to their village.

Eventually, however, this did come to pass, and the family came together once again under one roof. The father was especially pleased with his eldest son, for, in his place, the son had re-instilled the father's values within the children. The father could see that his children resembled him physically, but, once again, they acted like him as well.

All children resemble their Creator in their structural integrity. One can see something of the Divine in all persons. But that is where the resemblance ends. Children by nature do not behave as God's children. They, like the prodigal son, go off to seek their own pleasures. They not only *don't* image God in their walk, they *can't* image him, for they no longer know him. They need the Son of the Father, Jesus Christ, to reintroduce them to the Father. Jesus spoke to his disciples about being "the way" to the Father:

> "No one comes to the Father except through me. If you really knew me, you would know my Father as well. From now on, you do know him and have seen him."
>   Philip said, "Lord, show us the Father and that will be enough for us."
>   Jesus answered: "Don't you know me, Philip, even after I have been among you such a long time? Anyone who has seen me has seen the Father. How can you say, 'Show us the Father'? Don't you believe that I am in the Father, and that the Father is in me? The words I say to you are not just my own. Rather, it is the Father, living in me, who is doing his work. Believe me when I say that I am in the Father and the Father is in me. . . ." (John 14:6–11)

It is only through the Son, who is the very likeness of the Father, that profaned images can become renewed images.

This truth has several important implications. First, the only way of salvation—the only way to a renewed image—is through Jesus, the Way. The process of this salvation will be explained more fully in the next chapter. Second, salvation is not an end in itself; it leads, once again, to bearing the image of God—this time through imaging Christ. In fact, this was part of God's plan for his children before they were born: "For those God foreknew he also predestined to be conformed to the likeness of his Son . . ." (Romans 8:29). Third, not only are believers in Jesus to image him in their *beings,* but because they are a part of his body, they are to actively image him in their *doings* as well.

Christ—the Perfect Image of the Father

To understand how images of God can be renewed through Jesus, we must accept the fact that the Son is the perfect image the Father. The Bible is quite clear on this.

> The god of this age has blinded the minds of unbelievers, so that they cannot see the light of the gospel of the glory of Christ, who is the image of God. . . . For God, who said, "Let light shine out of darkness," made his light shine in our hearts to give us the light of the knowledge of the glory of God in the face of Christ. (2 Corinthians 4:4, 6)

> He is the image of the invisible God, the firstborn over all creation. (Colossians 1:15)

> The Son is the radiance of God's glory and the exact representation of his being. . . . (Hebrews 1:3a)

We see in these passages that even though God is invisible to us, in Christ the invisible God can be known; one who looks at the Son recognizes the Father. The glory that the Son radiates is not his own but that of the Father. Christ the Son is a perfect representation of God the Father; every trait, every characteristic, every quality found in the Father is also found in the Son.

The Renewed Image—in Direction

When Adam and Eve sinned, their hearts were redirected away from the one true God and toward false gods. Consequently, they turned their backs on God, ceasing to reflect his glory, and began walking away from him on the broad path that leads to destruction. They began functioning as profaned images of God. To reverse this and be transformed into renewed images, people must have regenerated, redirected hearts. This allows them to turn around, to face and reflect the glory of God once again, and to begin the sanctifying walk on the straight and narrow path toward God.

A redirected heart

I gave my heart to God the summer of my sixteenth birthday. I hadn't planned to. I had been reared in a Christian home, had attended church more times than I wanted, and had been enrolled in a Christian school from kindergarten on. Yet, my relationship with God was not very personal. The Bible didn't really speak to me. My prayer life was minimal. My vocabulary was crude. At best, I was practicing religion—just going through the motions. But one evening at a Youth for Christ campfire meeting held on the shore of a lake, I gave my heart to Jesus. The setting was moving. It was dark, except for the blazing fire. The speaker stood in the flickering flames and gave the invitation. It was really more of a challenge than an invitation. He challenged us to commit our hearts and lives to the cause of Christ. We could symbolize that "commitment to the cause" by coming forward and placing pieces of wood on the fire. The burning embers would represent our lives as living sacrifices. All I can say is that the Holy Spirit must have come over me, for I was led to do that which I had not planned to do. I stood up, went forward, picked up a piece of wood from the pile, and laid it on the flame. That evening I gave my heart to Jesus, and I haven't looked back since.

Remember the Covenant of Works? Back in the beginning, God covenanted with Adam that if he obeyed God perfectly, he would be given eternal life. Even though Adam blew the opportunity, the Covenant of Works was never abrogated—it continues to stand. The problem is that no *mere* human being can perfectly live out the God-given responsibilities of life. No one can love God perfectly, love one's neighbor perfectly, or exercise dominion perfectly. No one, that is, except Jesus Christ, God who became human, like us in all ways except for sin. He lived a perfect life, vicariously, in our place. Was he tempted? Yes. Did he sin? No. Because of Jesus, the Covenant of Grace allows profaned image bearers to meet the requirements of the Covenant of Works. A renewed image begins with renewed heart direction. The prophet Ezekiel wrote about this type of transformation, as it was to occur in the lives of the people of Israel:

> "Therefore say to the house of Israel, 'This is what the Sovereign LORD says: It is not for your sake, O house of Israel, that I am going to do these things, but for the sake of my holy name, which you have profaned among the nations where you have gone. I will show the holiness of my great name, which has been profaned among the nations, the name you have profaned among them. Then the nations will know that I am the LORD, declares the Sovereign LORD, when I show myself holy through you before their eyes.
>
> "'For I will take you out of the nations; I will gather you from all the countries and bring you back into your own land. I will sprinkle clean water on you, and you will be clean; I will cleanse you from all your impurities and from all your idols. I will give you a new heart and put a new spirit within you; I will remove from you your heart of stone and give you a heart of flesh. And I will put my Spirit in you and move you to follow my decrees and be careful to keep my laws. You will live in the land I gave your forefathers; you will be my people, and I will be your God.'" (Ezekiel 36:22–28)

The language used by Ezekiel parallels language used in describing the transformation from being a profaned image bearer of God to becoming a renewed image bearer of God. Israel no longer reflected the holiness of God, and, consequently, God's name was being publicly profaned. But in an act of grace, God would renew the hearts of his people, and through the power of his Spirit they would once again desire to obey him. They would be able to resume their responsibilities as image bearers of God—loving God, loving their neighbors, and exercising dominion.

Regenerated hearts direct renewed image bearers toward obedience. Their heart's desire is to please God as a response of love and gratitude. But the actions of renewed image bearers still contain the taint of sin; neither the motivations nor the actions themselves are without flaw. Here, too, Jesus intervenes and mediates with the Father. Claiming his atoning death on the cross, Christ presents the deeds of his bride to the Father and covers them with his own righteousness. Only then do works become acceptable to the Father. Only in the Covenant of Grace can the requirements and responsibilities of the Covenant of Works be met.

The act of presenting one's heart to God is to choose to love God with one's entire being, which is the first and great commandment. The Protestant Reformer John Calvin understood the central place of the heart in one's relationship with God. His coat of arms was a hand holding a flaming heart. His motto was: *"Cor meum tibi offero Dominie prompte et sincere."* Freely translated, this means: "My heart for thy cause I offer thee, Lord, promptly and sincerely."

In Chapter 3, we determined that the heart was both the unifying and direction-giving center of the soul or person. The heart functions as the "mini-me." Whoever or whatever has a person's heart has the person— totally. God desires to have the hearts of his children, for to have their hearts is to have them. But God refuses to "take" their hearts; rather, he has created his children with responsive hearts that can be offered to him as living sacrifices. God, however, does make the first move. He loves his children before they even think about loving him. Through the regenerating power of the Holy Spirit, the irresistible grace of God through Christ is made known to his children, and they respond by offering their hearts to the only One who can satisfy their awakened need.[1]

A heart that has been offered to God through regeneration by the Holy Spirit is a heart that will direct a person in a Christ-imaging way. Parents and teachers who want their children to "be like Jesus" and to profess his lordship over their lives need to concern themselves with their children's heart direction. I can remember an after-school meeting with several middle school teachers that was being held to discuss what to do with a boy for whom nothing seemed to be working. He was, to state it simply, incorrigible. Finally, after a lengthy but fruitless discussion, one of the teachers, with a hint of exasperation, blurted out, "That kid needs Jesus to get ahold of him!" The teacher was exactly right, for the primary motivator and direction-giver for children are their hearts. And the Spirit of Jesus is the Ultimate Change Agent of children. When a heart has been transformed by the Spirit, the vast majority of problems are taken care of.

What can parents and teachers do toward effecting heart change in their children? This topic will be dealt with more thoroughly later in the book, but two suggestions can be made here. One, from earliest childhood, share the Word of God with children. For God's Word softens and prepares the heart for the work of the Holy Spirit.[2] Paul referred to such biblical instruction when he wrote to his spiritual son, Timothy, ". . . how from infancy you have known the holy Scriptures, which are able to make you wise for salvation through faith in Christ Jesus" (2 Timothy 3:15). Second, pray specifically for the Holy Spirit to renew the hearts of children so that they will be born again, this time from above. Lord willing, that will take place at a young age, and the process of conforming to the likeness of Christ can begin early in their lives. The promises of the Lord are certain and need to be claimed.

A redirected walk

The Bible often speaks of the "way" a person should go. The word *way* could refer to either a direction or a path. In Proverbs, we read the following injunction for parents and teachers:

> Train a child in the way he should go,
>   and when he is old he will not turn from it. (Proverbs 22:6)

During the time of the early church, Christianity was sometimes referred to as "the Way" (Acts 9:2, 19:9, 23). Jesus called himself "the way" (John 14:6). Such references to the "way" illustrate an important theme of Scripture: One should turn one's face toward God in an act of loving relationship with him and then walk toward him in awe-filled obedience. It's a matter of direction and walk.

Moses issued a warning to the people of Israel along this line:

> [B]e careful to do what the LORD your God has commanded you; do not turn aside to the right or to the left. Walk in all the way that the LORD your God has commanded you, so that you may live. . . . (Deuteronomy 5:32–33)

A redirected heart allows one to walk in a right or righteous direction. Facing God in this manner and walking toward him is the pivotal aspect of imaging God.

An episode in the life of Moses provides an intriguing introduction to the imaging or reflecting of God in this way. While Moses was interacting with God on Mount Sinai, he asked to see God, or at least to see his glory. Read God's response:

> And the LORD said, "I will cause all my goodness to pass in front of you, and I will proclaim my name, the LORD, in your presence. I will have mercy on whom I will have mercy, and I will have compassion on whom I will have compassion. But," he said, "you cannot see my face, for no one may see me and live."
>
> Then the LORD said, "There is a place near me where you may stand on a rock. When my glory passes by, I will put you in a cleft in the rock and cover you with my hand until I have passed by. Then I will remove my hand and you will see my back; but my face must not be seen." (Exodus 33:19–23)

When Moses directed his focus upon God, his countenance became radiant, reflecting God's divine glory. We read:

> When Moses came down from Mount Sinai . . . he was not aware that his face was radiant because he had spoken with the LORD. When Aaron and all the Israelites saw Moses, his face was radiant, and they were afraid to come near him. . . . When Moses finished speaking to them, he put a veil over his face. (Exodus 34:29–30, 33)

When a bride turns toward the groom, her face reflects or radiates the love that she sees. Moses, representing the bride of Christ, God's chosen people of Israel, reflected in his countenance the glory of God. That radiance was evident to all who saw him.

This Shekinah, or glory of God, was cited in the Old Testament as evidence of God's presence, of his dwelling with his people, primarily in the Tent of Meeting and later in the temple. It is the nearest Jewish equivalent to the Holy Spirit.[3]

The Apostle Paul provides a wonderful link between the reflection of God's glory on the face of Moses and the indwelling Spirit of Christ[4] that conforms us to his likeness:

> We are not like Moses, who would put a veil over his face to keep the Israelites from gazing at it while the radiance was fading away. But their minds were made dull, for to this day the same veil remains when the old covenant is read. It has not been removed, because only in Christ is it taken away. Even to this day when Moses is read, a veil covers their hearts. But whenever anyone turns to the Lord, the veil is taken away. Now the Lord is the Spirit, and where the Spirit of the Lord is, there is freedom. And we, who with unveiled faces all reflect the Lord's glory, are being transformed into his likeness with ever-increasing glory, which comes from the Lord, who is the Spirit. (2 Corinthians 3:13–18)

The New King James Version translates the final verse above in the following way: "But we all, with unveiled face, beholding as in a mirror the glory of the Lord, are being transformed into the same image from glory to glory, just as by the Spirit of the Lord." The redeemed in the Lord mirror, or reflect, Christ. Others see Christ in and through us. And since Christ "is the radiance of God's glory and the exact representation of his being" (Hebrews 1:3), others see the Father through us as well.

At times I have used the analogy of the moon reflecting the light of the sun to describe image bearing, but in this day and age of satellite technology, we may be able to do one better. Plans are being considered to attach giant mirrors to satellites that would be able to reflect the light of the sun to places on earth that are dark twenty-four hours a day because of the winter solstice. People who live in such places as Siberia would no longer have to suffer through weeks of total darkness each winter. Whatever you think of this idea, it does provide an appropriate analogy of believers not only *reflecting* Christ, but actually *showing* Christ. That illustration comes close to the true meaning of being image bearers of Christ in our world. Just as people looking at the mirrors would not see the mirrors but rather the sun reflected in the mirrors, people should not first see us, but they should see Christ shining through us. God's purpose for redeeming the bride of Christ is that she should be fully conformed to the image of the bridegroom.

The bride of Christ is both an image-bearing *being* and an image-bearing *becoming*. She has been created structurally as an image bearer of God, and she has been called directionally to image or reflect the second person of the Godhead, her bridegroom. The former is a static—from the outside-in—proclamation; the latter is a dynamic—from the inside-out—transformation. It is the Spirit of Christ who accomplishes this transformation through the process of regeneration and progressive sanctification. In this way, one becomes genuinely new. One will become *totally* new only when the bridegroom returns to be with his bride for all eternity.

This aspect of image bearing has to do with direction, for one must face God uprightly to be able to reflect him. People who turn their backs on God cannot transmit or reflect his glory. That, in fact, is one way to describe the difference between a believer and an unbeliever. A believer is turned toward God, facing him with head and hands held upward, receiving the gift of grace bestowed through Christ Jesus. An unbeliever rejects the offer of life through Christ and continues, with back turned, to walk away, doing his or her own thing. The former seeks to do the will of the Father; the latter chooses a life of disobedience. A believer reflects Jesus; the unbeliever reflects the evil one. "The god of this age has blinded the minds of unbelievers, so that they cannot see the light of the gospel of the glory of Christ, who is the image of God" (2 Corinthians 4:4). People either reflect the light of God's glory or are blinded by the gods of this age.

All children are images of God in their unified structures, in their integral essences. That's a given. But children also are called to turn their heart direction toward God, through Jesus Christ. They are to face God and walk toward him in loving obedience. They are to actively image God through their lives.

The Renewed Image—in Structure

God's "good" creation remained "good" in structure or essence even after humankind's fall into sin. The structural integrity of God's image bearers remained intact. The dimmed and diminished light of image bearing never was fully extinguished. But the structure was profoundly infected and affected by the bondage of sin. The profaned images could no longer function in a God-honoring way. They had become prisoners of sin.

The first advent of Christ changed this, at least to a great extent. His resurrection in particular broke the chains of sin that held God's image bearers captive. Hear the words of Jesus as he read them from Isaiah:

> "The Spirit of the Lord is on me,
>   because he has anointed me to preach good news to the poor.
> He has sent me to proclaim freedom for the prisoners
>   and recovery of sight for the blind, to release the oppressed,
> to proclaim the year of the Lord's favor." (Luke 4:18–19)

Jesus then began his sermon with the words: "Today this scripture is fulfilled in your hearing" (v. 21). Jesus came to break the chains of bondage that had enslaved the human race for many centuries. The Apostle Paul wrote: "[T]hanks be to God that, though you used to be slaves to sin, . . . [y]ou have been set free from sin and have become slaves to righteousness" (Romans 6:17–18). Jesus bore testimony to this freedom found in himself with the words, "[I]f the Son sets you free, you will be free indeed" (John 8:36). Jesus has provided healing from the ravages of sin and restoration to some semblance of original image bearing.

But not all is the way it was in the beginning. Even with redemption and restoration through Jesus, the lingering residue of sin haunts us. Even with the Spirit of Christ residing in a renewed heart, and even though a person sincerely desires to do the will of God, the old sinful nature lingers on the periphery, waiting for an opportunity, a moment of weakness, when one may instinctively revert to her or his former sinful ways (Romans 7:21–23).

While the image-bearing structure of humankind did remain "good" after the Fall, it also became a captive to sin. This structure can now be redeemed from the insidious bondage of sin because of the life, death, and resurrection of Jesus Christ. But the effects of sin will not be fully eradicated until renewed images become glorified images, when Christ returns a second time.

The Renewed Image—in Responsibilities and Function

Responsibilities of image bearers: Renewed through Christ

What is it that a renewed image bearer should be busy doing? Did the redemption of Jesus usher in a whole new set of expectations, a new game plan for life? Not really. In the beginning, God commanded his images to love him totally—that was the most important thing to do. Next, his images were told to love other people as much as they loved themselves. And they were instructed to have dominion over creation. These three responsibilities have been in place from the dawn of creation. But the atoning work of Christ now makes it possible for those redeemed in the Lord to obey these commands. They still can't obey them perfectly, for even sanctified works are imperfect and require the grace of God in Christ. But one's heart direction or attitude can now be a proper one, for the Holy Spirit is the direction-giver and prime motivator.

Yes, the original commands are still in place. But because of sin, additional work must be done. Some of this is seen in the Great Commission, which was given by Jesus to his disciples shortly before his ascension:

> "All authority in heaven and on earth has been given to me. Therefore go and make disciples of all nations, baptizing them in the name of the Father and of the Son and of the Holy Spirit, and teaching them to obey everything I have commanded you." (Matthew 28:18–20)

Jesus followed this commission with the words: "[B]e my witnesses in Jerusalem, and in all Judea and Samaria, and to the ends of the earth" (Acts 1:8). These mandates are obviously evangelistic in nature. We have been commissioned to share the Gospel, the good news about Jesus, with a lost world. Souls need to be saved; the harvest is ripe and needs gathering. But there is more. We are to teach all that Christ commanded. We are to be his body on earth. We are to continue doing the kinds of things that Jesus did during his earthly ministry.

Early in his ministry, it was reported that "Jesus went throughout Galilee, teaching in their synagogues, preaching the good news of the kingdom, and healing every disease and sickness among the people" (Matthew 4:23). Just as Jesus did, renewed image bearers are to teach and live out the truth as prophets, bring healing and restoration to a hurting and broken world as priests, and administer justice and righteousness as kings. They are to image Christ as they function in his name throughout his world.

Functions of image bearers: Renewed through Christ

The responsibilities have now become obedient possibilities. The next and final dimension of becoming a *renewed* image bearer is functioning as one. For this, we return to the original threefold office and functions of prophet, priest, and king.

A basic distinction exists, however, between these functions as they were portrayed in the original images and those to be portrayed in renewed images. The three functions within renewed images are to reflect the three functions of Christ, who was ordained by God the Father and anointed with the Holy Spirit to be our chief Prophet, our only High Priest, and our eternal King. Renewed image bearers today are to reflect Christ as twenty-first-century prophets, priests, and kings at home, at church, at school, and in the public arena.

Reflecting Christ as prophets

People don't normally get to hear others eulogizing them following their deaths. But Christ did. On the road to Emmaus, Cleopas and his companion described Jesus of Nazareth as "a prophet, powerful in word and deed before God and all people" (Luke 24:19). They shared this with the person about whom they were speaking, for they did not recognize Jesus. In this one brief statement, the essence of Christ as our chief Prophet[5] is captured. For prophets, according to the examples in the Bible, are persons who know God's truth with their entire beings, speak God's truth on the issues of the day, and live God's truth both privately and publicly.

But what is truth? Sound like a familiar question? It was asked of Jesus some 2,000 years ago by the Roman governor Pilate.[6] But Jesus had already answered that question earlier in his ministry with the words: "*I am . . . the truth*" (John 14:6, emphasis mine). Truth is a person! This flies in the face of Greek thought that saw truth as an objective thing, an axiom to be known cognitively. It's the stuff you study for a test, head knowledge. But a person? Again, Hebrew thought comes into play here. The Hebrews' way of thinking, in contrast to that of the Greeks, was holistic and dynamic, reflecting their Covenant God. Truth, then, is embodied in the person of Jesus Christ. Truth is whole and alive. Truth is perfect integrity and total sufficiency. Truth is the *Alpha* and *Omega,* life's beginning and end. Truth involves more than the head; truth embraces the heart and hands as well. For Jesus Christ is the living Truth.

As chief Prophet, Christ was endowed with true knowledge. This knowledge, also, was holistic, involving heart, head, and hands. Christ "knew" people and gave himself to them totally. The Hebrew word for "knowing," *yadah*, involves the whole person: understanding the truth, believing the truth, and doing the truth. One who knows God's truth in the Hebrew sense becomes the embodiment of God's truth and, consequently, becomes the living testimony of God's truth, both privately and publicly. Just like Jesus!

God's children, as image bearers of Christ, are called to be prophets who know the Truth, have committed their hearts to the Truth, and live the Truth—Christ—in their own time, because they, too, have been endowed with true knowledge. They are to be ones who have taken off their old selves and put on their new selves, "which [are] being renewed in knowledge in the image of [their] Creator" (Colossians 3:10). Daily they are to be renewed through the sanctifying process of the Holy Spirit—transformed into the very likeness of Christ. Every facet of their lives must reflect the integrity, the wholeness, of the Truth. Their presence must be so Christlike that it decimates the kingdom of darkness, wherever it may be found, with the light of Truth. In this way, the kingdom of Christ on earth can be advanced.

Christian schools often pride themselves on the achievement test scores of their students. I believe that that focus, important as it may be, should be redirected to the question: How well do our students know and live out the Truth in their lives? I'm not advocating that Christian schools become evangelism academies, although coming to know the Truth who makes one free has a place in schools, too. This Jesus, the Truth, is the creation Word who holds all of reality together by his powerful word. Without his living presence, no curriculum can come close to being complete. And, neither can a student body. God's children are called to be twenty-first-century prophets, with prophetic voices, yes, but especially with prophetic lives. As image bearers of God, they are to reflect Christ both in their beings and in their doings. They are to *be* his responsive disciples—his body—in his world.

Reflecting Christ as priests

Throughout the ages, priests have done lots of things, but their work has always centered on ministering to people with needs. Often that would involve administering some kind of healing balm to the sick, broken, and wounded. Priests also have served as mediators and advocates, seeking to restore broken relationships.

Obviously, this definition of priesthood fits Christ perfectly. He, in fact, was anointed by God to be our only High Priest.[7] The book of

Hebrews has a lot to say about this. Hebrews 4:14 through Chapter 7 describes Jesus as the great high priest, and Chapters 8 through 10 speak of Christ in his priestly role as the mediator of the new covenant. Listen to the comforting words that introduce Jesus as our only High Priest:

> Therefore, since we have a great high priest who has gone through the heavens, Jesus the Son of God, let us hold firmly to the faith we profess. For we do not have a high priest who is unable to sympathize with our weaknesses, but we have one who has been tempted in every way, just as we are—yet was without sin. Let us then approach the throne of grace with confidence, so that we may receive mercy and find grace to help us in our time of need. (Hebrews 4:14–16)

Recently, I heard a sermon entitled "There's more to being well than not being sick." The point made by the sermon was that Jesus healed more than the illness or the maimed body of a person; he brought wholeness to the individual. He was in the business of healing souls. This is evidenced by the many times he forgave a person's sins as part of the total healing process. In doing so, Jesus demonstrated concern for the larger picture, for he had come "to destroy the devil's work" (1 John 3:8) and to reestablish the kingdom of God on earth. His healing had a greater purpose than simply allowing one more crippled person to walk and one more blind person to see. Jesus' miracles of healing were acts of destroying the devil's work—sickness and brokenness being a result of the Fall—and bringing the healing *shalom* of his kingdom to bear. Jesus' priestly activity never lost sight of the ultimate goal: the consummation of the kingdom of God in a new heavens and a new earth. His mediating role of bridging the chasm between humankind and God pointed to this goal, as will his role as advocate or defense attorney for his bride, the church, at the final judgment. Every accusation of Satan hurled at believers will be countered and covered by the life, death, and resurrection of Jesus. As our only High Priest, Jesus "stands in the gap" (Ezekiel 22:30) on behalf of his bride, from beginning to end.

Today, God's children are called to be imitators of Christ as priests for the twenty-first century. They, too, must keep their eye on the ultimate goal of reclaiming territory lost to Satan, planting the flag of Christ on territory that has always rightly belonged to him. They need to counter the evil that produces illness and brokenness. Since the Fall, there has been no shortage of opportunities for healing and restoration. That may involve healing bodies or uncovering a cure for cancer or AIDS. It may involve working with marriages and families or with those who are incarcerated. Whatever the avenue, however, the goal must be to bring wholeness—the healing touch of Jesus—to human souls. The cup of water needs to be given *in Jesus' name.* As mediators and advocates, God's children are to be the voices and presence for the marginalized and disenfranchised, for those who have little or no voice to speak or power to act on their own behalf. That includes the unborn child and the patient with Alzheimer's, those who are homeless and those in the minority.

As our only High Priest, Jesus was endowed with true holiness. Holiness has two elements: One is *consecration,* the other is *sanctification.* Both demonstrate the essence of holiness, that is, separating oneself from that which is secular and profane and being set apart for godly purposes and service. Consecration, however, is from the outside in, an action taken by another. Jesus was consecrated by the Father from the beginning, but its earthly manifestation took place at his baptism by John the Baptist. In the case of God's children, they have been declared holy, or consecrated by God.[8] God has a prior claim on them and has set them apart for his service and glory. This holiness is a fact, a done deal. But sanctification, on the other hand, must emerge from the inside out. It can only result from a heart that has been regenerated by the Holy Spirit. Again, God's children are called to put off their old selves and to put on their new selves, "created to be like God in true . . . holiness" (Ephesians 4:24). God says to his children, "Yes, I have consecrated you, declared you to be holy. You are not your own. You belong to me. Now I desire that you, in the power of my Holy Spirit, set yourself apart for me and my kingdom. Declare my Son, Jesus the Christ, to be lord of your life. Be sold out to him. Be holy as he is holy" (1 Peter 1:15–16). Jesus, the perfect image of the Father, has always been fully sanctified—committed to God and his kingdom. It is the responsibility of God's children in cooperation with the Spirit of Christ to grow daily in sanctification, conforming more and more to the likeness of Jesus.

An important point needs to be made here. Priestly holiness is more than simply doing priestly deeds because one has been consecrated or appointed to a priestly office. Holiness is more than acting in a certain way or doing certain things. True holiness must originate from one's *being* before it can be expressed through one's *doing.* People who are holy from the inside out can't help but imitate Jesus in their attitudes, thoughts, speech, and actions—for the Spirit of Jesus is living in them and is flowing through them. They are out of control—at least their own control! In response, then, to the person who asks, "Why are you being kind to me?" they reply, "I can't help it. Jesus is living in me. That's who I am, so this is what I do. It's just what I do. I can't help it." Priestly holiness is more than a halo glowing on the outside, it is a light shining from within that brings hope to a world crying out for someone to help. The light of God's glory, seen in Christ, is reflected through his holy, image-bearing priests.

Reflecting Christ as kings

I have long had a yearning to name a school "Christ the King Academy." I think that name is divinely cool. It captures the essence of what life is all about and certainly what education ought to be about. Christ's kingship, however, is somewhat of a "back to the future" story; to gain a proper perspective, we will need to return to events previously described.

At a time of his choosing, the sovereign God declared his Son to be King. Both the prophet Daniel and the Apostle John described this:

> "In my vision at night I looked, and there before me was one like a son of man, coming with the clouds of heaven. He approached the Ancient of Days and was led into his presence. He was given authority, glory and sovereign power; all peoples, nations and men of every language worshiped him. His dominion is an everlasting dominion that will not pass away, and his kingdom is one that will never be destroyed." (Daniel 7:13–14)

> After Jesus said this, he looked toward heaven and prayed: "Father, the time has come. Glorify your Son, that your Son may glorify you. For you granted him authority over all people that he might give eternal life to those you have given him." (John 17:1–2)

All authority was given to Christ so that he could defeat the evil one, who was holding his bride captive, and redeem and prepare a kingdom home for her. Jesus spoke to his disciples about conferring this kingdom on them: "And I confer on you a kingdom, just as my Father conferred one on me, so that you may eat and drink at my table in my kingdom and sit on thrones . . ." (Luke 22:29–30). Then, in the end times, the kingdom will be returned to the Father. The Apostle Paul tells us:

> Then the end will come, when [Christ] hands over the kingdom to God the Father after he has destroyed all dominion, authority and power. For he must reign until he has put all his enemies under his feet. The last enemy to be destroyed is death. For he "has put everything under his feet." Now when it says "everything" has been put under him, it is clear that this does not include God himself, who put everything under Christ. When he has done this, then the Son himself will be made subject to him who put everything under him, so that God may be all in all. (1 Corinthians 15:24–28)

Christ is King. Someday everyone will acknowledge this fact, and "at the name of Jesus every knee should bow, in heaven and on earth and under the earth, and every tongue confess that Jesus Christ is Lord . . ." (Philippians 2:10–11).

God's children, called to be image bearers of Christ, are to be viewed as children of the King. The children we parent and the students we teach are image-bearing royalty. And just as princes and princesses are nurtured for the task of someday ruling over a kingdom, so our children are to be nurtured toward assuming their kingdom responsibilities given by God in the beginning. Originally, that task centered on the Cultural Mandate. That mandate was reaffirmed by Paul for the New Testament church: "For we are God's workmanship, created in Christ Jesus to do good works, which God prepared in advance for us to do" (Ephesians 2:10). Because of the Fall, the original mandate has been expanded to include a redemptive dimension. The Gospel is to be shared with the lost. Those of us who have a voice and power within society must seek to rectify with justice and righteousness the wrongs that have been done to those with no voice and power. The activities of the marketplace need to be reclaimed for Christ and reconciled with his way of doing things.

Just as Christ was anointed by God to be our eternal King,[9] so the children who image Christ are called to rule as kings over society, culture, and the natural world.[10] And as Christ the King was endowed with true righteousness, so those who rule in his name are expected to exercise godly righteousness. Paul tells us that they are to put on their new selves, created "like God in true righteousness" (Ephesians 4:24). Righteousness in this context means doing what is right—according to God's definition of rightness. It is seeking justice. The prophet Micah captured this thought in his answer to the question: "And what does the LORD require of you?" He replied: "To act justly and to love mercy and to walk humbly with your God" (Micah 6:8). This admonition was given most often to kings and others who held positions of power, for they were entrusted with protecting the rights of the powerless. Persons who have been placed in positions of authority are to serve—to seek the welfare of—those who are under their authority, "for [the one in authority] is God's servant to do . . . good" (Romans 13:4). Ruling with true righteousness, then, is using one's authority to do what is right and helpful for those who fall under the realm of one's authority. It is ruling as Christ would rule.

Christ mandated that, rather than seeking first to fulfill our human needs, we are to "seek first his kingdom and his righteousness" (Matthew 6:33). He promised that if we put first things first, the hand of God will cover all of our cares and worries and needs. That arrangement seems paradoxical, however, for we often feel better equipped to earn a paycheck and thus provide for our own needs than to resolve kingdom and righteousness issues. Those sound more like God's business. But God says, "I have chosen to advance my earthly kingdom of righteousness through you. When I call you to a task or tell you to do something, don't be immobilized by fear of failure or by words of ridicule or threat and say that you can't do it. For, as Moses and Paul both discovered,[11] I will provide for all of your needs, if you will face your fear in faith, rather than by the sinful responses of fight or flight. Do what is right, and I will take care of you." That "command with a promise" is one of the most important kingdom truths that we can teach kids of the kingdom. Those born to royalty need to be people of faith if they are to rule rightly in the name of their King.

Imaging in a Fourth Relationship—Self-Image

We have examined what it means to image God in the three basic relationships of life—with God, with others, and with creation. But a fourth relationship remains—the one we have with ourselves. The mental image or picture a person has of him- or herself can be called self-perception, self-concept, or self-image. These terms refer to how one sees oneself through one's mind's eye. It is a perceptive and cognitive activity. Self-esteem, on the other hand, refers to how one *feels* about oneself. The creation of positive self-esteem in children is a prominent goal for many parents and educators today.

The preoccupation that some adults have with enhancing the self-esteem of their children draws me to the second of the Ten Commandments, the one that warns against the creation of images to worship. An inordinate amount of attention placed on developing positive self-esteem in children can, in fact, border on idolatry. Some might point to Christ's command to "love our neighbors as much as we love ourselves" as the justification for this self-focus. But this commandment *assumes* self-love; it does not mandate it. It is descriptive rather than normative. The Bible tells us to love God and others. Nowhere does it instruct us to love ourselves in a narcissistic fashion.

Self-image is a legitimate area of concern, however; for the manner in which children perceive themselves does have a direct bearing on how ably they carry out their responsibilities in the relationships of life. The following goals for an informed self-image relate to the three functions of image bearing: loving God, loving one's neighbor, and exercising dominion. All children should be able to say:

- *I am loved, thus I feel lovable.* I am valued for who I am as an image bearer of God, not because of what I do or don't do.
- *I am in healthy relationship with others.* I am a contributing member of a community. Because of this, I feel a sense of dignity.
- *I am capable.* I have talents and gifts that have been identified and are being developed and used.

Even though each goal begins with the pronoun *I,* the ultimate purpose is to focus on God and bring glory to his name. The image of oneself must always point to the One who is to be imaged.

The formation of self-image

Two concepts important to the formation of self-image are *persons of significance* and *self-fulfilling prophecy.*

Persons of significance

The self-images of children are formed primarily through the way they perceive the persons of significance in their lives perceiving them. It's as though children send out radar impulses that bounce off the important people in their lives and return to them for processing. This concept has several nuances.

First, the type of people who are perceived by children as important tends to depend on the age of the children. For young children, persons of significance are usually their parents. As children grow older, teachers tend to become persons of value. And adolescents usually view their peers as persons of great importance to them. Children value the opinions of these people. Consequently, a statement made to a child by a person of significance is taken much more seriously than one made by a person of little or of no importance to the child. The effect of such communication depends on the significance of the relationship—as viewed by the child.

A second distinction needs to be made as well: The *actual* perceptions by the persons of significance are not as important as the way children *perceive* the views of others. For example, parents may view their children as being very capable but seldom verbalize this in words or actions. Thus, the perception or message received by the children could easily be inaccurate. They might view themselves as being incapable, while the parents actually view them as being quite capable. If children seldom hear the words *I love you,* and if that lack is coupled with a minimal display of affection, it is quite possible for children to perceive that they are unloved and, consequently, unlovable. Parents and teachers may love and accept their children, but that love must be communicated through both words and actions. The message must actually be received and processed by the children, not simply assumed by the adults.

Self-fulfilling prophecies

Self-fulfilling prophecies often contribute to the formation of self-images. Children tend to live out the visions that they perceive significant others have for them. To put it more simply, children often become in reality that which they think important people in their lives want them to be or perceive them to be. For instance, a boy for whom a football is purchased before he is out of diapers will probably be playing football in high school and college some day. The message will have been received that playing football is a desirable activity and that he should be and actually is capable of doing rather well in that sport. On the other hand, children who are put down, constantly criticized, and called "ugly," "stupid," or "clumsy" will also tend to live out those roles rather accurately. Many of them will not discover that they are not ugly, stupid, or clumsy until they reach adulthood. But by then it can take years to heal the wounds, and emotional scars often remain.

Although self-fulfilling prophecies can be detrimental to children if agendas other than God's are followed, the formative influence of parents and teachers can be a powerful tool for good as well. Adults must communicate to children how *God* views them. This communication has two primary forms: telling children verbally who they are, and telling children nonverbally who they are. Both are necessary, for sometimes our actions speak so loudly that our children can't hear what we are saying. Actions must authenticate words. If we love our children unconditionally, we should say so. Often. But we must also communicate our love through our tone of voice, hugs, quality time, and the like. Actions make words real for children.

A list of loving actions that parents and teachers can take is listed on pages 51–52. These actions tell children that in God's view, they are loved and they are lovable.

Self-image—from profaned to renewed

A profaned self-image

Since the Fall, the self-perception of people has tended to fall into one of two extremes—triumphalism or reductionism. Persons either succumb to the sin of pride and become gods to themselves,[12] or they wallow in their shame and guilt.[13]

Both extremes are wrong, for a biblical self-image is one that is accurate, balanced, and God-related. First, self-image should be accurate in the sense of being truthful—emerging from and being in harmony with God's Word. An accurate or truthful picture of oneself is meant to set one free to be all that God intended. Second, self-image should be balanced in that an accurate view of self contains both positive and negative features. On the positive side, we could cite that children have been created by God, are image-bearers, possess talents and gifts, and are redeemable. On the negative side, children are sinners, experience shame and guilt, have limitations, and can be plagued by their "old natures." Third, self-image should always be God-related, by seeing God as the source of the positives and the answer for the negatives. Both the positive and negative features of oneself should direct a person to God.

A renewed self-image

A self-image renewed by the redemptive acts of Christ and his Spirit creates a picture that calls for celebration. The burden and bondage of sin have been removed and replaced by freedom and victorious power. Redemption is not simply a cosmetic change or cognitive acceptance of a different belief system; it is the total transformation of a person, a complete makeover. A heart that was directed by sin has now become a heart that is directed by the Spirit of Christ. Paul wrote, ". . . if anyone is in Christ, he is a new creation; the old has gone, the new has come!" (2 Corinthians 5:17). Hoekema elaborated on this:

> The person who is in Christ is to be seen as a member of God's new creation, as someone who belongs to the new era ushered in by Christ. . . . These words were written in the present tense. To those who are in Christ Paul says, "You are new creatures *now!* Not *totally* new, to be sure, but *genuinely* new." And we who are believers should see ourselves in this way: no longer as depraved and helpless slaves of sin, but as those who have been created anew in Christ Jesus.[14]

A renewed self-image is a Christ-reflecting image. God's secret to a positive self-image is found in Jesus Christ, who "emptied himself" for us. Augustine labeled pride as "the root sin of man." Indeed, pride is the central ingredient in many self-images. The surest antidote to pride is humility, the kind exemplified by Christ and one that Paul told us to imitate:

> Your attitude should be the same as that of Christ Jesus:
> Who, being in very nature God,
>   did not consider equality with God something to be grasped,
> but made himself nothing,

taking the very nature of a servant, being made in human likeness.
And being found in appearance as a man, he humbled himself
and became obedient to death—even death on a cross! (Philippians 2:5–8)

The Bible tells us, "Do not think of yourself more highly than you ought, but rather think of yourself with sober judgment . . ." (Romans 12:3). In God's economy, a person must be willing to lose oneself to gain oneself, to die before living. The Christlike walk is one of personal denial. The more one gives oneself away to the cause of others, the greater the sense of personal fulfillment.

Christ-reflecting humility is demonstrated, first, in an honest awareness of both our strengths and limitations, to give us a realistic picture of ourselves. Second, humility includes an acceptance that we are no better than others. Third, humility involves recognition that all of our talents and gifts come from God, not from our own efforts. This acknowledgment deals with pride at its very roots. Finally, humility includes a willingness to use our gifts for God in the service of others.[15]

In summary, then, the formation of a biblical self-image in children is a valid area of focus for parents and teachers. Biblical anthropology should be taught to children, answering the "Who am I?" questions. God's love for children needs to be vicariously lived out with them. They must experience this instruction on who they are and whose they are daily. Self-image that is right before God is accurate, balanced, and God-related. The ultimate path to a biblical self-image is the "way of the cross." Self-surrender to Christ followed by the self-denial of Christ leads to true humility, a self-image that has been emptied of self and replaced by Christ.

Chapter Conclusions

Now that you've completed the last three chapters, can you answer the question: What does it mean to bear the image of God? The answer is both simple and complex, isn't it? Simply stated, *all* people image God in their structure, and *some* people also image God in their function and direction. But the details contained within structure, function, and direction can get a bit complex. That may be understandable, however, since the God who is being imaged is beyond our understanding. In that sense, no one will ever say the final word on image bearing. The divine Original transcends finite comprehension.

Even though this topic can be a bit difficult to understand, it is, nonetheless, a matter that parents and teachers should spend some time thinking about. The *nurture* of God's children must be in harmony with the *nature* of God's children. Adults who work with children need to develop a biblically accurate picture of who these kids of the kingdom really are as they seek to guide them in a godly direction.

The next section of the book deals with this nurturing process.

Chapter 5: Further Thoughts to Consider

1. What difference in impact might there be between informing children that they have been created in the image of God and instructing children that they are called to image Christ? Are both messages valid? Is one more effective than the other?

2. What are the similarities and differences between the original image and the renewed image?

3. The author cites a specific time in his life when he gave his heart to Jesus. Should all believers be able to point to similar specific times in their lives? Why or why not?

4. What are some implications of the fact that the Covenant of Works has never been abrogated?

5. What do you make of the statement by the teacher who said: "That kid needs Jesus to get ahold of him!"?

6. What is the difference between reflecting Christ and showing Christ? Are both good things?

7. What happens when Jesus frees the structure of a person's being?

8. Biblically clarify the distinction between God being Sovereign and Jesus being King. Should we speak of God's kingdom or Christ's kingdom—or both?

9. How can a focus on self-image be compatible with Scripture?

10. Can you now answer the question: What does it mean to bear the image of God?

Chapter 5: Notes and References

1. Matthew 16:15–17; John 3:5; Acts 16:14.
2. James 1:18; 1 Peter 1:23. Anthony Hoekema, in his book *Saved by Grace,* stated: "New spiritual life . . . is bestowed *immediately* by God; but the new birth is produced *mediately* (italics mine), through the [preaching, teaching, or reading of the] word" (Grand Rapids, MI: Eerdmans, 1989, 110 [emphasis mine]).
3. After Pentecost, God no longer limited himself to "temples made with hands" (Acts 7:48; 17:24), but God, as the Holy Spirit, now dwells in the hearts of the bride of Christ, his church.

4. The terms *Holy Spirit* and *Spirit of Christ/Jesus* are used interchangeably in the New Testament. See Acts 16:6–7; Romans 8:9–10; 2 Corinthians 3:17; and Galatians 2:20. This may help explain the popular concept of "receiving Jesus into one's heart." Since Jesus is in heaven, that is not possible. But most assuredly, his Spirit dwells in the hearts of believers.

5. Deuteronomy 18:15–22; John 1:1, 18; 6:14.

6. John 18:38.

7. Romans 5:10–11; Ephesians 2:13–17; Hebrews 7:17, 25; 1 John 2:1–2.

8. 1 Corinthians 7:14.

9. Psalm 9:7–9; Luke 1:32–33; 1 Timothy 1:17; Revelation 17:14.

10. Romans 13:1–7; 1 Peter 2:9, 13–14.

11. Exodus 3:11–14; 4:1–17; 2 Corinthians 12:7–10; Philippians 4:10–13.

12. Genesis 3:5.

13. Genesis 3:7–10.

14. A. A. Hoekema, *Created in God's Image* (Grand Rapids, MI: Eerdmans, 1986), 110.

15. Hoekema, 106–7.

SECTION THREE

THE BIBLICAL NURTURE

OF

GOD'S CHILDREN

Chapter 6

SPIRITUAL DEVELOPMENT

Introduction

In the beginning—*God;* once again, this is a proper place to begin. As we transition into dealing with the nurture of children, several fundamental questions about God come to mind. What reasons has God given for the bearing of children? In fact, from his vantage point, why should parents have children? Has he ever told us? Another question: What does God want from children? What are his expectations? Toward what end or goals should they be nurtured? Are the answers to these questions the same today as they were for Adam and Eve? Will they be the same for our children's children? Before moving into this chapter on the spiritual development of children, it may be important to address some of these key issues, for the answers to these questions will provide the context necessary to explore both the spiritual development and the biblical nurture of God's children.

What reasons has God provided for the bearing of children?

The initial answer to this question is provided up front in Scripture, in the very first chapter of Genesis; it's part of the Cultural Mandate: "Be fruitful and increase in number; fill the earth and subdue it" (Genesis 1:28). The first part of God's mandate "to bear children" was necessary to accomplish the second part, that of "subduing the earth." In the beginning of time, additional people simply were required to get the dominion task done! Some might argue that we have been more than successful in the "filling" part and, consequently, should have fewer or no children. But we still have quite a ways to go in "subduing" creation; so God continues to provide this kingdom answer to the childbearing question. His sovereign rule has yet to be acknowledged within every dimension of society and culture. The first answer, then, for the "Why bear children?" question is: to provide the workers necessary for the establishment of God's earthly kingdom.

A second answer is provided in the book of Malachi: The Lord desires "godly offspring" (Malachi 2:15). The term *godly* within this context probably means "holy"—separated from the profane world and belonging to the community of God's people. God has consecrated—made holy—his children for his divine purposes. This type of language is found in the covenant established with Abraham, which will be dealt with more completely later in this chapter. Let it suffice to say that this second answer to the question of bearing children is covenantal in nature.

The psalmist provides a third answer with the words: "Sons are a heritage from the LORD, children a reward from him. Like arrows in the hands of a warrior are sons born in one's youth. Blessed is the man whose quiver is full of them" (Psalm 127:3–5). Reading somewhat between the lines, we can say that children are a blessing from God and are to be enjoyed—the more the merrier. But the psalmist does hint that being a youthful parent might be helpful!

What does God desire of his children?

The biblical answer to this question is that God desires the hearts and lives of his children. He wants their hearts—their trust, submission, and commitment. He also wants them to walk in his ways. He desires responsive discipleship and thankful obedience. Proverbs captures both of these thoughts rather well:

> Trust in the LORD with all your heart
>   and lean not on your own understanding;
> In all your ways acknowledge him,
>   and he will make your paths straight. (Proverbs 3:5–6)

This is, indeed, the goal for nurture that could have been given to our first parents in the Garden of Eden and to all parents ever since.

Children are important to God. He has mandated that parents have children, many of them. He has consecrated the children of believers—declared them to be holy (1 Corinthians 7:14)—for his own divine purposes, one of which is exercising dominion over his creation. His children are to be nurtured toward commitment to him; he wants their hearts and their lives.

Ideally, the spiritual development of believers' children should be seamless. Children who have been reared in Christian homes should, ideally speaking, be able to state that there never was a time when they did not know that God was their Heavenly Father and that they were his children. Such a seamless or smooth transition through the stages of spiritual development does not always happen, but that is a proper goal toward which Christian parents and teachers can pray and work.

The children of believers are called "covenant" children because they have a place within the Covenant of Grace that informs virtually everything about their spiritual development and nurture.

Holy Children Have a Place within the Covenant of Grace

God's answer for a fallen bride and her fallen creation home was to establish a *new* covenant called the Covenant of Grace. This covenant was unfolded in progressive stages as God covenanted with and through individuals during the Old Testament era. God's covenant with Noah included the promise never again to destroy humankind and the earth "as long as the earth endures" (Genesis 8:22).[1] The earthly setting for God's kingdom was reestablished and secured. Work on the home for the bride of Christ could resume. God's covenant with Abraham established a people through whom "all peoples on earth will be blessed" (Genesis 12:3). Jesus Christ would be born a Jew, a descendant of Abraham, the patriarch of the Hebrew people. Abraham would also be the spiritual father of all believers.[2] The identity of the bride of Christ was reestablished. Next, God's covenant with Moses reestablished standards for the relationship between God and his chosen people. They were to love God and their neighbors—perfectly.[3] Since this would be impossible for a sinful people, the bridegroom Jesus Christ would have to meet the bride's responsibilities within this covenant. Later, God's covenant with David promised that a Savior-King would come through his royal line and that this King would establish a kingdom that would never end.[4] The kingdom of God on earth was, indeed, on its way to being reestablished. All of these covenants, however, pointed to and were subsumed in God's ultimate covenant, the Covenant of Grace, established with his chosen people through Jesus Christ.[5] The author of Hebrews wrote: ". . . Christ is the mediator of a new covenant, that those who are called may receive the promised eternal inheritance—now that he has died as a ransom to set them free from the sins committed under the first covenant" (Hebrews 9:15).

What is the place of children within this covenant structure? For the answer to this question, we must examine the portion of the covenant established specifically with Abraham, for the sign of that covenant involved children.

The Covenant of Grace is a family affair

Each of God's covenants with humankind included a sign or visual symbol. With Noah, God provided the rainbow.[6] With Moses, the Sabbath was given as the covenantal sign.[7] God's covenant with David required no special symbol, since David's offspring were its visible token.[8] And the Lord's Supper was instituted as the sign of the new covenant that Christ mediated.[9] When God began unfolding the details of his Covenant of Grace with Abraham, he provided a visual sign as well: circumcision.[10] The act of circumcision was not uncommon in Abraham's day. Some Near Eastern cultures circumcised their children as a rite of passage from childhood to manhood. But God commanded Abraham to circumcise the males within his family or household when they were only eight days old. The children of believers were to be under the umbrella of the Covenant of Grace from their earliest years. In this way, God declared himself to be Lord of the entire family.

The sign of circumcision—the cutting away of the foreskin of the organ of procreation—symbolized that male babies, as future leaders of their families and clans, had been consecrated by God. Through the circumcision of newly born male children, God illustrated his commitment both to helpless babies and to succeeding generations. God reached out in sovereign grace and declared the children of believers to be holy, set apart from the profane world and placed within the covenant community of believers.[11]

It is important to note that the act of circumcision was God speaking, not the child. It was God declaring that the children of believers belonged to him as kids of his kingdom and that they were to be treated accordingly. Royal offspring would require special nurture to prepare them for their kingly responsibilities. The central theme of that nurture was guidance toward responsive discipleship. God did, in fact, desire a response from the child, not at the time of circumcision, but later in life when he reached the age of discretion. Indeed, the symbolism of circumcision reached beyond the physical act. Its focus was ultimately on the spiritual relationship between God and the child. God was reaching out, declaring the child to be his, but the child, upon reaching the age of understanding, would need to respond personally in faith to that claim. God's ultimate desire was a heart that was circumcised. Already in the Old Testament, the scriptures speak of this:

> The LORD your God will circumcise your hearts and the hearts of your descendants, so that you may love him with all your heart and with all your soul, and live. (Deuteronomy 30:6)
>
> This is what the Sovereign LORD says: No foreigner uncircumcised in heart and flesh is to enter my sanctuary, not even the foreigners who live among the Israelites. (Ezekiel 44:9)

This emphasis on the circumcision of one's heart in a faith relationship with Christ is clarified in the New Testament, as circumcision of the flesh is fully replaced by circumcision of the heart. The Jerusalem Council of A.D. 50 declared that the physical act of circumcision was not a requirement for becoming a follower of Christ.[12] Later, in his letter to the Colossians, Paul wrote:

> For in Christ all the fullness of the Deity lives in bodily form, and you have been given fullness in Christ, who is the head over every power and authority. In him you were also circumcised, in the putting off of the sinful nature, not with a circumcision done by the hands of men but with the circumcision done by Christ, having been buried with him in baptism, and raised with him through your faith in the power of God, who raised him from the dead. (Colossians 2:9–12)

Even though circumcision, the visual sign of the covenant made with Abraham, was abrogated by the New Testament church, the covenantal relationship between God and the children of believers continued. Paul stated that the children of even one believing parent are holy, consecrated by God for his kingdom purposes.[13] They are his "godly offspring" (Malachi 2:15). As the words of Peter declare, "The promise is for you and your children and for all who are far off—for all whom the Lord our God will call" (Acts 2:39). God continues to be God of the entire Christian family.

Some Christian parents acknowledge this holy consecration of their children by God through *paedobaptism,* or infant baptism.[14] This is based on their belief that the New Testament sacrament of baptism replaced the Old Testament practice of circumcision. Other parents respond to God's claim on their children through infant dedication. Whatever the mode of response or lack thereof, *all* children of believing parents are consecrated children.

The children of believers receive special blessings from God

There are at least two special blessings for the children of believers that accompany being consecrated by God: one, membership within the body of Christ, and two, the expectation of regeneration.

Membership within the body of Christ

First, as we have noted, both the Old and New Testaments teach that the children of a believer in Christ belong to God. They have been declared by God to be his kids. In that regard, they are legal members of and heirs within the body of Christ. They have been declared by God to be in legal relationship with him as not-yet-professing children of believers. Their believing parents, on the other hand, are in living fellowship with God; they have been regenerated, have exercised saving faith, and are living for God. Pierre Marcel captures the unique essence of this relationship of believers' children to their Heavenly Father: "In God's eyes parents and their children are one. By divine right parents are the authorized representatives of their children: they act for them; they engage in spiritual obligations because of them, and also in their name. Such is the order of God."[15] The children of believers stand in the shadow of the reality of the Covenant of Grace. They are "in" (or "under") the covenant, but they are not yet "of" the covenant. They are legal heirs of the promises of God, but that is, however, no guarantee of salvation. These children of the covenant must personally appropriate the promises when they reach the age of responsibility. It is as though God signs the top signature line of his covenant agreement with his children when they are born. When they come to understanding, they are invited to personally sign the bottom signature line of the covenant agreement and profess faith in Jesus, thus accepting the free gift of salvation offered by God to them many years before.

The greatest benefit a child within a Christian family can receive is the nurture and admonition in the Lord mandated in Ephesians 6:4 (KJV). From the moment of birth, children of believers are to be taught the revealed truth of God through example and word. Bible stories are to be told and read, prayers are to be said, and biblical standards on right and wrong are to be taught. The redemptive promises of God are to be shared, and parents are to pray that their children will personally claim these promises. In brief, God's norms for life and the world are to be both lived out visually and taught verbally on a daily basis. That is, indeed, a great benefit!

A vital part of Christian nurture is formal instruction—schooling. While it is true that the Christian home and the Christian church play central roles in the nurturing of children, the time spent in formal education soon begins to eclipse the nurturing time spent elsewhere. As noted above, the act of holy consecration by God of the children of believers calls for special preparation for service to God and to his kingdom. Provision of this type of special preparation is not found in the mission statements of secular schools, and, consequently, an alternate approach to schooling must be found. Home schooling or kingdom-oriented Christian schools are such alternatives. It is imperative that the instruction provided God's children be in harmony with their consecrated status. It is part of their rightful inheritance.

In addition to Christian nurture, being a member of the covenant community includes the benefit of protection—from evil and from the evil one. The body of Christ provides a support system of guidance and correction. It has a vested interest in the welfare of its young. It takes steps to insure that no ill befalls them. Prayers are given on their behalf. There is a spiritual canopy, or umbrella of the covenant, under which the children of believers live. The vulnerable young children within the body of Christ are protected from that which would harm them, especially spiritually.

Finally, there is the benefit of corporate access to the Holy Spirit. Strictly speaking, unregenerate children do not yet have the Holy Spirit residing in their hearts. Their inherent sinful natures continue to guide them intrinsically, while the counterbalancing nurture by more mature people in their lives guides them extrinsically. Children who are in a legal rather than in a faith relationship with God nonetheless experience the presence of the Holy Spirit within their lives vicariously, through both their parents and the broader body of believers. According to 1 Corinthians 7:14, all family members of a believing parent are under his or her holy influence and, in that sense, are sanctified. The Holy Spirit is present in their midst. The same is true within the Christian church, which is called the temple of the Holy Spirit.[16] Here, too, the special manifestations of the Holy Spirit can be observed and experienced by young children.

In summary, one of the primary blessings of being the child of a believer in Christ is being a legal member of Christ's body, the church, and enjoying the benefits of biblical nurture, protection from evil, and access to the Holy Spirit.

Expectation of regeneration

Over a hundred years ago, Horace Bushnell wrote:

> The godly home is to be the organic channel of Christian nurture to the growing child so that Christ himself, by that renewing Spirit who can sanctify from the womb, shall be practically infused into the child's mind; in other words that the home having a domestic spirit of grace dwelling in it, should become the church of childhood, the table and hearth of holy rite . . . the liveliness of a good life, the repose of faith, the confidence of righteous

expectation, the sacred and cheerful liberty of the Spirit—all glowing about the young soul, as a warm and genial nurture and forging in it by methods that are silent and imperceptible, a spirit of duty and religious obedience to God. This only is Christian nurture. The nurture of the Lord.[17]

As stated earlier, the goal of Christian nurture is the personal appropriation of the promises of God by his children. There is to be movement from a legal relationship to that of a living fellowship. According to Geerhardus Vos:

> The presumption is that the children of the covenant who are in covenant relationship will also be led into the fellowship of the covenant. Hence we say: of those who are born under the covenant it is only demanded with double force that they repent and believe, but it is also expected and prayed for with double confidence that they will be regenerated so that they will be enabled to repent and believe.
>
> Only in this way can we maintain the organic connection between being (in or) under the covenant and being (of) the covenant, between the covenant relationship and the covenant fellowship. The first is, as it were, the shadow cast by the second. The covenant relationship into which a child of believing parents is born is the image and the likeness of the covenant fellowship, which he is later expected to live. Being under the covenant, therefore, not only precedes the covenant fellowship in the case of believers' children, but is also instrumental in bringing it about.[18]

Christian parents who have faithfully nurtured their children in the Lord can rightfully expect them to be regenerated by the Holy Spirit, for the cultivating groundwork of regeneration is the teaching, preaching, and reading of the Word of God.[19] The godly instruction found within the Christian home, church, and school *does* bears fruit. Even though regeneration is solely the work of the Holy Spirit, the holy nurture provided by these institutions can legitimately give rise to the expectation that the children in their care will at some point receive regenerated hearts. Given the God-ordained role of Christian parents to instruct their children in the things of God, and given their faithful fulfilling of that role over their children's formative years, parents should prayerfully expect that the sovereign work of regeneration will take place in the lives of their children at an early age.[20]

Holy Children Need to Experience Salvation through Jesus

The children of believers belong to God. He has declared them to be holy, consecrated to himself and to his kingdom purposes. That is God's initiative. But these children have a part to play as well. When they reach an age at which they can understand the ways of God, they must respond in faith to the gracious offer of salvation found only in Jesus. For "all have sinned and fall short of the glory of God" (Romans 3:23). There are no exceptions.

Even holy children need a Savior

The amount of progress in a child's physical growth or cognitive development is always measured against some baseline or previous status. Spiritual development is no different. A baseline or point of departure needs to be established. That point is at conception, for God's breath provides a new life at that very moment.[21] The spiritual nature and status of the children of believers at the time of conception form a mixed bad-news, good-news picture. The bad news is that all children are conceived and born with sinful moral natures.[22] A sinful inclination dominates their hearts, hearts that in turn direct their thinking, speaking, and actions. A taint of sin can be found in each thought, word, and deed of children. And "the wages of sin is death" (Romans 6:23a). Were nothing to happen to transform their sinful hearts, they would find themselves eternally lost.

The good news for the children of believers, from their very moment of conception, is that God says: "You are mine, and I desire to be your God." He gives them his word that even though they deserve eternal death—for that is the wage they have "earned," his gift to them "is eternal life in Christ Jesus our Lord" (Romans 6:23b). Salvation is offered to them as a costly but free gift. Consequently, these children are to receive godly instruction and be provided every encouragement to respond to God and his promises for them. There is, as described above, likelihood that at some point in their lives their hearts will be transformed from being sin dominated to becoming Spirit directed. But for them to move from being legal heirs of the kingdom of God to becoming actual recipients of that which has been held in trust for them, several steps in spiritual transformation and development must be experienced personally. These are *regeneration, saving faith,* and *sanctification.*

Regeneration—being born again

When children experience physical birth, their hearts are controlled by sin. They have a sinful nature that originated with Adam, the representative head of the entire human race. They are not sinners because they sin; they sin because they are born sinners. For God's children to gain their inheritance of perfect *shalom* in God's eternal kingdom, they must experience spiritual rebirth. This is the message that Jesus shared with Nicodemus some 2,000 years ago: "I tell you the truth, unless a man is born again [or born of the Spirit], he cannot see [or enter] the kingdom of God" (John 3:3). Children must be born from above. The Holy Spirit must transform their hearts from sin domination to God orientation. The Spirit of Jesus needs to be on the throne of their hearts. They are to become new creations—firstfruits of the ultimate consummation of Christ's kingdom.[23] In theological terminology, this renewing of one's heart is called *regeneration*.

Regeneration is *God's* work. In grace, God's Spirit reaches out, touches, and transforms self-centered hearts into God-centered hearts. Regenerated hearts change from selfishly wanting to do one's own thing to passionately desiring to please God. This is no cosmetic alteration; it is a total makeover from the inside out. God, speaking through Ezekiel, describes this heart renewal:

> I will give you a new heart and put a new spirit within you; I will remove from you your heart of stone and give you a heart of flesh. And I will put my Spirit in you and move you to follow my decrees and be careful to keep my laws. (Ezekiel 36:26–27)

Even though regeneration is solely a work of God to which humankind contributes nothing, parents and teachers can do certain things to prepare the hearts of their children for the new birth. When children hear the Word of God at home, in church, or at school, their hearts are spiritually cultivated and softened. Scripture speaks of this:

> [God] chose to give us birth through the word of truth, that we might be a kind of firstfruits of all he created. (James 1:18)

> For you have been born again, not of perishable seed, but of imperishable, through the living and enduring word of God. (1 Peter 1:23)

In addition to telling the story of Jesus to our children from their earliest years, we also must serve as their advocates before God's throne of grace. We are to pray without ceasing for the regeneration of our children's hearts. God hears the heartfelt prayers of Christian parents, preachers, and teachers.

How can we tell whether our children have been regenerated? The simple answer is that only God knows for certain. John wrote in his gospel, "The wind blows wherever it pleases. You hear its sound, but you cannot tell where it comes from or where it is going. So it is with everyone born of the Spirit" (John 3:8). But as is true of any person touched by God's Spirit, there are evidences in the way a Spirit-filled individual thinks, speaks, and acts. One's heartfelt desire is to please God. One's words and actions tend to exhibit the fruit of the Holy Spirit: love, joy, peace, patience, kindness, goodness, faithfulness, gentleness, and self-control (Galatians 5:22–23). Yes, it is true that one's sinful nature lurks in the background of one's being and will raise its ugly head if given opportunity,[24] but the dominant heart-direction of a born-again child will be toward God and not toward self or any other idol.

When does regeneration take place in the life of an individual? Again, we don't know. Only God knows his perfect timing, and it differs with each person. There are, however, a few considerations that may be helpful to our understanding.

There is biblical evidence that regeneration *can* occur before one is born. This is possible because regeneration is solely a sovereign work of God. God's word to Jeremiah was:

> "Before I formed you in the womb I knew you,
>   before you were born I set you apart;
>   I appointed you as a prophet to the nations." (Jeremiah 1:5)

The angel who spoke to Zechariah said that his son John (the Baptist) would "be filled with the Holy Spirit even from birth" (Luke 1:15). Indeed, when Mary, pregnant with Jesus, visited her cousin Elizabeth, who was pregnant with John, it is recorded that "when Elizabeth heard Mary's greeting, the baby leaped in her womb, and Elizabeth was filled with the Holy Spirit" (Luke 1:41).

These occurrences appear to be quite rare, however, and may apply only to persons who have received a special calling by God to a specific kingdom task. Even in these cases, it is not clear whether regeneration actually took place at that time in their lives, although God is certainly capable of such activity.[25]

Given the mediating role that the Word of God normally has preceding regeneration, it would seem plausible to expect regeneration to occur sometime between the ages of five and twelve or thirteen for children within Christian families and at some older age for other children. One may legitimately expect that in the case of a child of a believing parent, the life of God will be implanted many years before the child can fully understand or appreciate it. During that time period, one can often see the effects of this implanting in the child's life and behavior, years before a conscious decision is made to place one's faith and trust in Christ. This will differ, however, depending on the families and children. In some families, the walk with the Lord is so natural, real, alive, and inviting that the hearts of the children are made ready at an age of earliest awareness. Some children also seem to be born with a special sensitivity that makes spiritual receptivity as natural as breathing. Girls often precede boys in spiritual development, as they do in other developmental areas. Again, only God knows the moment regeneration occurs. The responsibility of parents and teachers is to nurture their children in the things of God and to pray that the Holy Spirit will transform the hearts of their children, preferably at a young age.

Saving faith—placing one's trust in Jesus

Typically, theologians cite conversion as the step that follows regeneration in the order of salvation. Conversion is described as both a "turning away" *and* a "turning toward."

The turning away from sin

Conversion normally requires a turning away from a life of sin, self-centeredness, and rebellion. Scripture often admonishes people to stop sinning. In fact, it tells them to *flee* from sin! Both the desire and the ability to do this come from the Holy Spirit, who now resides in a person's regenerated heart. It is in this process of "turning away" from sin, however, that the conversion experience for children from the community of faith typically differs from those children (and adults) from outside of that community. Let me explain.

First, children within Christian families usually have not lived such sin-filled lives that a turning away from sin is a primary focus. Indeed, either because of parental influence and/or the indwelling of the Holy Spirit through regeneration, these children may actually be leading rather godly lives. The point to be made here is that the conversion process for children within Christian families probably focuses more on "saved for" than "saved from," more on the positive than on the negative, and more on the future than on the past. Children who "from infancy . . . have known the holy Scriptures" (2 Timothy 3:15) may, and ideally should, experience such a seamless relationship with their Heavenly Father that they cannot remember a time when they did not love him and seek to serve him. For them, the *turning* toward God in the conversion process is more of a *continuing* toward God that may have little turning away from sin involved. The children of believers are not to be viewed as pagans or unbelievers who need to do a 180-degree turnaround in their lifestyle; rather, they are to be dealt with as consecrated not-yet-believers (or not-yet-professors of faith) who may already be serving God in their own childlike way.

Second, the New Testament writings on "turning away" from lives of sin were addressed primarily to adults, most of whom were, indeed, pagan unbelievers. They had much to repent from. Consequently, their conversion or "turning around" was often quite radical. The Apostle Paul is a classic example. What is virtually absent from New Testament teachings, however, is a description of how children within Christian households came to faith in Christ. The closest illustration may be found in Jesus' own words as he held and blessed the children: "Let the little children come to me, and do not hinder them, for the kingdom of heaven belongs to such as these" (Matthew 19:14). Elsewhere he stated: "I tell you the truth, unless you change and become like little children, you will never enter the kingdom of heaven" (Matthew 18:3). It appears from these words that the road that the children of believers must travel to the kingdom of God requires less "change" and "turning around" than that required for most adults.

The turning to Christ in faith

The "turning to" or "continuing toward" dimension of conversion must be fully embraced by all children if they are to receive eternal life. Every child, including those born to believing parents, must consciously and personally place her or his faith in Jesus as Savior from the penalty of sin. They must sign the "bottom line" of the covenant that God established with them before they were born. God's offer of an eternal relationship with him through Christ must be personally appropriated. Saving faith needs to be exercised. The Apostle Paul writes: "[I]f you confess with your mouth, 'Jesus is Lord,' and believe in your heart that God raised him from the dead, you will be saved. For it is with your heart that you believe and are justified, and it is with your mouth that you confess and are saved" (Romans 10:9–10). God's Word is to be believed; Jesus is to be trusted as the only way to God the Father and, subsequently, to the abundant life in him.

The answer to the question "What must I do to be saved?" needs to include "*You* must do something." Whereas regeneration is solely a work of God, conversion involves participation—a personal response of saying "Yes!" to Jesus.

I'll never forget the testimony of a prison inmate from Mexico whom I met during a Prison Fellowship weekend in South Dakota. He shared that he had been arrested in a small town in the western part of the state. While he was being held in the town jail, a local preacher visited him and posed the question: "Are you a Christian?" The man answered, "Yes," for he wasn't Jewish, Muslim, or Buddhist and he was a member of a Christian church back in Mexico. The pastor then asked, "Have you ever given your life to Jesus?" The inmate answered, "No, I never was told I had to do anything. I thought just being a member of my church was enough." The pastor then proceeded to explain what the man had to do to be saved and led him through each step. This was now possible, because the man understood that something was expected of him. He had to respond to God's gracious gift. He had to believe. He had to accept. He had to give his heart. He had to exercise saving faith.

While regeneration is always instantaneous, for children within Christian families the resultant turning toward God though a personal faith commitment in Christ can take years to develop. That process begins, however, immediately following regeneration, just as water flows immediately following the turning of the tap. It culminates when a child reaches her or his age of understanding. The faith development of the boy Samuel provides a helpful biblical example of this process. Samuel was God's child from conception. He was also formally dedicated to the Lord by his parents at a young age. Interestingly, the Bible states that he ministered before the Lord even before he knew God personally.[26] For Samuel was known by God from the beginning, and God's Spirit probably claimed his heart through regeneration at a young age. He could minister because he was being nurtured by God though the Holy Spirit and in God by Eli's instruction and example. But even though he knew about God, he had not yet given his heart and life to God in a formal sense. He did not "know" God in the full Hebrew manner of knowing (*yadah*), which always involved cognitive understanding, heart commitment, and an active response. Samuel had not yet reached the age of spiritual maturity at which time he could consciously give himself to God as a living sacrifice, for "the word of the LORD had not yet been revealed to him" (1 Samuel 3:7). Up to that time, he had heard the Word of God through others, probably his parents and Eli. Then, when God deemed Samuel personally ready to hear and understand his Word, God called Samuel and spoke to him directly. And Samuel's response was the response that God desires from all his children who have reached their ages of understanding: "Speak, for your servant is listening" (1 Samuel 3:10). Samuel was able to say "Yes!" to God and commit his heart to him in an act of saving faith.

Not every child of believers, however, proceeds through the faith development process in as seamless a manner as Samuel. That is the ideal, however. The more godly the home and loving the nurture within it, the more likely the journey of faith will be connected and smooth. Unhappily, however, sin exists within all families, and the consequent dysfunction can create gaps and rough spots for some of God's children. The commitment problems that result can occur for a number of reasons. Some children may not be transformed by the Holy Spirit through regeneration until they are teenagers or even older. When they do receive the new birth, however, the time span before a conscious commitment is made will usually be brief. In fact, the two often go hand in hand, as was probably true in the case of the Apostle Paul. The downside of delayed regeneration, though, can be kids getting into stuff they shouldn't, which can create scars that may haunt them later in life. Some children, for a number of reasons (e.g., anger over abuse that took place within a religious home) fight the work of the Holy Spirit in their lives. Although this time period of spiritual limbo can be difficult and damaging, the Spirit of God is more powerful than human resistance and can ultimately prevail.

Sadly, however, some children of believing parents never come to a faith commitment. Christian parentage is no guarantee of life from above. The Bible notes several cases of godly parents who had ungodly children. Eli and Samuel were such parents. The Apostle Paul told us: "not all who are descended from Israel are Israel" (Romans 9:6). In other words, physical descent is no guarantee of life in God's kingdom. Normally, however, as mentioned previously, Christian parents who nurture their children in the things of the Lord can be assured that there is a strong likelihood that their children will come to saving faith.

The age of understanding

At what age can one consciously exercise saving faith? When can children or young people understand the things of God in a way that would allow them to personally respond to God's claim on their lives? We would all agree that children under five years old do not normally understand existentially—apart from others—the need for a Savior, the need to submit to the lordship of Christ, or the call to service in the kingdom of God. At that time in a child's spiritual and moral development, acts of wrongdoing are identified more by their immediate and concrete negative consequences than as failures to love God perfectly. These things are beyond the understanding and experience of very young children. The concepts are too abstract. Young children can accept many of the tenets of the Christian faith simply because parents and other adults in their lives teach them, but they cannot yet personally believe these tenets of faith. At what age does moral understanding and personal accountability begin? The Bible does not say precisely. The answer differs for each child and depends on several factors.

Expectations set by parents and/or the Christian community, the nature and degree of previous religious instruction, and developmental maturity all differ for each child. In some instances, experience has shown that an appropriate time period for deliberate and conscious response by children nurtured in the Lord is as young as five to ten years old. John Inchley stated:

> For children brought up within a Christian home the reality of intelligent response, with or without a crisis experience, is likely to occur at any time between the ages of six and eleven, or maybe even earlier. It will be a culmination of much that has gone before, whether unconsciously or subconsciously in the mind of the child. The question to ask such children, and adults, for that matter, is not, "Have you believed?" but rather, "Do you believe?" or "Are you believing?"[27]

On the other hand, the age span from ten to fifteen years old is consistent with the physical development of a child entering puberty. It also matches, according to Jean Piaget, the mental and moral development of a child entering the stage of formal operations—having the ability to think abstractly. And it agrees with the social and emotional development of children as they begin making more independent decisions about issues, activities, and friends. All in all, within Western culture, the age range from ten to fifteen years old appears to be a fertile time period for spiritual understanding and response.

The ages of twelve and thirteen have been viewed historically as being of significant religious importance for Jewish youth (e.g., the bar mitzvah for boys and the bat mitzvah for girls).[28] As guardians of the laws of God, the Jews taught that there was an age of accountability before the law and set the limit of legal innocence at age twelve. Today, the legal age range in which contributory negligence (i.e., being responsible for one's actions) begins to be a consideration is from eight to fourteen, and even then, personal negligence will be considered only a possibility. Children who are under eight years old are not considered by the courts to be at all legally responsible for their actions.

What takes place at the age of understanding? Before reaching this age, children cannot willfully rebel against God. To believe otherwise would be to negate the concept of an age of understanding, discretion, or accountability. Charles Spurgeon once said, "When a child knowingly sins, he can savingly believe." (Another expression states that when a child or young person is able to doubt, he or she is able to believe.) To "knowingly" sin requires moral awareness, something young children typically do not possess.

There are several descriptors for this age that may help to clarify what happens to children when they reach this place of moral and spiritual development in their lives. It can be viewed as the:

- *Age of moral consciousness.* A child has understanding—forethought or consciousness—and knows the difference between right and wrong; "When I do right or wrong, I am quite aware of what I am doing and the difference between the two."
- *Age of understanding.* A child can conceptually comprehend the very nature of a sinful act, the inherent, existential wrongness of it; "I can recognize sin apart from simply negative consequences; I understand sin to be an offense to a holy God."
- *Age of accountability.* A child becomes personably answerable to God for choices made; "I know the laws of God, and I understand that I have freedom to choose to obey or disobey them. I cannot blame others for my choices."
- *Age of moral separateness.* A child has *personal* belief versus belief based on what others say; "The pieces have come together for me personally. I believe because *I* believe."
- *Age of choice.* The child makes a choice between believing or not believing the Gospel message; "I understand that I can walk away from God saying that I no longer accept that which I have been taught about him, or I can walk toward God and embrace him."
- *Age of belief.* The child believes with her or his heart, not solely with her or his head; "I have committed my total life to Jesus and his way of doing things. Jesus is not just my Savior; he is the Lord of my life."

To summarize, there comes a time, a point of maturity, when children personally—not simply because some adult said so—are given enough insight into the things of God to understand and to believe. It is a time when the pieces of the pattern of life begin to come together, to make sense in a new, personally meaningful way. The child's view of the world or belief system is formed independently from that of parents or teachers. It is of a personal nature. Sin becomes more than just a bad choice followed by negative consequences. It is understood as an offense to a holy God. Children become personally accountable for the nature of their response, for they possess moral awareness of right and wrong according to God's standards, and they have the ability to choose between the two. The need to accept Jesus into their hearts and lives as

Savior and Lord is understood and acted upon, and the desire to love and obey God with one's entire being is deeply felt.

The appropriate response upon reaching one's age of understanding is both a personal and public (i.e., within the church) profession of faith in Jesus Christ as Savior and Lord. Within some churches, such a public profession of faith is accompanied by believer's baptism.

> Over the years, I have asked a question of students from Christian colleges in which I have taught: "At what age did you commit your heart to Christ?" A number of them told me that they were four or five years old. Several said that they came to this decision point during a devotional time before they were tucked into bed. I then asked whether the "decision" or "profession" held up over the years, especially as they entered adolescence. Usually, they said that it did.
>
> Four or five years old is really a young age for this type of commitment to be made! What is one to think? Were these commitments for real? My response is that the students themselves—most of whom were females—attested to their validity, and I believed them.
>
> Interestingly, this reminds me of the verse in the King James Version of the Bible that reads: "Suffer little children, and forbid them not, to come unto me: for of such is the kingdom of heaven" (Matthew 19:14). Jesus rebuked his disciples when they tried to keep the children from him. If Jesus says it's okay for them to come, who are we to stop them?

Sanctification—becoming more and more like Jesus

Children who have been regenerated and have exercised saving faith, in one sense, have returned "back to the future." The image-bearing capabilities that were lost with the introduction of sin into the world, to a great degree, have been restored because of Christ. Things are back on track. There has been restoration to a spiritual state that had been lost. Paradise lost has become Paradise regained. Once again, the redeemed in the Lord can reflect God in structure, function, and moral direction. They can stand upright, facing and reflecting the holiness of God, this time, however, through mirroring the likeness of his Son, Jesus Christ. For before the creation of the world, God's children were "predestined to be conformed to the likeness of [God's] Son" (Romans 8:29).[29]

Sanctification means holiness, separating oneself from the things of this world and attaching oneself to the things of God. It is the flip side of consecration. Both consecration and sanctification have the same goal—that of imaging God—but as consecration works from the outside in through others, sanctification works from the inside out, through one's renewed heart. Sanctification, then, really begins with the new birth. This growth in holiness, becoming more and more like Jesus, continues throughout one's life until physical death, at which time one becomes glorified, fully conformed to the likeness of Christ. Unhappily, some people don't grow much in holiness after they have been saved. That is sad, and it grieves God, for he desires that there be holy compatibility between the bride—the church—and his Son, the bridegroom.

Growth in sanctification takes place, if you will, through double indwelling. First, Christ dwells within the hearts of his redeemed children. They, in turn, dwell in or become a part of his body, the church.

Christ dwells within the hearts of redeemed children

Some people describe their newly found relationship with God as "having Jesus in their hearts." That is both an inaccurate and an accurate description. It is inaccurate in that Jesus ascended to heaven where he is preparing a place for us and from where he will return someday.[30] Jesus is physically in heaven with the Father. It is an accurate description, however, in that the Holy Spirit, also called the Spirit of Christ,[31] resides in the hearts of true believers. Sometimes we tell others that we will be "with them in spirit" even though we cannot be with them in person. Jesus did much better when he promised that he would always be with his disciples by having his Spirit reside in them.

> "I will ask the Father, and he will give you another Counselor to be with you forever—the Spirit of truth. The world cannot accept him, because it neither sees him nor knows him. But you know him, for he lives with you and will be in you. I will not leave you as orphans; I will come to you. Before long, the world will not see me anymore, but you will see me. Because I live, you also will live. On that day you will realize that I am in my Father, and you are in me, and I am in you." (John 14:16–20)

There are several places in the Bible that speak of the Holy Spirit dwelling within us.

> Don't you know that you yourselves are God's temple and that God's spirit lives in you? If anyone destroys God's temple, God will destroy him; for God's temple is sacred, and you are that temple. (1 Corinthians 3:16–17)

> Do you not know that your body is a temple of the Holy Spirit, who is in you, whom you have received from God? You are not your own; you were bought at a price. Therefore honor God with your body. (1 Corinthians 6:19–20)

> Do not be yoked together with unbelievers. For what do righteousness and wickedness have in common? Or what fellowship can light have with darkness? What harmony is there between Christ and Belial? What does a believer have in common with an unbeliever? What agreement is there between the

> temple of God and idols? For we are the temple of the living God. As God
> has said: "I will live with them and walk among them, and I will be their God,
> and they will be my people." (2 Corinthians 6:14–16)

In the first reference cited, Paul is referring to the church, the corporate body of Christ, as the temple within which God dwells. In the second and third references, Paul speaks of individual Christians as temples of the Holy Spirit. Christians, as individuals filled with the Holy Spirit, are a part of the church filled with the Holy Spirit.

God has always dwelled with his people, for he is a God of covenantal relationship. In the Old Testament, God walked with the saints;[32] he also dwelt in a tabernacle and, later, in a temple built with human hands. The Revelation of John speaks of a New Jerusalem in which there will be no need for a temple, whether created by humans or by God:

> "Now the dwelling of God is with men, and he will live with them. They will
> be his people, and God himself will be with them and be their God." . . . I did
> not see a temple in the city, because the Lord God Almighty and the Lamb
> are its temple. (Revelation 21:3, 22)

When the kingdom of God is established in fullness, a separate dwelling place for God will not be necessary, for he will be all and in all. Until then, however, redeemed people are the temple—the dwelling place—of God.

Growth in sanctification—becoming progressively more like Jesus—comes with a price, that of self-surrender. Only when we have died to ourselves will we be able to live for Christ and bear the fruit of his Spirit.

a. Growth in sanctification comes through brokenness—no pain, no gain

Too often, the process of sanctification is viewed a process akin to going on a diet—if we just try a little harder, we will be able do it. So we resolve to make a greater effort to be good and kind and loving. And, of course, we fail every time—for good reason. First, conforming to the likeness of Christ is a cooperative venture between the Holy Spirit and us. We cannot do this by our own power. Second, the pathway to holiness is one of pain and suffering, for we must have "a broken and a contrite heart" (Psalm 51:17) before God will do anything with us. Self-sufficient pride is the greatest enemy of sanctification, for it leaves little room for the Spirit of Christ in our hearts. The sinful nature of people seeks independence from God; they want to do it themselves, much like young children. And the "old man" within the redeemed often continues to promote that desire. But God tells us that he wants us totally, 100%, and for that to happen we must be stripped of all pride, self-righteousness, and self-sufficiency. We are to lose everything (at least we think it's everything) so that we can gain everything.[33] All of our human crutches must be removed so that we can fall flat on the ground in utter helplessness. Only then will we be able to look up to see the hand of Jesus reaching down to help us—in his power and in his way. All Christians know that salvation comes through grace and not through works. Well, sanctification is a product of God's grace as well. We cannot do it in our own power, and we should stop trying.

The Apostle Paul speaks of this road of brokenness in several of his letters. To the church in Rome, he wrote:

> And we know that in all things God works for the good of those who love him, who have been called according to his purpose. For those God foreknew he also predestined to be conformed to the likeness of his Son, that he might be the firstborn among many brothers. (Romans 8:28–29)

Sometimes Christians view "the good" that God works in "all things" to be a Disneyland kind of existence for the redeemed in the Lord: no pain, only good stuff. But the "good" of which Paul is speaking is growth toward "his [God's] purpose," which is being "conformed to the likeness of his Son." Given our natural bent to do it our way, the conforming process is often painful. Paul wrote to the Corinthians:

> To keep me from becoming conceited because of these surpassingly great revelations, there was given me a thorn in my flesh, a messenger of Satan, to torment me. Three times I pleaded with the Lord to take it away from me. But he said to me, "My grace is sufficient for you, for my power is made perfect in weakness." Therefore I will boast all the more gladly about my weaknesses, so that Christ's power may rest on me. That is why, for Christ's sake, I delight in weaknesses, in insults, in hardships, in persecutions, in difficulties. For when I am weak, then I am strong. (2 Corinthians 12:7–10)

Elsewhere, Paul continued to explain the relationship between suffering and growth in sanctification: " . . . we also rejoice in our sufferings, because we know that suffering produces perseverance; perseverance, character; and character, hope" (Romans 5:3).

For us to be become like Jesus, then, we must walk a pathway of suffering just as Jesus did.[34] Peter wrote: ". . . since Christ suffered in his body, arm yourselves also with the same attitude, because he who has suffered in his body is done with sin" (1 Peter 4:1). Indeed, a vital part of sanctification is being "done with sin." Peter continues:

> Dear friends, do not be surprised at the painful trial you are suffering, as though something strange were happening to you. But rejoice that you par-

ticipate in the sufferings of Christ, so that you may be overjoyed when his glory is revealed. If you are insulted because of the name of Christ, you are blessed, for the Spirit of glory and of God rests upon you. . . . [I]f you suffer as a Christian, do not be ashamed, but praise God that you bear that name. (1 Peter 4: 12–14, 16)

For people to be usable by God for his purposes, they must be sanctified, and to be sanctified one must be broken, in a manner not dissimilar to a horse's being broken.[35] We must be brought to our knees or flat on our faces in utter dependency as our human props and support systems are removed. A. W. Tozer is quoted as saying, "It is doubtful that God blesses man greatly until he has been hurt deeply." The true God wants us to let go of all of the false gods upon which we depend.

While it is true, then, that sanctification requires the presence of the Holy Spirit in our hearts, it does not depend on how much of the Holy Spirit we have; growth in holiness actually depends on how much of us the Holy Spirit has. Granted that a special measure of the Holy Spirit can be poured out on those who are called to a unique area of service for which special equipping may be necessary (e.g., Samson), all Christians are filled with the Holy Spirit at the time of their new birth. From then on, it is a matter of appropriating the divine resource that has been provided, for the Holy Spirit dwells fully within every believer. Rather than praying for a filling of the Spirit, then, we need to pray for a cleansing of our hearts and souls, our entire beings, so that the Holy Spirit can function fully and freely. The words of David come to mind:

Wash away all my iniquity and cleanse me from my sin.
Cleanse me with hyssop, and I will be clean;
     wash me, and I will be whiter than snow.
Create in me a pure heart, O God,
     and renew a steadfast spirit within me.
Do not cast me from your presence
     or take your Holy Spirit from me.
Restore to me the joy of your salvation
     and grant me a willing spirit, to sustain me. (Psalm 51:2, 7, 10–12)

The major difference between David and his predecessor Saul was not a matter of who sinned the most or the least, for both sinned greatly. God rejected Saul as king because he would not humble himself. David, on the other hand, searched his innermost being and was horrified at what he saw. He cried out for cleansing, to be made whiter than snow, so that he would be able to fellowship in the presence of the holy God once again. God was then able to use David for his purposes. David understood brokenness. He was teachable; he was moldable. This same lesson was taught to the people of Israel years before. Listen to the words of Moses:

> Remember how the LORD your God led you all the way in the desert these forty years, to humble you and to test you in order to know what was in your heart, whether or not you would keep his commands. He humbled you, causing you to hunger and then feeding you with manna, which neither you nor your fathers had known, to teach you that man does not live on bread alone but on every word that comes from the mouth of the LORD. Your clothes did not wear out and your feet did not swell during these forty years. Know then in your heart that as a man disciplines his son, so the LORD your God disciplines you. (Deuteronomy 8:2–5)

The discipline lessons of God come through humbling tests and trials, for God wants our entire being, not just portions of it. He wants full surrender; the white flag renouncing self-sufficiency must be raised. For many of us that doesn't come voluntarily; we must be broken by God. Then his Holy Spirit can have free rein—or reign—to bear fruit through us.

b. Transformed hearts produce transformed lives: The fruit of the Spirit

A Christian song from the 1960s declared: "They will know we are Christians by our love." Indeed, authentic Christianity is identifiable by the spiritual fruit being produced, and sacrificial, or *agape,* love is the primary fruit of the Holy Spirit. Other fruits are joy, peace, patience, kindness, goodness, faithfulness, gentleness, and self-control (Galatians 5:22–23). *Being* a Christian and *acting like* a Christian go hand in hand, for being conformed to the likeness of Christ means reflecting him in attitude, thinking, speaking, and actions.

There is a vitally important truth about the fruit of the Spirit that is often not understood, however. The fruit of the Spirit is the fruit *of the Spirit.* Christians bear the fruit; they do not produce it. It is not a matter of what we can do for God, but what God can do through us. The free gift of God's grace is as present in sanctification as it was in regeneration and conversion.

This has definite implications for nurture within the home and the school: The fruit of the Spirit cannot be taught or learned in a formal sense! They can be described, they can be reinforced, and they can be mandated, but they cannot be taught, for they are the rightful jurisdiction of the Holy Spirit. The only way children can love as God wants them to love is to surrender their own self-centered hearts to God and allow the Vine, Jesus Christ, to give life to them as his branches. Then, and only then, can fruit be borne on the child-branches. The Apostle John summarized this truth with the words of Jesus:

"Remain in me, and I will remain in you. No branch can bear fruit by itself; it must remain in the vine. Neither can you bear fruit unless you remain in me. I am the vine; you are the branches. If a man remains in me and I in him, he will bear much fruit; apart from me you can do nothing." (John 15:4–5)

What does this mean for children? It means that they are to "let go" and "let God." It means looking upward for answers rather than inward. Humanistic "christianity" must be replaced with theistic Christianity. Life must move from only-the-rational to include supernatural possibilities. It's at this point that the Christian life gets really exciting. It becomes the abundant life in Jesus, empowered by his Holy Spirit.

To act like Jesus, then, one must be like Jesus. Sanctification by the Holy Spirit produces the fruit of the Holy Spirit. To grow in sanctification, one must personally surrender and bend one's knee in homage to Jesus Christ as Savior and as Lord. Parents and teachers are to teach these lessons often, through example and verbal instruction. They need to challenge their children to commit their hearts, minds, and lives to Jesus. They should encourage them to remain in the Vine. They must pray for all of this daily, for it cannot be learned cognitively; it must be experienced from above.

Redeemed children are "in Christ" as members of his body, the church

Just as Christ told his disciples, "I am in you," he also told them, "You are in me" (John 14:20). Christ dwells within those who place their trust in him, but believers also dwell within Christ as members of his body, the church, of which he is the head. This arrangement is one of perfect, reciprocal unity, symbolized by the "two becoming one" in marriage. The bride of Christ is in intimate relationship with the bridegroom. This union with Christ includes two modes: *community* and *gifts*.

a. Membership in Christ's body involves community

The children of believing parents are consecrated members of Christ's church from the moment of their conception. When they respond personally to Christ in saving faith, they become professing members of his church. They are moved from a legal relationship with their Heavenly Father to a relationship of living fellowship. From being members "in" or "under" the Covenant of Grace, they become members "of" the Covenant of Grace. God's children are always part of something bigger than they. They are always in relationship with God but also with other members of the body of Christ. Membership initially provides nurture and protection; later, it provides opportunities for fel-

lowship and ministry. But the body is continually seen as a place of relationship, called to function within unity—i.e., to be a community.

The unity of the church is very important to Christ, its head. In his
high-priestly prayer recorded in John 17, Jesus first prayed for his disciples, then he prayed for all believers:

> My prayer is not for them alone. I pray also for those who will believe in me
> through their message, that all of them may be one, Father, just as you are in
> me and I am in you. May they also be in us so that the world may believe that
> you have sent me. I have given them the glory that you gave me, that they
> may be one as we are one: I in them and you in me. May they be brought to
> complete unity to let the world know that you sent me and have loved them
> even as you have loved me. (John 17:20–23)

Unhappily, the community desired by Christ is too often much-talked-
about and too-little-practiced. The reason may be that the formula for
community that is provided through these verses is not being followed.
The ability to be in unified relationship comes not from human effort
but through a supernatural, trinitarian Source—the Father who is in the
Son who gives us his Spirit. The genesis for unity is God, living in and
through believers. Just as it is true in sanctification, being in relationship
with brothers and sisters in Jesus means "letting go" and "letting God."
This distinction is illustrated through two ways of describing the church.

The church—the unified body of Christ, of which God's children are
members—is both an *organism* and an *organization*. As an organism, the
church is alive. It receives direction from its living head—Christ—and it
is empowered by the Spirit of Christ who dwells within it. As an organization, however, the church comes alive only when its members become
active. It becomes a *living* organization only when it begins to function as
a unified whole with each diverse part fulfilling its task. Christ's church
is a living organism, and this living organism is called to become a living
organization.

The Apostle Paul showed the way for the church to become a living
organization by connecting the concept of "unity" with the concept of
"gifts":

> Make every effort to keep the unity of the Spirit through the bond of peace.
> There is one body and one Spirit—just as you were called to one hope when
> you were called—one Lord, one faith, one baptism; one God and Father of
> all, who is over all and through all and in all. . . .
>   But to each of us grace has been given as Christ apportioned it. . . . It was he
> who gave some to be apostles, some to be prophets, some to be evangelists, and
> some to be pastors and teachers, to prepare God's people for works of service,

> so that the body of Christ may be built up until we all reach unity in the faith
> and in the knowledge of the Son of God and become mature, attaining to the
> whole measure of the fullness of Christ. (Ephesians 4:3–6, 7, 11–13)

Unity within the body of Christ is achieved through each member exercising his or her spiritual gift in service to other members. This brings us to the second aspect of union in Christ—gifts of the Spirit.

b. Membership in the body of Christ involves identifying and exercising spiritual gifts

The church of Christ exists in both unity and diversity. Community demonstrates the former; spiritual gifts are evidence of the latter. Just as the human body has many different parts that must function harmoniously as one system, so the body of Christ has many parts that are designed to function in an interrelated and interdependent manner. Paul described the "diversity within unity" that marks the body of Christ:

> The body is a unit, though it is made up of many parts; and though all its
> parts are many, they form one body. So it is with Christ. For we were all bap-
> tized by one Spirit into one body—whether Jews or Greeks, slave or free—
> and we were all given the one Spirit to drink. . . .
>
> Now you are the body of Christ, and each one of you is a part of it. And in the
> church God has appointed first of all apostles, second prophets, third teach-
> ers, then workers of miracles, also those having gifts of healing, those able to
> help others, those with gifts of administration, and those speaking in different
> kinds of tongues. Are all apostles? Are all prophets? Are all teachers? Do all
> work miracles? Do all have gifts of healing? Do all speak in tongues? Do all
> interpret? But eagerly desire the greater gifts. (1 Corinthians 12:12–13; 27–31)

When children and young people profess their faith in Jesus Christ as Savior and Lord, their role within the church begins to shift, at least to some degree. Rather than solely being served and nurtured by others, they are to begin serving and nurturing other members. As professing members, they become part of the diverse mosaic that constitutes the body of Christ. In that, they are called to be active body parts exercising their particular spiritual gifts "for the building up of the body."

What are spiritual gifts? They are "special abilities given by Christ through the Holy Spirit to empower believers for the ministries of the body."[36] Each member of the body has a gift, and, consequently, each has a special ministry to other believers. The Apostle Paul explained this:

> Now about spiritual gifts, brothers, I do not want you to be ignorant. . . .
>
> There are different kinds of gifts, but the same Spirit. There are different
> kinds of service, but the same Lord. There are different kinds of working, but
> the same God works all of them in all men.

> Now to each one the manifestation of the Spirit is given for the common good. To one there is given through the Spirit the message of wisdom, to another the message of knowledge by means of the same Spirit, to another faith by the same Spirit, to another gifts of healing by that one Spirit, to another miraculous powers, to another prophecy, to another the ability to distinguish between spirits, to another the ability to speak in different kinds of tongues, and to still another the interpretation of tongues. All these are the work of one and the same Spirit, and he gives them to each one, just as he determines. (1 Corinthians 12:1, 4–11)

Persons who have been transformed by the Holy Spirit through regeneration have been given at least one spiritual gift that they are to exercise. This gift can, but not necessarily must, relate to one's natural talents.

Natural talents and spiritual gifts, indeed, are alike in some ways. Both are given by God. Both are possessed by believers. Both can be used to the glory of God. But they are not the same.[37] First, the purpose of natural talents and spiritual gifts differs. The purpose of natural talents relates to the cultural mandate of Genesis 1:28 as one "exercises dominion" through such things as vocations and avocations. The purpose of spiritual gifts is focused more narrowly on serving, equipping, and edifying the body of Christ, the church.

The characteristics of natural talents and spiritual gifts differ as well:

Talents: are provided by God at the time of natural birth.
Gifts: are provided by God through his Holy Spirit at the time of spiritual birth.

Talents: are inclusive; everyone has a measure of all available talents.
Gifts: are exclusive; each person has at least one "unique" gift.

Talents: are given in differing amounts.
Gifts: are given in full amounts but are appropriated only in proportion to one's faith.

Talents: are manifested as potential to be developed.
Gifts: are already fully developed when given.

Talents: are divergent. The focus is on individuals functioning in the world.
Gifts: are convergent. The focus is on the church as varied members of the body seek to function in unity.

Talents: are self-recognizable. Thus one may seek "office" on one's own.

Gifts: are confirmed by others. Thus one is "called" to office by God through other believers.[38]

Talents: usage-accountability is directly to God.

Gifts: usage-accountability is to God but through the body of believers.

Because natural talents and spiritual gifts differ in the ways cited above, it is important not to carelessly blend them into one as we work with children. All children have talents. They were born with them, and they need to be recognized and developed. But not all children possess spiritual gifts. Only those who have been born again and have had their hearts transformed by the Holy Spirit have been equipped with such gifts. These, too, must be identified, usually with the assistance of other members of the body. Then they must be exercised within the body for its edification. Both natural talents and spiritual gifts are realities that need to be acknowledged and encouraged within our children and young people.

A listing of the gifts of the Holy Spirit named in the New Testament can be organized under three headings: equipping gifts, service gifts, and sign gifts. Additional gifts may be listed elsewhere in Scripture (e.g., intercession and creative ability—see Exodus 35:30–36:2 and 1 Chronicles 25:6–7), or they may not be listed in Scripture at all. There is also a debate within Christian circles whether all of the gifts present during the early church (e.g., tongues, healing, and miracles) are still present in the church today.

Equipping gifts: apostleship, prophecy, evangelism, shepherding, and teaching

Service gifts: administration, leadership, knowledge, wisdom, helps/service, encouragement, mercy, hospitality, giving, faith, discernment, and interpretation of tongues

Sign gifts: tongues, healing, and miracles

In summary, spiritual gifts are a primary avenue through which to achieve unity within the church. They reflect the diversity that is necessary if the church is to accomplish its kingdom task. Each gift and its related task are vital. When every member does her and his task, the body of Christ can function in unity as intended.

Chapter Conclusions

Return to the question cited earlier in this book: What do we desire most for our children? The answer to that question will dictate the spiritual pathway that we as parents and teachers will lay out for them. As stated previously, the greatest desire we should have for our children is that they acknowledge Jesus as Lord with their total beings. As we nurture our children toward that goal, they face both a barrier and blessings. The barrier is sin. They are born with sinful natures, and if nothing changes, they will become eternally lost. The blessings are the presence and promises of God, who has included them under the canopy of his Covenant of Grace.

Because they are sinners, all children need a Savior. Their Heavenly Father has provided them with this Savior, his Son Jesus. Our children, at a time in their life when they have reached spiritual discernment and understanding, must respond to the quickening of the Holy Spirit in their hearts and say "Yes!" to Jesus. They must be born again; they must exercise saving faith. At that time, they will be personally able to declare Jesus Christ as Lord of their hearts, minds, and bodies.

Happily, this spiritual development toward personal faith does not depend solely on them. From the moment the breath of life enters their beings, the children of believers are claimed by God to be his. He consecrates them, setting them apart for himself and his kingdom service. He promises to be a God to them. He provides them with the blessings of a Christian home and a Christian community. He sends his Spirit to transform their hearts from being oriented to sin to seeking to please him. This same Spirit then begins the lifelong sanctification process of transforming them into the very likeness of Jesus.

Scripture declares that someday, when the name of Jesus is heard, "every knee should bow . . . and every tongue confess that Jesus Christ is Lord, to the glory of God the Father" (Philippians 2:10–11). Lord willing, the first fruits of the consummation of Christ's kingdom will be our children, as they are transformed into new creations for the glory of God!

Chapter 6: Further Thoughts to Consider

1. What evidences can you cite that children are important to God?

2. What is the goal of biblical nurture? Can you support your answer with Scripture?

3. What are the key tenets of "covenant theology"? Is there a biblical basis for each tenet?

4. What does a noncovenantal view of children look like? How might these two differing theological positions also differ in their approaches to the spiritual development of children?

5. What does it mean that the children of a believing parent are holy? What implications of this are there for parents and teachers?

6. Why would holy children need a Savior? Are all covenant children saved?

7. What does it mean that "the Covenant of Grace is a family affair"?

8. What justification exists for the concept of "an age of understanding"? For "an age of accountability"?

9. Can parents and teachers help their children in the sanctification process? If not, why not? If so, how?

10. Should teachers be concerned with the spiritual development of their students? Why or why not?

Chapter 6: Notes and References

1. Genesis 9:9–17.
2. Genesis 15 and 17; Galatians 3:6–9.
3. Deuteronomy 6:4–6.
4. 2 Samuel 7:12–17; Luke 1:30–33.
5. Acts 2:29–36.
6. Genesis 9:12–17.
7. Exodus 31:13, 17.
8. 2 Samuel 7:11b–16.
9. Luke 22:17–20.
10. Genesis 17:9–14.
11. Romans 11:16; 1 Corinthians 7:14.
12. Acts 15:1–35.
13. 1 Corinthians 7:14.
14. Infant baptism does not save (i.e., baptismal regeneration), nor does it "forecast" salvation (i.e., presumptive regeneration). It is God speaking symbolically about a holy child upon whom he has placed a claim.
15. J. Inchley, *Kids and the Kingdom: How They Come to God* (Wheaton: Tyndale, 1977), 67.
16. 1 Corinthians 3:16–17.
17. Inchley, 54.
18. P. De Klerk, and R. R. De Ridder, eds., *Perspectives on the Christian Reformed Church* (Grand Rapids, MI: Baker, 1983), 189.
19. James 1:18; 1 Peter 1:23.
20. A book devoted to this topic and worth reading is *Will My Children Go to Heaven?* by Edward N. Gross (Phillipsburg, NJ: Presbyterian & Reformed, 1995).
21. Actually, God "knows" his children even before conception. See Romans 8:29, Ephesians 1:4, and 2 Timothy 1:9.

22. Psalm 51:5.
23. 2 Corinthians 5:17.
24. Romans 7:21–23.
25. There are two other views on the timing of regeneration worth noting: a) Roman Catholics and Lutherans teach baptismal regeneration, "the remission of original and actual sin and of the punishment due to them and regeneration in Christ or adopted sonship." Both churches also teach that the regeneration received in baptism may again be lost. b) Dutch theologian and statesman Abraham Kuyper viewed prebaptismal regeneration as the ground for the baptism of the infants of believing parents and thus a seal of a grace presumed to be already present. This "presumptive regeneration" of "covenant" children made the assumption that the children of a believing parent were saved unless in later life they proved otherwise. (A. A. Hoekema, *Saved by Grace* [Grand Rapid, MI: Eerdmans, 1989], 108–9.)
26. 1 Samuel 3:1, 7.
27. Inchley, 25–26.
28. Luke 2:42.
29. Ephesians 1:4; 2 Timothy 1:9.
30. John 14:2; Acts 1:9–11.
31. Acts 16:6–7; Romans 8:9–10; 2 Corinthians 3:17; Galatians 2:20.
32. Genesis 5:24 states that "Enoch walked with God."
33. Matthew 10:37–39; John 12:24–25.
34. Philippians 2:1–8.
35. Matthew 21:44.
36. A. J. Vander Griend, *Discover Your Gifts and Learn How to Use Them* (Grand Rapids, MI: CRC Publications, 1996), 15.
37. Vander Griend, 36.
38. Acts 1:21–26; 6:3; and 13:1–3.

Chapter 7

Nurture and Admonition
within the Family

Introduction

What's a parent to do? That's a good question. Bearing children is not usually the difficult part; it's the rearing of children that is the great unknown. Hospitals don't issue an instruction booklet with each child born. Parents are pretty much on their own to figure out what to do next. And, typically, they rear their children the same way they themselves were reared. After all, virtually the only instruction parents receive on the care and feeding of children is that which their own parents provided through example. That can be a good thing, and often it is. But that can also be a bad thing, for, because of sin, *every* home is dysfunctional to some degree. Consequently, parents may not want to repeat some of the parenting they themselves received. A cycle may need to be broken.

What's a parent to do? As stated before, the starting place for finding answers to this question must be God and what he has revealed about child rearing in his Word. But this introduces a new question: Where in the Bible can we find godly examples of child rearing? Certainly, the Bible must be chock-full of them! But, interestingly, there are few, if any, examples in the Bible of families that functioned in a God-honoring fashion. A quick sampling verifies this. Beginning with the Old Testament era, the first child ever born, Cain, was a murderer. Later, Jacob and Esau also exhibited severe sibling rivalry. Indeed, Jacob was a liar and a cheat, and his mother, Rebecca, joined him in collusion against her husband Isaac. Continuing on, we see that Eli's family was removed from the priesthood because he failed to discipline his sons. Samuel was reared in the ways of the Lord, but he was raised by Eli rather than by his own parents. And he, too, had sons who did not follow God's ways.

Finally, even David, the "man after God's own heart," had all sorts of troubles with his children. He was not a very good father. Continuing into the New Testament era, we note that neither Jesus nor Paul was married, so we can't learn from their example as parents. The account of Timothy as Paul's spiritual son, perhaps, comes closest to being a success story. Paul wrote about him: "I have been reminded of your sincere faith, which first lived in your grandmother Lois and in your mother Eunice and, I am persuaded, now lives in you also" (2 Timothy 1:5). Even here, however, it is likely that Timothy had an unbelieving father.

The lack of family role models in the Bible is something of a mystery. Perhaps the dysfunctional families of Scripture are meant to serve as a warning. Eli's family certainly does that. David's family also provides the warning that even godly parents can fail to produce godly offspring. On the other hand, a measure of comfort can be drawn from the fact that even the saints of old messed up on a regular basis, just as we do. Ultimately, it is not our feeble efforts but God's grace that prevails.

The Bible does, however, provide parents with guidance on rearing children. The model is laid out in Old Testament Israel. Parents are instructed on numerous occasions to be examples to their children and, simultaneously, to explain what they are doing and why. It is also obvious in Scripture that the family is God's primary instrument for nurturing children. Paul acknowledges this when he tells parents, fathers in particular, to bring their children up "in the nurture and admonition of the Lord" (Ephesians 6:4b). Each of these themes will be further developed in this chapter.

The Biblical Model for Child Rearing Is "Show and Tell"

The model family cannot be found in Scripture, for all have sinned and fallen short. Rather, we must look to the people of Israel corporately, the Jews as a whole, to provide us with key tenets for child rearing. Parents shared the ways of God with their children through example and explanation. This sharing also included symbolism and ceremony. Moses summarized this approach to child rearing when he addressed the Israelites:

> These commandments that I give you today are to be upon your hearts. Impress them on your children. Talk about them when you sit at home and when you walk along the road, when you lie down and when you get up. Tie them as symbols on your hands and bind them on your foreheads. Write them on the doorframes of your houses and of your gates. (Deuteronomy 6:6–9)

This model for child rearing could be labeled "show and tell." Parents are instructed both to show, or demonstrate, to children how to live and at the same time to tell, or explain, the rationale and significance of their actions. This approach is illustrated several times in the Old Testament.

> Then the LORD said to Moses, "Go to Pharaoh, for I have hardened his heart and the hearts of his officials so that I may perform these miraculous signs of mine among them that you may tell your children and grandchildren how I dealt harshly with the Egyptians and how I performed my signs among them, and that you may know that I am the LORD." (Exodus 10:1–2)

> [The LORD said:] "Obey these instructions as a lasting ordinance for you and your descendants. When you enter the land that the LORD will give you as he promised, observe this ceremony. And when your children ask you, 'What does this ceremony mean to you?' then tell them, 'It is the Passover sacrifice to the LORD, who passed over the houses of the Israelites in Egypt and spared our homes when he struck down the Egyptians.'" (Exodus 12:24–27)

> So Joshua called together the twelve men he had appointed from the Israelites, one from each tribe, and said to them, "Go over before the ark of the LORD your God into the middle of the Jordan. Each of you is to take up a stone on his shoulder, according to the number of the tribes of the Israelites, to serve as a sign among you. In the future, when your children ask you, 'What do these stones mean?' tell them that the flow of the Jordan was cut off before the ark of the covenant of the LORD. When it crossed the Jordan, the waters of the Jordan were cut off. These stones are to be a memorial to the people of Israel forever." (Joshua 4:4–7)

The parents in ancient Israel taught their children through object lessons; they illustrated and they explained. Psalm 78 summarizes this approach to nurture. It instructs parents to tell their children about the faithful and powerful acts of God in the past so that they and their grandchildren and their great-grandchildren may trust God in the future.

> O my people, hear my teaching; listen to the words of my mouth.
> I will open my mouth in parables, I will utter things hidden from of old—
>   things we have heard and known, things our fathers have told us.
> We will not hide them from their children; we will tell the next generation
>   the praiseworthy deeds of the LORD,
>   his power, and the wonders he has done.
> He decreed statues for Jacob and established the law in Israel,
>   which he commanded our forefathers to teach their children,
>   so the next generation would know them,
>   even the children yet to be born, and they in turn would tell their children.
> Then they would put their trust in God
>   and would not forget his deeds
>   but would keep his commands. (Psalm 78:1–7)

How does this model for family life fit in today's scene? Frankly, not as well as one might hope. Family life has become far too disconnected in today's frenetic world. But there are bits and pieces of this model that may be helpful to share for the sake of illustration. I think of my high school friend's small church that I attended with him on occasion. In contrast to my home church, where adults and children had separate programs and, consequently, had very little interaction, the parents in my friend's church often sponsored and/or joined in the recreational activities of their adolescent children. They actually did things together and enjoyed each other! The lasting impression was that these parents *really* liked being a part of their kids' lives. I also remember the Christian school principal who would take four of his children to a local supermarket after school each afternoon to sweep out the back storage rooms. As "pay," they would be given the vegetables that were no longer saleable, which would then be fed to the animals that this family was raising. The father taught his children by doing and explaining. It was a togetherness thing that bonded them as a family unit. I observed another family that spent a lot of time together camping and attending the athletic events of the children. It was obvious that the children were assimilating the values of their parents as they shared those real-life experiences. Finally, I also was blessed through a visit with a family that had devotions together in their living room after dinner each evening, led by the father. When it came time to pray, we all got down on our knees. It was powerful imagery that I can still see and feel to this day.

My most personal example of show-and-tell child rearing was homeschooling my fourteen-year-old daughter. I can see two huge benefits of the experience. One, I observed both the strengths and limitations of my daughter as a student, information that I wish I had known a number of years before. The second benefit was the bonding and instructional time that we had together. I was with her virtually all day every day, not always in a teaching mode, but we shared the four walls of our home more than we ever had before. In a real sense, I lived life with and in front of my daughter. The instructional portion of our day had several meaningful dimensions. The biblical studies program unfolded each morning with joint devotions. We each had different study Bibles from which we read one chapter a day. We alternately read and explained the verses. This was followed by a time of prayer. My daughter first shared about the spiritual needs of a country listed in *Operation World*—a guide for praying for the world. She then prayed for the needs of that country, and I followed by praying for other needs. I also incorporated into the Western Civilization course a heavy dose of church history as we proceeded through the various time periods. Both God's faithfulness to his church and the church's influence in the world were noted. Finally, each Friday we had family video night. I tried to select edifying films, such as *A Man for All Seasons, Martin Luther,* and *Roots.* Those types of experiences allowed me to live out and instruct on my value system. If I had not homeschooled my daughter, creating the time for this would have been far more difficult.

In summary, the Hebrews of old had the right idea on how to rear children in the ways of God: Get next to your children and teach them as though they were apprentices learning a trade. Teach them how to live the Christian life by living it before them and with them, always talking, always explaining. Personally introduce them to God and to his way of doing things.

The Family Is God's Primary Agent for the Nurture and Admonition of His Children

Effective CEOs tell us that every enterprise needs a plan—a long-range plan. All long-range plans, on the other hand, need to emerge from a mission statement with plainly stated goals. In a similar manner, families, too, need to establish desired outcomes. The roles and responsibilities of the various members of the family need to be developed. The concepts of honor, obedience, and authority should be mutually understood.

The family—its nature, its mission, and its goals

The family is the oldest and most basic of human institutions. It was established at the dawn of history, following God's decision that "It is not good for the man to be alone. I will make a helper suitable for him" (Genesis 2:18). God formed Eve from Adam's side and presented her to him as a companion, partner, and helper. The institution of marriage was formally established with God's mandate that "For this reason a man will leave his father and mother and be united to his wife, and they will become one flesh" (Genesis 2:24). In this manner, the covenant of companionship called marriage was formed, a covenant designed to serve as the foundational element of the family. A family begins with the loving relationship between a husband and a wife, formed for mutually fulfilling companionship.

It is difficult to know how much to make of "a man leaving his father and mother to be united with his wife." Certainly, the husband's highest priority must be his wife. And there may be some truth to the saying that "the parents of the groom lose a son, while the parents of the bride gain a son-in-law." Daughters, perhaps because they tend to be more relational, do often experience more difficulty in "leaving and cleaving." Yet they, too, must view their spouse as the number one person in their lives, for a new and separate family unit has been formed.

Following the joining together of a man and woman in the institution of marriage, families can experience completion through the bearing and rearing of children. As already noted, the issue of procreation was included in the Creation Mandate. Reproduction is a creation norm. The first parents, Adam and Eve, obeyed God's command and bore children. Upon the birth of her first child, Eve responded: "With the help of the LORD I have brought forth . . ." (Genesis 4:1). Every child born thereafter has been a gift from God as well.

God's purposes for childbearing were outlined above in Chapter 6: kingdom development, covenant fulfillment, and sheer enjoyment. The family is a God-ordained institution through which these purposes can be fulfilled. God's creation norms for children—the way things are supposed to be for them—are to have a father and a mother who jointly create and rear them as godly offspring. Marrying an unbeliever, divorce, parenting by persons of the same gender, and single parenting (although sometimes necessary) are not a part of God's original plan for the family. This type of antinormativity in marriage is alluded to as the prophet Malachi lamented Judah's unfaithfulness to Yahweh, their Covenant God:

> Have we not all one Father? Did not one God create us? Why do we profane the covenant of our fathers by breaking faith with one another?
>
> Judah has broken faith. A detestable thing has been committed in Israel and in Jerusalem: Judah has desecrated the sanctuary the LORD loves, by marrying the daughter of a foreign god. As for the man who does this, whoever he may be, may the LORD cut him off from the tents of Jacob—even though he brings offerings to the LORD Almighty.
>
> Another thing you do: You flood the LORD's altar with tears. You weep and wail because he no longer pays attention to your offerings or accepts them with pleasure from your hands. You ask, "Why?" It is because the LORD is acting as the witness between you and the wife of your youth, because you have broken faith with her, though she is your partner, the wife of your marriage covenant.
>
> Has not the LORD made them one? In flesh and spirit they are his. And why one? Because he was seeking godly offspring. So guard yourself in your spirit, and do not break faith with the wife of your youth.

> "I hate divorce," says the LORD God of Israel, "and I hate a man's covering himself with violence as well as with his garment," says the LORD Almighty. So guard yourself in your spirit, and do not break faith. (Malachi 2:10–16)

God hates divorce, and most people involved with divorce, especially the children, hate divorce as well. For any departure from God's creation norms is antinormative to his kingdom and covenant purposes for the family, and all such variances tend to produce pain within relationships. The best advice that can be given to any couple contemplating marriage or having children is to do it God's way. Anything less has built-in problems.

Finally, what are appropriate biblical goals for the nurture of children within a family? Again, answers to this question have already been provided, but God's words through Moses summarize them well:

> These are the commands, decrees and laws the LORD your God directed me to teach you to observe in the land that you are crossing the Jordan to posses, so that you, your children and their children after them may fear the LORD God as long as you live by keeping all his decrees and commands that I give you, and so that you may enjoy long life. Hear, O Israel, and be careful to obey so that it may go well with you and that you may increase greatly in a land flowing with milk and honey, just as the LORD, the God of your fathers, promised you.
>
> Hear, O Israel: The LORD our God, the LORD is one. Love the LORD your God with all your heart and with all your soul and with all your strength. (Deuteronomy 6:1–5)

Years later, Christ encapsulated with just two commands the law of which Moses was speaking: Love God and love your neighbor.[1] Simply stated, parents are to teach their children how to love. One way to demonstrate love for God is through obedience.[2] Willing obedience, in turn, is the product of a heart that has been broken and is in submission to Jesus as Lord and King—another legitimate goal for the nurture of children.

The mission and goals of the Christian family might best be summarized by the words of Joshua as he laid it on the line for the people of Israel: ". . . choose for yourselves this day whom you will serve . . . . But as for me and my household, we will serve the LORD" (Joshua 24:15). Parents are encouraged to take time to search the Scriptures and to think through, pray about, and write a similar mission statement for their own families, for families need to know where they are going if they hope ever to arrive at their destination.

The family—its roles and responsibilities

When God said that it was "not good for the man to be alone," he did not say that Adam was lonely, for he did have fellowship with God and he had the animals. The word *alone* seems to indicate that something or someone was missing, thus producing a "not good" aspect of creation. Eve was created to be a companion for Adam, as one who would complement or "complete" him. Adam needed Eve. She was "suitable" (i.e., tailor-made) for him. They were to be companions *and* partners in the fullest sense. Eve fulfilled Adam relationally, but she also was created to partner or "help" him fulfill the Cultural Mandate to "be fruitful" and "rule" (Genesis 1:28).

The key provision of the marriage ordinance upon which to focus, however, is the concept of unity. Two must become one—the miracle of marriage. This unity, which does include a physical and sexual component, is, in essence, spiritual in nature. The spirits of two separate persons meld together in a unified desire to serve God and find fulfillment in him. This "becoming united," however, can be achieved only through mutual submission. The preface to the Apostle Paul's exhortation to wives and husbands reads: "Submit to one another out of reverence for Christ" (Ephesians 5:21). Within the marital relationship, submission presupposes unity. Unhappily, as a consequence of the Fall, submission was replaced by competition. God's statement to Eve following her fall into sin could be paraphrased: "Your desire will be to dominate and control your husband, but your husband will, in fact, dominate and control you."[3] This message has held true for marriage in all succeeding generations. While the marriage ordinance remains in place as a creation norm, the "battle of the sexes" has tended to frustrate it ever since the Fall. Only when a husband and a wife submit themselves to God through Christ in the power of the Holy Spirit are they able to submit to each other as mandated.

While it is true that in Christ "there is neither . . . male nor female" (Galatians 3:28) and that males and females are called to be full partners in fulfilling the Cultural Mandate, in God's economy, or way of doing things, he has ordained distinctive roles and responsibilities within the family. To the husband and father, he has given the role of head or spiritual leader.[4] Understood correctly, this role is not one of dominance but, rather, one of servanthood and of taking spiritual initiative, much like Christ's role as the groom of his bride, the church.[5] It is fathers who are addressed by Paul to nurture and admonish their children in the Lord;[6] consequently, fathers are held specially accountable for the spiritual direction of their families. Understandably, husbands and fathers need both cooperation and help with these awesome responsibilities, and that is where wives and mothers are to assume a God-given role as well. But this support role is based on submission to the husband's role as spiritual leader of the home.[7] The wife serves as a vital partner and helper in the nurturing of the children. The Bible tells children to obey both parents and to honor both their father *and* their mother.[8] The nurturing task within the family is a shared responsibility.

But, you may ask, how does this *really* work in practice? What is meant by "spiritual direction," and what role does the wife have in decision making? The direction issue revolves around the Joshua pledge to "serve the Lord." That is the goal. Many (but not all) family decisions have spiritual ramifications that either direct a family toward the Lord or away from him. Where shall we live (the "Abraham-Lot" question)?[9] Which church shall we attend? To which school should we send the children? What will we watch on TV or the VCR? Should I stop working outside of the home when we have children? Should we have a family altar? Do we care whom our children date and where they go? What rules should be established for our children, and how should we discipline them? We could go on and on with similar spiritual-direction questions. Families are faced with direction questions, both large and small, virtually every day. If someone doesn't provide leadership, things tend to drift, and everyone does her or his own thing. God knew that that would happen, so he gave the spiritual leadership role to the husband. Only God knows why males received the nod, for they aren't always the ones best equipped for the task. But they did receive the responsibility, so they must try to figure out how to exercise leadership that seeks to serve others and not themselves.

Ideally, all issues that affect the family to any significant degree should be thoroughly discussed by both the husband and the wife. As children get older, they, too, should be asked for input into decisions that affect them. Common sense acknowledges that each family member has some level of expertise on issues and should be heard. Sometimes the husband-father will know more and sometimes the wife-mother or the children will. Each needs to be heard if they have something substantive to say. Most times, a husband and wife can arrive at a mutually satisfying answer—a win-win answer, if you will. This should be particularly true if both are believers. For those few instances when an impasse is reached after all views have been shared, the husband-father, as spiritual leader and head of his family, will have to make the call. He must not defer or abdicate (as much as he might like to), for it is he whom God has appointed for those times.[10]

The person responsible for any nonspiritual-direction tasks should typically be allowed to decide how to accomplish those tasks. How a job is done (e.g., loading the dishwasher or cutting the grass) should be left to the person doing the job, as long as it gets done satisfactorily. That's called empowerment, which is a demonstration of respect.

The key to all of this is the sacrificial agape love that the husband shows his wife and the respect that the father shows his children. The Apostle Paul spoke directly to men about their responsibilities:

> Husbands, love your wives, just as Christ loved the church and gave himself up for her to make her holy, cleansing her by washing with water through the word, and to present her to himself as a radiant church, without stain or wrinkle or any other blemish, but holy and blameless. In this same way, husbands ought to love their wives as their own bodies. He who loves his wife loves himself. After all, no one ever hated his own body, but he feeds and cares for it, just as Christ does the church—for we are members of his body. . . . Each one of you . . . must love his wife as he loves himself. (Ephesians 5:25–30, 33a)

> Husbands, love your wives and do not be harsh with them. (Colossians 3:19)

> Fathers, do not exasperate your children; instead, bring them up in the training and instruction of the Lord. . . . (Ephesians 6:4)

> Fathers, do not embitter your children, or they will become discouraged. (Colossians 3:21)

Husbands who actively and sacrificially (to the point of death?) seek the welfare of their wives and cherish them, as Christ does his bride, engender in their wives the love and trust that allows them to willfully submit to their husbands, for they know that their husbands would do them no harm, only good. Paul had this to say to wives:

> Wives, submit to your husbands as to the Lord. For the husband is the head of the wife as Christ is the head of the church, his body, of which he is the Savior. Now as the church submits to Christ, so also wives should submit to their husbands in everything. (Ephesians 5:22–24)

> Wives, submit to your husbands, as is fitting in the Lord. (Colossians 3:18)

Believing wives should find "submission" spiritually palatable, for they submit "as to" or "in" the Lord. That makes all the difference to a person who has already submitted all to her Savior and Lord.

It is curious that husbands are told to "love," whereas wives are told to "submit." Shouldn't wives love their husbands, and, as mentioned above, shouldn't a believing husband be willing to submit to his sister in Jesus? Both of these statements are probably true, but Paul may have simply been focusing on the particular foibles of fallen husbands and wives—husbands tending to be self-centered and harsh (to use Paul's word) and wives tending to seek control through manipulation and seduction. In Christ, these traits are tempered but, at times, still tempting.

This brings us to the responsibilities of children within the family setting. Two words are operative here—*honor* and *obey*.

Children are to honor and obey their parents

Children learn how to relate to their Heavenly Father through their relationships with their earthly parents. God gives two commands to children on how they are to relate to their parents: They are to honor, and they are to obey. These same two commands summarize the response God ultimately desires from his children as well.

What does it mean to "honor"?

The word *honor* is a substantive word. The Hebrew word for honor in the Old Testament is *kabed/kabod,* which means "to make heavy or weighty" or, in the figurative sense, to consider something or someone to be important.[11] The Greek word for honor in the New Testament is *timao/time,* which seems to indicate a sense of deference, recognition, reverence, and respect mingled with love.[12] Honoring is holistic in that it involves volition, attitude, and action. It is more than outward conformity, merely "showing" honor; it is "doing" or "living" honor. To honor someone, then, is no insignificant or incidental thing. It is an attitude of the heart.

Children are told in both the Old and New Testaments to honor their parents. The fifth of the Ten Commandments states: "Honor your father and your mother, so that you may live long in the land the LORD your God is giving you" (Exodus 20:12; Deuteronomy 5:16). The New Testament version repeats this command, but modifies the promise a bit: "'Honor your father and mother'—which is the first commandment with a promise—'that it may go well with you and that you may enjoy long life on the earth'" (Ephesians 6:2–3). To honor one's parents is to honor and respect God, in whose place they serve and from whom they derive their authority. Children are also to honor those who serve in the place of their parents, such as teachers and others in authority over them.

The often-overlooked promise that accompanies this command deserves some attention as well. The Old Testament version deals with the quality and length of life in the soon-to-be-occupied land of Canaan. The New Testament version, since it was written to the church in Ephesus, had to be modified slightly to fit the intended audience, but the essence of the promise is the same: Children who honor their parents will be blessed by God with his *shalom* during their lifetime, which under normal circumstances will be lengthy. The reason for this is that living life God's way always produces the quality of life intended at the beginning. The Creator of life knows how life is to be lived for maximum meaning, enjoyment, and longevity.

What does it mean to "obey"?

The New Testament command for children to obey their parents is less holistic but more directive than the command to honor. Twice children are told to obey. In Ephesians 6:1, we read, "Children, obey your parents in the Lord, for this is right," and Colossians 3:20 states, "Children, obey your parents in everything, for this pleases the Lord." The Greek word for "obey," *hypakouo,* derives from *akouo,* which means to "hear" or "listen"; with the prefix *hypo* it intensifies into "listening" in the sense of "obeying."[13]

When parents speak to children, children are to listen attentively. Based on personal public observation, that appears to be a rarity today. But there is more. To paraphrase James, children are not only to be hearers of the word; they must be doers of the word as well (1:22). Obeying involves actually doing that which the parents have requested—promptly. But the ball is not totally in the child's court on this command. Disobedient children are usually the product of parenting that is less than it should be. Any parent (or teacher) who continues to speak while a child is obviously not listening is an accessory to the sin of disobedience. And any parent (or teacher) who allows a child to get away with not doing what was requested is guilty of reinforcing sin in the child. The primary focus is not on the unfinished or poorly done task, for many tasks given to children could be done more easily by the adult. The key issue is obedience, something God takes really seriously, and parents and teachers must take it seriously as well.

Children are to listen and submit. That almost sounds like "Children are to be seen and not heard," an adage about children from days long ago that is rightly rejected by most people today. Yet there is a kernel of truth in that saying that needs to be revisited, for a common practice of children today is to first, listen (hopefully); second, argue or debate; and third, submit (perhaps). The additional activity of "argue or debate" has been wrongly inserted into the biblical mandate. All too often, the first response of a child after being told to do something is not a "Yes, Sir" or "Yes, Ma'am"; rather, it is a "Yes, *but . . .*" Instead of obeying first and discussing later, which is an appropriate sequence of events, children often try to dissuade parents and teachers from following through on their requests.

One classic illustration of a "Yes, but . . ." answer involved King Saul and the prophet Samuel.[14] Saul had been given explicit instructions to totally destroy the Amalekites and all of their possessions. But Saul, thinking he knew a better way, decided to save the best of the animals— for sacrifices, of course! Samuel's response was, "To obey is better than sacrifice, and to heed is better than the fat of rams" (1 Samuel 15:22b). Sinful people simply want to do it their way rather than God's way. And it's not just a matter of thinking they are smarter than God, which would be bad enough; it is straightforward rebellion and disobedience. Often, children are not much different when it comes to obeying those in authority over them. They, too, like to leverage some control, so they offer seemingly plausible alternatives to up-front obedience (such as being *really* nice). Parents and teachers need to be aware of traps that soft-pedal obedience. Without sounding too authoritarian, it must be said that the Bible really does mandate children to keep two ears open and one mouth shut when they are told to do something by their parents or teachers. And the reason for this is that the concept of submitting to and obeying authority is a big deal to God.

Obedience is, in fact, one of the operative themes throughout Scripture. Already in the Garden of Eden, obedience was given as the test of Adam and Eve's love for God. God selected only one tree of many from which they were not to eat—the tree of the knowledge of good and evil. Perfect obedience to that command would have been the gateway to eternal life, for the covenant that God originally established with Adam was one of works. Obedience, indeed, is important! It has been from the beginning. Our children need to understand and accept this.

Perhaps with this difficult pill to swallow in mind, Paul added a few clarifiers to his command to obey. In the Ephesians portion, he said: "Children, obey your parents *in the Lord. . . .*" The "in the Lord" phrase is explained by the Colossians' account that states: "obey . . . , *for this pleases the Lord.*" What is being said is that obeying parents is a God-thing, not just a parent-kid thing, for obeying parents is really obeying God. God placed parents in authority over children, and parents speak on his behalf. Besides, God really likes seeing obedience from his children.

This introduces the question of blind obedience, for the Colossians' portion instructs children to obey their parents "in everything." Is there a parental command that a child should not obey? The answer is "Yes." Any request by any person that is contrary to God's moral law must be disobeyed. Several biblical precedents exist on this issue. The Hebrew midwives "feared God" and did not obey the king of Egypt's command to kill all Hebrew boy babies.[15] Daniel and his three friends disobeyed royal commands to worship gods other than Yahweh.[16] Peter and the other apostles summarized this principle well in their response to the order of the Sanhedrin to stop preaching in Christ's name: "We must obey God rather than men!" (Acts 5:29).[17] Stated positively, children are to obey their parents in all things that are not in conflict with God's directives and norms for conduct.

Parents and teachers should expect children to obey, but they should not expect children always to agree with them. Children can be allowed the right to disagree, if this is done in a respectful manner. Adolescents, in particular, often seek to question ideas, not out of rebellion, but as a means to develop their own values and belief systems. Parents and teachers need to allow children and young people opportunities to discuss issues, if this is handled responsibly. Respect, however, is a two-way street, so a line must be drawn clearly between questioning ideas and questioning the authority of the person with the ideas.

Parents are to exercise biblical authority

A biblical understanding of headship, submission, honor, and obedience rests on a biblical view of authority. An improper view of authority is often the rub that irritates and, consequently, harms relationships. In Scripture, husbands are admonished *not* to "be harsh with [their wives]," and fathers are told *not* to "embitter [or exasperate] their children" (Colossians 3:19 and 21; Ephesians 6:4). These warnings are given because, since the Fall, authority has often been used for self-centered purposes.

The thirteenth chapter of Romans contains several principles that define biblical authority. First, "there is no authority except that which God has established" (Romans 13:1). Second, "he who rebels against the authority is rebelling against what God has instituted, and those who do so will bring judgment on themselves" (v. 2). Third, don't be afraid of the one in authority, "[f]or he is God's servant to do you good" (v. 3, 4). This third point reflects the crux of authority instituted by God (which is *all* authority): Authority is given to persons for the purpose of service. It is the servant-leader who best represents biblical authority.[18] It is the blending of legitimate power (i.e., the right or position to make and implement decisions), based on insight (knowing God's truth on a matter), for the purpose of service (seeking the welfare of others). The exercise of power alone is authoritarianism. The exercise of power for service, but without insight, is paternalism. Insight without power is impotence. Insight with power that is not directed toward service creates a benevolent dictatorship. Only when power, insight, and service are blended in proper balance can one exercise "authoritative" or biblical authority.

Christ was the perfect example of such authority. "The people were amazed at his teaching, because he taught them as one who had authority" (Mark 1:22). He also "amazed" his disciples, who asked, "What kind of man is this? Even the winds and the waves obey him!" (Matthew 8:27). The "authoritative" authority exercised by Jesus included truthful insight into the nature of the situation, was based on rightful power, and was used for the welfare of others.

The Primary Task of Parents and Teachers Is Discipling God's Children

There is a saying that "Charity begins at home." The same is true for the mandate in the Great Commission that calls for the discipling of all nations—it begins at home. The final words of Jesus before his ascension into heaven fleshed out this previously stated commission: ". . . you will be my witnesses in Jerusalem, and in all Judea and Samaria, and to the ends of the earth" (Acts 1:8b). The act of discipling operates from concentric circles, beginning with the core circle and moving outward. Discipling begins at home. The Apostle Paul made this clear when he listed requirements for church officers. To Timothy he wrote, "[An overseer] must manage his own family well and see that his children obey him with proper respect. (If anyone does not know how to manage his own family, how can he take care of God's church?)" (1 Timothy 3:4–5). To Titus, he wrote, "An elder must be . . . a man whose children believe and are not open to the charge of being wild and disobedient" (Titus 1:6). The first and primary responsibility of parents, fathers in particular, is to disciple their own children. This is done though providing "the nurture and admonition of the Lord."

In response to the question, "What's a parent to do?" Scripture answers, "And, ye fathers, provoke not your children to wrath: but bring them up in the nurture and admonition of the Lord" (Ephesians 6:4. The King James Version of the Bible is quoted here because it is the only version that uses the words *nurture* and *admonition*, words that most adequately capture the intended meaning). Fathers, as the God-ordained spiritual leaders within their homes, are given two commands regarding their children—to *nurture* them and to *admonish* them. But this nurture and admonition must not be in the power or from the agenda of the father; rather, it must be *of the Lord.* Anything less will anger and embitter his children, which will lead to discouragement.[19] God tells parents to rear his children his way! The same holds true for teachers. Indeed, there is a God-normed way to instruct, correct, and guide children, and those who have been given this authority and responsibility had better do their homework on nurturing in God's way. Otherwise, such efforts will be frustrating to the children. If the insight or the service component of biblical authority is missing, nurture will degenerate into manipulation and control. Parents or teachers will have promoted their own agenda rather than God's agenda. And kids know the difference.

What is the biblical definition of "nurture"?

The New Testament Greek word *paideuo/paideia* can be translated to mean either "nurture" or "discipline." In Scripture, nurture and discipline are one and the same, a fact worth pondering. *Paideuo/paideia* is used in various ways in the New Testament, and to better understand the meaning of nurture or discipline, one should note its two primary uses.

First, this word can refer to instruction and education in the sense of moral training:

> Moses was *educated* in all the wisdom of the Egyptians and was powerful in speech and action. (Acts 7:22, emphasis mine)

> Then Paul said: "I am a Jew, born in Tarsus of Cilicia, but brought up in this city. Under Gamaliel I was thoroughly *trained* in the law of our fathers and was just as zealous for God as any of you are today." (Acts 22:3, emphasis mine)

> And the Lord's servant must not quarrel; instead, he must be kind to everyone, able to teach, not resentful. Those who oppose him he must gently *instruct,* in the hope that God will grant them repentance leading them to a knowledge of the truth. (2 Timothy 2:24–25, emphasis mine)

Second, this word can refer to the chastening or correcting that is commonly associated with discipline:

> When we are judged by the Lord, we are being *disciplined* so that we will not be condemned with the world. (1 Corinthians 11:32. emphasis mine)

And you have forgotten that word of encouragement that addresses you as sons:
> "My son, do not make light of the Lord's *discipline,*
>   and do not lose heart when he rebukes you,
> because the Lord *disciplines* those he loves,
>   and he punishes everyone he accepts as a son."

Endure hardship as discipline; God is treating you as sons. For what son is not *disciplined* by his father? If you are not *disciplined* (and everyone undergoes *discipline*), then you are illegitimate children and not true sons. Moreover, we have all had human fathers who *disciplined* us and we respected them for it. How much more should we submit to the Father of our spirits and live! Our fathers *disciplined* us for a little while as they thought best; but God *disciplines* us for our good, that we may share in his holiness. No *discipline* seems pleasant at the time, but painful. Later on, however, it produces a harvest of righteousness and peace for those who have been trained by it. (Hebrews 12:5–11, emphases mine)

This word can also refer to whipping or chastising in the sense of punishment rather than correction, but this usage is unusual. The only time it is used in this manner in the New Testament is the time Christ was before Pilate:

> Therefore, I will *punish* him and then release him. (Luke 23:16, emphasis mine)

> For the third time he spoke to them: "Why? What crime has this man committed? I have found in him no grounds for the death penalty. Therefore I will have him *punished* and then release him." (Luke 23:22)

The closest Old Testament Hebrew equivalent to *paideuo* is *yisser/musar,* which is defined to mean "admonish, correct, discipline, chastise, instruct." It generally refers to discipline in the sense of teaching or even warning a person to obey God's law, often as a corrective response to improper behavior. Following are two passages that reflect this.

> Know then in your heart that as a man *disciplines* his son, so the LORD your God *disciplines* you.
>   Observe the commands of the LORD your God, walking in his ways and revering him. (Deuteronomy 8:5–6, emphases mine)

> Hold on to *instruction,* do not let it go; guard it well, for it is your life.
> Do not set your foot on the path of the wicked
>   or walk in the way of evil men. (Proverbs 4:13–14, emphasis mine)

It is clear, then, that the biblical definition of nurture and discipline are synonymous. This nurture or discipline contains two primary emphases, that of instruction or education and that of chastening or correcting.

What is the biblical definition of "admonition"?

The second part of the directive found in Ephesians 6:4 calls for admonition, or *instruction that carries a warning.* This is the Greek word *noutheteo/nouthesia.* Several other Scripture passages that use the word *noutheteo* shed light on its meaning:

> I myself am convinced, my brothers, that you yourselves are full of goodness, complete in knowledge and competent to *instruct* one another. (Romans 15:14, emphasis mine)

> These things happened to them as examples and were written down as *warnings* for us, on whom the fulfillment of the ages has come. (1 Corinthians 10:11, emphasis mine)

> Let the word of Christ dwell in you richly as you teach and *admonish* one another with all wisdom, and as you sing psalms, hymns and spiritual songs with gratitude in your hearts to God. (Colossians 3:16, emphasis mine)

> Now we ask you, brothers, to respect those who work hard among you, who are over you in the Lord and who *admonish* you. (1 Thessalonians 5:12, emphasis mine)

> Yet do not regard him as an enemy, but *warn* him as a brother. (2 Thessalonians 3:15, emphasis mine)

> *Warn* a divisive person once, and then *warn* him a second time. After that, have nothing to do with him. (Titus 3:10, emphasis mine)

This word *noutheteo* appears to have several meanings that are different from the word *paideuo.* This word appeals more to the reasoning ability and understanding of a mature Christian, which distinguishes *noutheteo* from *paideuo* and reflects the different origins of the two words. While the former derives from *nous,* which means "mind" or "intellect," the latter comes from *pais,* which means "child." Accordingly, subordination gives way to coordination. The one being confronted in counseling is dealt with as a responsible person whose level of understanding renders her or him accountable. It seems to speak to older people rather than to younger children. It does not seek to coerce or manipulate. It treats the person as one who is responsible and accountable, having reached the age of understanding.

Like *paideuo,* the word *noutheteo* can describe instruction that comes from above. Thus, in 1 Corinthians 10:11 and 1 Thessalonians 5:12, the believer is tutored by God and the appointed church leaders. But *noutheteo* is not limited to that perspective, as is evident from the remaining texts. Christians are told to admonish and instruct one another in mutual sharing of their knowledge of the faith. It is a word for biblical confrontation or counsel.

It should be remembered, however, that instruction, correction, and admonition are interrelated and interdependent acts that will often be taking place simultaneously. They are dealt with separately only for purposes of analysis.

It appears, then, that the nurture or discipline of *paideuo/paideia* is most applicable to younger children. This includes both instruction and correction. The admonition of *noutheteo/nouthesia* becomes more applicable as children mature in the faith and become more accountable for their actions. The transition will, of course, be a gradual one, occurring at various rates depending on the persons and the circumstances.

Chapter Conclusions

God tells us that he desires Godly offspring.[20] To accomplish that end, he consecrates his children from conception, setting them apart for service in his kingdom. At that point, he entrusts them to parents who are mandated to nurture them toward sanctification, which is a holiness that will begin in their hearts and permeate their entire beings from the inside out. This nurture is to take place within a family context and is to be led by the father, who serves as the spiritual head. The wife and mother assists in this as the covenantal partner of the husband and father. They jointly are called to nurture their children in God's ways *and* in God's way. The children, on the other hand, are to honor and obey their parents, for this is pleasing to God. The primary responsibility of parents, then, is to rear their children in the nurture and admonition of the Lord with the goal of leading them toward responsive discipleship of Jesus Christ. The next two chapters will explore what it means in practice to nurture and admonish children toward this discipleship.

Chapter 7: Further Thoughts to Consider

1. Why do you think the Bible contains so few models of godly nurture of children?

2. Do you agree that the most prominent model of godly nurture in the Bible is that of "show and tell?" What other models might there be?

3. What are some ways in which this "apprenticeship" model could be implemented in today's busy world?

4. Write (and share) what you believe to be a biblically based mission statement and set of goals for a Christian family.

5. Why is it important for a family to have a designated spiritual head?

6. Do you believe that divorce could be eradicated if husbands would love and cherish their wives as Christ loves and cherishes his bride, the church? Explain your answer.

7. Why is obedience such a crucially important concept to teach children?

8. Is obeying one's parents a lifelong obligation? Is honoring one's parents a lifelong obligation?

9. What examples can you provide of authority that did not include a proper balance of insight, power, and service?

10. Do you agree that "the primary task of parents and teachers is discipling God's children"? Why or why not?

Chapter 7: Notes and References

1. Matthew 22:34–40.
2. John 14:15; 1 John 5:3.
3. Genesis 3:16b. Susan Foh, in her book *Women and the Word of God: A Response to Biblical Feminism* (Phillipsburg, NJ: Presbyterian & Reformed, 1979), develops this thought by comparing Genesis 4:7, which uses the same word structure, with Genesis 3:16b.
4. 1 Corinthians 11:3; Ephesians 5:23. Jim Hurley, in his book *Man and Woman in Biblical Perspective* (Grand Rapids. MI: Zondervan, 1981), presents a biblically balanced view of male headship within the home. See Chapter 6 in particular.
5. Ephesians 5:24–33.
6. Ephesians 6:4.
7. Ephesians 5:22–24.
8. Ephesians 6:1–3.
9. Genesis 9.
10. J. B. Hurley, *Man and Woman in Biblical Perspective* (Grand Rapids, MI: Zondervan. 1981), 150ff.
11. 1 Samuel 2:30; 1 Kings 3:13; Proverbs 3:9–10; Malachi 1:6.
12. Romans 12:10; 1 Timothy 5:17; 1 Peter 2:17.
13. Mark 1:27, 4:41; Hebrews 11:8.
14. 1 Samuel 15.
15. Exodus 1:17.
16. Daniel 3:18, 6:10.
17. The word *obey* here translates the Greek verb *peitharcheo*. That it means the same as *hypakouo* is evident from its use in Titus 3:1.
18. Mark 9:35, 10:42–45; John 13:12–17.
19. Colossians 3:21.
20. Malachi 2:15.

Chapter 8

INSTRUCTIVE NURTURE

Introduction

QUESTION 1: *What is it that God wants parents and teachers to tell his children?*
ANSWER: *"God loves you!"*

QUESTION 2: *What is it that God wants his children to tell him in response?*
ANSWER: *"I love you, too!"*

Sometimes it is a good exercise to try to distill complex ideas down to their most elementary form. I recently had to do that during a Prison Fellowship weekend that I was leading for the inmates of a state penitentiary. My time was limited, but the good news of Jesus Christ had to be communicated in a simple but total way so that the inmates could understand their need to respond to the claims of Christ on their lives. I began with the same two statements written above: God loves you, and God wants you to love him back.

Those are the essentials, aren't they? Everything we do with our children must communicate that God loves them. But that is only the front half of the message. God expects an in-kind response from them, for to love God is the first and greatest of commandments. It is the bottom line, the starting place, for how we and our children must live.

Returning Children to God through Biblical Nurture

Children are gifts from God, and they are to be returned to God through the process of biblical nurture. The prayer of Samuel's mother, Hannah, reflected this: "O LORD Almighty, if you will . . . not forget your servant but give her a son, then I will give him to the LORD for all the days of his life . . ." (1 Samuel 1:11).

God directs parents and teachers: "Train a child in the way he should go, and when he is old he will not turn from it" (Proverbs 22:6). This verse can be paraphrased to read: "Start a child off along the proper path, and when he is older he will not turn off onto another pathway." The analogy is that of one walking with a person to give the individual a proper start on a journey. At some point along the way, the person is allowed to continue on his or her own, but the guide is always watchful in case the person needs additional direction or assistance.

The Hebrew word in Proverbs 22:6 for "train" is *chanak*. This same word is used for the dedication of a house (Deuteronomy 20:5) and of Solomon's temple (1 Kings 8:63; 2 Chronicles 7:5). The noun form of this verb is *chanukkah,* and it is used in reference to the dedication of an altar to God (Numbers 7:10, 84, 88), the temple (Psalm 30), and the wall of Jerusalem (Nehemiah 12:27–30). In the last passage, it is associated with purification. Thus, in the use of *chanak* in Proverbs 22:6, there are overtones of dedication and purification. Children are to be trained or nurtured in the sense of dedicating them in purity to God.

Parents and teachers who seek to nurture their children in the Lord must be people who have traveled the road themselves and know first-hand the pathway with its pleasures and its dangers. To be able to guide children along the path of godliness, parents and teachers must already know Jesus as Savior, have committed to him as Lord, and understand how he has revealed himself through his Word and his world.

This nurturing journey is to be intentional; parents and teachers are to take the initiative. They are to grasp the hands of their children and not only lead them but also instruct them so clearly that the children will eventually be able to navigate the pathway by themselves. The goal is self-direction or, if you will, Christ-direction.

Instruction *in the Lord* is a primary ingredient of biblical nurture. Many parents, at the time of infant dedication or baptism, promise before God and humankind to "tell their little ones about Jesus and his love for them," with the goal that, someday, their children will love Jesus back. But this simplest of all messages has a way of becoming complex in the world of the twenty-first century. Immediately, questions arise. Who is responsible for communicating this message? Parents? Preachers? Teachers? What form should this message take? One cannot simply repeat the phrase "God loves you" thousands of times and expect that to be sufficient. Where should this instruction take place? How does it differ for children at differing stages of development? And, given the rapid changes in society and culture, how does it differ from the instruction that parents and teachers themselves received as children? Is there a special way to instruct the "children of this millennium?"

This chapter seeks to provide answers to these and other questions about the instruction of God's children. First, it explores both "truth" and "knowing" in this day and age. Secondly, it examines the "divine tripod" of the Christian family, church, and school to see how each has roles and responsibilities in the instruction of children.

Truth and Knowing through the Ages

Every so often as I taught my college classes, I came across new and difficult vocabulary terms that I thought the students should know. Not wanting to lose them by using big words that might turn them off, I told them that if they were to sound like college graduates someday, they would need to be able to include words in their speech that contain more than one or two syllables. After all, they were paying big bucks for a college education that should allow them at least to *sound* highly educated! Plus, the next time they called home, they could try to impress their parents by including in their conversation a few of the multisyllabic words that they had learned in class. Well, I need to introduce a few words here, too, that could be challenging. But for us to understand the finer points of biblical instruction, certain terms that come from the field of philosophy can be useful.

The discipline of philosophy revolves around the seeking of answers to three basic questions: What is real?—which is answered in the study of ontology (also called metaphysics); What is true?—which is answered in the study of epistemology; and What is good?—which is answered in the study of axiology. The first two of these questions need to be addressed here, for children must understand and be committed to the biblical answers to these questions if they are to be transformers of the world rather than conformers to the world. The first (ontological) question can be applied to the nature of *truth;* the second (epistemological) question can be applied to the nature of *knowing,* or the way(s) in which one comes to know the truth. Because today's children are growing up in an age that appears to be in transition from modernity to postmodernity, it is important to trace the ways in which perceptions of truth (the *what* it is) and knowing (the *how* we can know it) have changed over the years. Finally, we need to arrive at some conclusions about a biblical approach to both truth and knowing.

Truth and knowing during the premodern age

During the Middle Ages, the nature of truth was determined primarily by the Roman Catholic church. Truth was whatever the church said it was. Transcendent truth was brokered by the Catholic church to its members through three modes: Jesus, the Truth incarnate; the Latin Vulgate version of the Bible, the written truth; and the truth present in the sacraments. But "truth" also was found in the temporal realm, in papal pronouncements and church tradition.

One came to know the truth *only* through the teachings, pronouncements, and actions of the Catholic church. Truth could not be proven; it had to be accepted by faith—trusting and obeying the clergy who spoke for the Bishop of Rome who spoke for Christ. Stated most simply, the minds of parishioners were viewed as *tabula rasa,* blank slates, to be written upon by the church. There was no interactivity and no questioning; only trusting acceptance.

Truth and knowing during the modern age

The eighteenth-century Enlightenment spawned the age of modernity. Vertical or transcendent truth was replaced by horizontal or temporal truth alone—only that which could be observed and measured. The church was viewed as being irrelevant, as was the God it served. Science and, later, technology became the new "saviors" of humankind. The universe was seen as being structured and lawful and, thus, predictable and knowable. Humankind was viewed, in a corresponding manner, as being capable of rational, logical, and organized thought. Science became the broker between the knowable universe and the knower. The five senses, the scientific method, and empirical research became the epistemological avenues to knowing the truth. It was both the age of science and the age of reason. And truth was something on which people could still agree.

Truth and knowing during the postmodern age

Beginning during the 1930s in Europe and the 1960s in North America, postmodernity emerged as the next dominant "spirit of the age." While it is still in a transitional stage, since individuals change more rapidly than institutions, postmodernists reject universal order and objective meaning. They deny the possibility of a metanarrative, a universal story that binds all humankind together. Rather, postmodernists focus on the individual, the subjective, and the fragmentary. Truth that is external, absolute, or objective gives way to truth that is internal, relative, and subjective. Ontologically, truth is that which each individual holds to be true for a particular time and place. Epistemologically, truth is "constructed" within the schemata or cognitive structures of a person. One actively "builds" an internal conceptual framework or view of the world, primarily though personal experience. Today, people no longer find agreement on what is true. Every person does "that which [is] right in his [or her] own eyes" (Judges 21:25b, KJV).

Truth and knowing—a Christian response

Imagine for a moment that you are a student in a secular institution and the professor asks your class: How do you know (or arrive at) whatever you believe to be the truth? The politically correct answer of the day would no doubt reflect the postmodern views outlined above. There may even be a hearty soul who would make claims for the modernist view that the empirical data of research are still the avenue to truth. But neither answer is sufficient for the Christian student.

Before developing a biblically faithful response to this inquiry about determining truth, however, we need to give credit to whom credit is due. Each of the three views described above actually contains a nugget or two that is true; unhappily, however, their proponents have tended to absolutize each nugget so that, for them, the part has become the whole. This is like taking one piece of a jigsaw puzzle and stating that it is the entire picture.

Looking first at postmodernism, several positive things can be said. This position states that there are additional ways of knowing beyond the cognitive, such as the emotional, experiential, social, and intuitive, to name a few. That is true. And, while the postmodernist would claim that the process of knowing the truth is totally subjective, we agree that knowing does, indeed, have a subjective dimension. Constructivism, the leading learning theory of the postmodern age, rightly states that the mind has basic structures or schemata that organize information and that the learner does, in fact, actively process, reformulate, and "construct" an internal conceptual framework or view of the world.

The modernist, too, contributes a piece to the big picture. In addition to having a subjective dimension, knowing the truth also has an objective dimension. All truth originates externally, outside of the individual, and truth can find expression in propositional, observable, and measurable forms. Truth, indeed, is absolute and unchanging; thus, different people can agree on what is true.

Finally, the premodern inclusion of the transcendent resonates with the Christian, for God is the source of all truth.

Each of the three dominant approaches to truth and knowing in the Western world contains that which is true, but none has captured the total picture. For that, one must go to God's revelation of truth, which indeed is transcendent, objective, and experiential and calls for a subjective or personal response. This revelation-response paradigm is an important component of instruction in the Lord.

Revelation

God has revealed his character, his acts, and his will through several modes: first, through creation; second, through the written Word—the Bible; and, ultimately, in the Incarnate Word—Jesus Christ. In addition, for understanding to take place, God illuminates hearts and minds through his Holy Spirit.

a. The creation is God's general revelation

The creation reveals truths about God in the same manner that a cathedral tells much about the architect, a painting about the artist, and a book about the author, for God was the architect, the artist, the author, and the Creator of the world in which we live. To know something about God, one needs only to look around! A psalm written by David expresses it well:

> The heavens declare the glory of God;
>   the skies proclaim the work of his hands.
> Day after day they pour forth speech;
>   night after night they display knowledge.
> There is no speech or language
>   where their voice is not heard.
> Their voice goes out into all the earth'
>   their words to the ends of the world. (Psalm 19:1–4)

The natural order proves that there is a mighty and majestic Creator. The Apostle Paul affirmed this: ". . . what may be known about God is plain to [humankind], because God has made it plain to them. For since the creation of the world God's invisible qualities—his eternal power and divine nature—have been clearly seen, being understood from what has been made . . ." (Romans 1:19–20).

God's revelation of himself through creation is called general revelation because it is accessible to all people. Even the unbeliever can't help but "bump into" God's presence—his design and will—in his world. Some would label these as "common grace insights," but for the unbeliever it is a "grace" that condemns. There is no excuse for not having knowledge of God, for he has actively disclosed himself through his creation from the very beginning.

b. The Bible is God's special revelation

The advent of sin into the world created the need for a more explicit form of revelation than that found in creation. The world became too dark to see without a light; the eyes of humankind became too clouded to see without a pair of divine spectacles. Consider the following:

> [Christianity] is a religion that rests on revelation: nobody would know the truth about God, nor be able to relate to him in a personal way, had God not first acted to make himself known. But God has so acted, and the sixty-six books of the Bible, thirty-nine written before Christ came and twenty-seven after, are together the record, interpretation, and expression of His self-disclosure. God and godliness are the Bible's unifying themes.[1]

God chose to communicate his unified Word though chosen human instruments. The words are God's; the style belongs to the writers. Moses was the first writer. Following the formal presentation of the Ten Commandments, written by the very finger of God himself, Moses recorded the history of humankind from creation up to the claiming of the promised land of Canaan. The Bible continues as an historical-redemptive account of God's interaction with humankind, ending with the apocalyptic book of Revelation, written by the Apostle John.

An important point needs to be made here: The Bible is to be used as a means to an end, not as an end in itself. Because the fall into sin both blinded humankind and subjected creation to "frustration" and "bondage" (Romans 8:20–22), one function of the Bible is to act as a light that breaks through the sin-caused gloom in creation. The psalmist wrote: "Your word is a lamp to my feet and a light for my path" (Psalm 119:105). Another psalmist, David, adds, ". . . in your light we see light" (Psalm 36:9b). By shining the Bible as a light on creation, we are able to discern God's truth from Satan's lie.

The Bible also functions as a pair of eyeglasses. The Protestant reformer John Calvin, in dealing with the knowledge of God as Creator, stated:

> Just as old or bleary-eyed men and those with weak vision, if you thrust before them a most beautiful volume, even if they recognize it to be some sort of writing, yet can scarcely construe two words, but with the aid of spectacles will begin to read distinctly; so Scripture, gathering up the otherwise confused knowledge of God in our minds, having dispersed our dullness, clearly shows us the true God.[2]

Perhaps referring to Calvin's "most beautiful volume" statement, the *Belgic Confession of Faith* describes creation as the "universe [that] is before our eyes like a beautiful book."[3] The eyeglasses of Scripture allow us to read and understand this "beautiful book," and it provides us with the insights necessary to get on with our original kingdom task. By viewing creation through the eyeglasses of Scripture, we are able to make sense of the world in which we live and recognize our place and purpose within it.

Instructing children in the Lord begins with the Bible, for the Bible explains God's story more clearly than any of the other modes of revelation. From their earliest years, children need to be immersed in Scripture. They need to become biblically literate. But instruction in the Bible must not be done in a willy-nilly fashion. There are several important things to remember as one studies God's written Word.

(1) The Bible is God speaking. Thus the focus must remain on what God is saying and not on what humankind is doing. The Bible is more than a guidebook on moral living. Its lessons must be more than "have the patience of Job," "be wise like Solomon," or "exhibit the courage of Daniel." In each of these stories we must ask: What is God saying? and Why did he include this in his Holy Canon?

(2) The entire Bible is God's Word and continues to be relevant today. God's story of humankind in time and space began in a garden (Genesis 1 and 2) and will culminate in a city (Revelation 21 and 22). The focal point throughout this story is Jesus Christ. To fully understand the significance of Christ's first and second comings, one must begin with Genesis. To quote Francis Schaeffer, "Take away the first three chapters of Genesis, and you cannot maintain a true Christian position nor give Christianity's answers."[4] We must begin at the beginning, then, and take what sometimes is called an historical-redemptive approach to reading the Bible. There is a sequence that should be understood. There is continuity and discontinuity as the redemptive story unfolds historically.

(3) The entire Bible is to be used to explain particular passages of the Bible. As is sometimes said, the Bible can be used to prove anything. Anyone can take a text out of context and absolutize it—letting it stand alone, speaking with binding authority. But the Bible is a whole book, inspired by one God who speaks with one voice. Apparent contradictions are a result of finite interpretation, not the fragmentation of the message. Each portion of Scripture must be understood within concentric circles, beginning with the immediate text and moving out into a Scripture-wide context.

(4) Each portion of Scripture is to be examined within at least four settings to gain the most accurate understanding of what God is saying. First, there is the historical-cultural setting. Should the passage under study be applied literally in the same way for all times and places, or should it be applied conceptually, in different ways for different cultural settings? Next, since

the entire Bible points to Jesus, what connections are there with the first advent of Christ? Then, in a similar manner, what connections are there with Christ's second advent, when he will return to establish his kingdom in fullness? Does the Scripture passage under consideration speak to that event as well? Finally, each portion of Scripture should be examined within a contemporary setting. What is God's Word saying to us (e.g., as the church) today in our particular situation?

(5) The Bible must be viewed as the final authority for all matters of faith and practice. If, for instance, findings from general revelation appear to conflict with what Scripture is saying, the problem is with the interpretation skills applied to general and/or special revelation, not with the inconsistency of the message. Again, God speaks with one voice. It is vitally important to remember that the Bible is to interpret and transform culture; culture is never to interpret and transform the Bible. As the most understandable form of God's revelation, the Bible must serve as the bottom line of authority when differences of interpretation and application arise.[5]

In summary, the Bible, of all the modes of God's revelation, most clearly tells his story. It is his metanarrative account of human history—the story that explains all other stories. It is a seamless, coherent account of life from the beginning to the end of time and into eternity—written from God's perspective. It is the story that transcends all others.

All of God's children, in one sense, need to become biblical scholars, for everything else in life depends on their understanding of the meaning of God's Word for them and for their world. They need to be nurtured in biblical study skills and in understanding the big picture with its eternal themes.

c. Jesus Christ is God's personal revelation

In addition to revealing himself through creation and the Bible, God has revealed himself most fully through his Son, Jesus Christ, his exact representation. The Bible, the Inscripturated Word, points us to Christ, the Incarnate Word, the pivotal focus of both the Old and New Testaments. Jesus is the ultimate revelation of God to humankind. His own words bear testimony to this: "I and the Father are one" (John 10:30), and "Anyone who has seen me has seen the Father" (John 14:9). If we want to know God intimately, in a personal relationship, Jesus tells us that he is "the way and the truth and the life. No one comes to the Father except through me. If you really knew me, you would know my Father as well" (John 14:6–7).

For one to understand the Bible, one must first know Jesus person-ally. The Spirit of Christ must dwell within individuals for them to understand the meaning of God's written words.[6] Instructing children toward a heart commitment to Christ, then, is valid in the home, the church, and the (Christian) school, for such commitment is a requisite for understanding God's special and general revelation.

d. The Holy Spirit is God's agent for revelation

Typically, the Holy Spirit is not designated as one of the modes of God's self-revelation, as are creation, the Bible, and Jesus. Yet to accept Christ as Savior and Lord, one must be regenerated by the Holy Spirit. To understand both special and general revelation, one must receive the illu-mination of the Holy Spirit. And the leading of the Holy Spirit in revealing the will of the Father is a vital part of the Christian experience. Indeed, the Holy Spirit is intricately entwined in God's revelatory activities.

In essence and in action, the Spirit is characterized by truth. He brings people to the truth of God. Note the words of Christ:

> And I will ask the Father, and he will give you another Counselor to be with you forever—the Spirit of truth. The world cannot accept him, because it nei-ther sees him nor knows him. But you know him, for he lives with you and will be in you.
> ... the Counselor, the Holy Spirit, whom the Father will send in my name, will teach you all things and will remind you of everything I have said to you....
> When the Counselor comes, whom I will send to you from the Father, the Spirit of truth who goes out from the Father, he will testify about me.
> ... when he, the Spirit of truth, comes, he will guide you into all truth. He will not speak on his own; he will speak only what he hears, and he will tell you what is yet to come. He will bring glory to me by taking from what is mine and making it known to you. (John 14:16–17, 26; 15:26; 16:13–14)

The Holy Spirit functions as the Spirit of truth, God's agent for revelation.

In summary, God has revealed himself to humankind through several different modes: creation, the Bible, Jesus Christ, and the Holy Spirit. Each shows God's story through a different set of lens. Each is impor-tant in the instruction of children. For a person to see God through creation, the Bible is needed. To understand the Bible, one needs both Jesus and the Holy Spirit. These facts are important to recognize as we seek to instruct children about God's world and their place in it.

Response

God's revealed truth always demands a response. That fact is not, however, accepted by all people. The Greek world during the time of the Apostle Paul didn't believe that truth demanded anything; rather, truth was viewed as something objective, a thing that could be controlled and even owned. Truth to the Greeks was static rather than dynamic. Truth could be mastered through the rational mind. To know truth, for the Greeks, was solely a cognitive process.

Much of education today reflects this view of and approach to truth (assuming one accepts the premise that truth exists!). Skills are "mastered," tests and courses are "taken," credits or units are "accumulated," degrees are "earned" and "awarded." Typically, course content is memorized and given back on a pencil-paper test. Different labels are provided for differing degrees of cognitive knowledge. An "A," a 4.0 GPA, a diploma on the wall are indicators of an educated person. There is even closure to knowing—terminal degrees.

The Hebrews differed from the Greeks in the way that they viewed truth itself as well as how one came to know the truth. This perspective is reflected throughout the Old Testament in particular and finds its fulfillment in the person and teachings of Christ.

a. What is truth?

The Hebrews believed that truth is living, active, dynamic, and relational rather than dead, passive, static, and individualistic. Truth masters, controls, and transforms. One doesn't own the truth; one is owned *by* the truth. One doesn't know truth as one "knows stuff"; rather, one *is known by* the truth. The answer to the "What is truth?" question, posed by the Roman governor Pontius Pilate many years ago (John 18:38), is centered in Christ. Jesus' words "I am . . . the truth" (John 14:6) really say it all. Truth is a person, not an object. This is the view of truth that belongs within Christian homes and schools, a very different view from the dominant one of our society.

One may rightly ask, however, how this biblical view of truth "plays out" through the curriculum of a school. A school's curriculum must be more than "simply knowing Jesus," shouldn't it? The answers to this question are both "yes" and "no," depending on one's perspective. If "knowing Jesus" is viewed narrowly as personal salvation and not much more, then that as the curriculum of a school is insufficient. But if "knowing Jesus" is viewed as a "full-orbed gospel," then a school needs no more. The Cosmic Jesus is all encompassing and, thus, all sufficient. But this thought needs to be unpacked a bit more fully.

Jesus Christ, the second person of the Trinity, was an active participant in the creation of the world. First, Jesus was the Word spoken by

God through whom "all things were made" (John 1:3; Colossians 1:16; Hebrews 1:2). Second, Jesus is the Word, or *Logos,* of creation, the one in whom "all things hold together" (Colossians 1:17). He is the unifying power of the universe, the one who brings order and harmony, without whom there would be ultimate fragmentation and chaos. He is the Truth in the fullest sense of the word.

To the Hebrew mind, the faithful sustaining presence of God was viewed as God's truthfulness, in this case, truthfulness-within-creation. When students examine created reality within their classrooms, they come face-to-face with the Truth, who seeks to transform them through the encounter. Truth always has a transcendent quality about it and must not be confronted in a casual or blasé manner. It is living, active, dynamic, and relational. It is life changing, always demanding a response.[7]

b. How does one know?

The Hebrew word for "to know" (*yadah*) is holistic, dynamic, and relational as well. First, one understands truth cognitively, based on God-given insight. Second, one accepts and commits to truth within one's heart. And third, one responds to truth in active obedience. Knowing in the Hebrew sense, then, could be compared to religious belief, in which both understanding and an active faith response are expected. It also corresponds well with the biblical view of truth. Knowing in this way is very different from the Greek model that is so prevalent in schools today. Christian teachers who are serious about teaching biblically will approach their lessons and their students' responses to those lessons in quite a different manner—one that is holistic and transforming.

It is interesting to note that each theory of learning tends to focus on one aspect of biblical knowing and absolutize it—building the entire theory around the one aspect or facet of what, indeed, is true. From the Middle Ages well into the 1900s, the "mental discipline" approach to learning was in vogue. The mind was viewed as a muscle that would grow stronger through mental exercise. Memorizing, solving problems (e.g., math), and thinking logically were means toward that end. The cognitive dimension reigned supreme. The weakness of this theory is that it tends to ignore heart commitment, the emotions, the physical, and, at times, even higher-level thinking itself. The Greek view of learning truth was dominant in this theory. The practice of mental discipline within the Christian community can result in a cognitive orthodoxy that fails to produce responsive orthopraxy. Unhappily, much of today's education continues to emphasize the teaching of low-level cognitive skills. While memorizing facts has a place in the learning process, it is far from the entire answer.

The mental discipline theory of learning was followed in the 1900s by behavioral learning theory, which focused solely on outward behavior. No concern was shown for anything internal or intrinsic. Learning was seen as an observable and measurable change toward desired behavior. External or environmental stimuli were used to elicit desired behavioral responses. In this case, the physical dimension reigned supreme. The weakness of this theory is that it ignores the mind, heart, and all other inner workings of the learner. It is, essentially, a mindless approach to learning, which within the Christian community can result in legalistic religious conformity. That is not to deny the fact that many of the learner's stimulus-response functions are quite useful. Driving a car or reciting the math tables in an automatic, "unthinking" manner are quite acceptable actions. In fact, behavioral learning theory has much to offer in the skill areas in particular. But it ignores the decisive issues of life, matters for students inwardly to contemplate and evaluate before acting upon.

During the 1960s and 1970s, "third force," or humanistic psychology, emerged as an alternative to the cognitive and physical approaches and focused instead on the "inner" person—the emotions or affect. Self-actualization became the goal for learning. Although Christians can find much in common with this learning theory, it has one decided weakness: It is centered solely on the self. There is no accountability to norms, absolutes, or persons outside of oneself. This is evident in the fact that humanistic learning theories do not require outward evidence that learning has taken place. Such evidence, while desirable, is not considered necessary for (inner) learning to exist.

An interesting parallelism exists between the development of these three theories of learning and the handling of truth during the premodern, modern, and postmodern eras. Classical education of the premodern era was "handed down" from an outside source, the church, and was received in catechetical style as verbatim truth. Mental discipline fit this approach to learning quite nicely. Modernity, however, focused on scientific predictability—the lawful universe could be comprehended by the rational mind, and a "scientific" approach to learning was needed to support this. Behavioral operant conditioning met this need. Finally, self-centered, existential postmodern thinking is reflected well in humanistic learning theory. No outside norms or absolutes are required, simply self-actualization, each in her or his own way. Today, cognitive learning theory is dominant once again, but with a dash of behaviorism and humanism mixed in. This time, however, the existential self continues to reign supreme as meaning is "constructed" uniquely by each individual. The *why, what,* and *how* of learning have become totally subjective.

Secular learning theorists don't really get it! Knowing or learning in the biblical sense emerges from a religious heart and involves the mind, the emotions, and the body. It is holistic in the fullest sense of the word. It is relational, as a deep and intimate association is established with someone or some part of created reality. It is manifested through an active response, both internal and external, to the truth revealed by the Source of all truth.

The Bible contains a number of examples of being both hearers *and* doers of the Word.[8] The mirroring concepts of faith-works, commitment-obedience, revelation-response, knowing the truth–acting on the truth are continual themes throughout Scripture. Biblical knowing calls for humankind, as a responsible agent, to respond. Christ provided the perfect example through his atoning death on the cross. He understood what was necessary for him to do; he was committed to this act. But for us to live, he actually had to die. He had to be a doer of the Word.

The instruction of God's children must be in a truth that is alive and dynamic and in a way of knowing that demands an obedient response. When God speaks, humankind *must* respond. If instruction within the home, church, and school actually required such responses, education would, indeed, become a transformed and transforming enterprise!

c. What is wisdom?

The first nine chapters of Proverbs state the goal and purpose of "knowing the truth"—acquiring wisdom that comes from above. The chapters are introduced by the prologue, which captures their essential message for the young:

> The proverbs of Solomon son of David, king of Israel:
> for attaining wisdom and discipline; for understanding words of insight;
> for acquiring a disciplined and prudent life,
>   doing what is right and just and fair;
> for giving prudence to the simple, knowledge and discretion to the young—
> let the wise listen and add to their learning,
>   and let the discerning get guidance—
> for understanding proverbs and parables, the sayings and riddles of the wise.
> The fear of the LORD is the beginning of knowledge,
>   but fools despise wisdom and discipline. (Proverbs 1:1–7)

Wisdom begins with a responsive and obedient relationship with the living Truth. It is knowing God relationally; it is placing one's trust in Christ, "in whom are hidden all the treasures of wisdom and knowledge" (Colossians 2:3). The writer continued:

> Trust in the LORD with all your heart
>   and lean not on your own understanding;
> in all your ways acknowledge him,
>   and he will make your paths straight. (Proverbs 3:5–6)

Professor John Van Dyk applies these verses appropriately to the educational setting:

> What is wisdom? According to the Bible, a wise person both *understands* and *does* the will of God (Ephesians 5:15–17). In other words, wisdom is not merely collecting and amassing theoretical or factual knowledge; nor is it simply gaining technical skills. Wisdom is knowledge and understanding deepened into spiritual insight and expressed in loving service (James 3:13). Wisdom originates in the fear of the Lord and is enhanced by faith, hope, love, knowledge, spiritual insight, and active discipleship. "The fear of the Lord," the Bible teaches, "is the beginning of wisdom; all who follow His precepts have good understanding" (Psalm 111:10).
>
> Thus . . . Christian educators refuse to be satisfied with providing only factual knowledge and marketable skills. Rather, [they] . . . seek to transform all activities and studies into an expression of biblical wisdom, training the students to walk as disciples of Jesus Christ.[9]

Given this biblical definition of wisdom, it is increasingly necessary in this Information Age and Day of the Internet for a distinction to be made between assembling data and possessing wisdom. One of the stark characteristics of the world in which our children are growing up is the constant bombardment of information. Information on everything is everywhere, whether one is seeking it or not. This is especially true on the Internet with its easy-linking process.

Not too long ago, teachers encouraged their students to expand their research beyond the books, journals, and readers' guides of the school library and become more familiar with the resources found on the Internet. Today, most students go intuitively to cyberspace for information and struggle with assignments that require them to use the hard-copy resources of the library. But the worst part is that students are tending to accept uncritically whatever the Internet offers, assuming that whatever someone placed on the Web must be true. The postmodern dictum that all views are equally valid is finding carte blanche acceptance by many young surfers of the Web, including too many of God's children. Consequently, the type of instruction that is required for today's youth must adjust accordingly. Sources must be closely examined and documented.

A biblical worldview needs to be understood and applied. The skills of logical and critical thinking must be learned. Biblically based discernment must become a vital tool for any information-gathering activity.

There may be roughly three levels of cognitive activity to reckon with in today's world. First, there is the cornucopia of data, information, and unrelated "stuff" that floods every avenue of the media. Second, there are the themes and concepts found in higher-level thinking (e.g., analysis, synthesis, evaluation) that reflect a unified, coherent, meaningful universe. And third, there is wisdom, as defined by the writer of Proverbs. We need to help our children transition from the first level into the second and third levels, for God's children need to be equipped with minds that can think deeply, critically, and Christianly.

The special kind of instruction required for God's special kids of the kingdom is primarily the responsibility of the parents, but the church and school are to assist as contributing members of God's divine tripod for educating his children.

God's Divine Tripod for Instructing His Children— the Home, the Church, the School

James Dobson has it right in regard to the nurture of children: The focus must be on the family. Parents—fathers in particular—are mandated throughout Scripture to instruct and correct their children in the ways of God.[10] The family is *the* primary unit ordained by God to produce "godly offspring" (Malachi 2:15). But the family is not alone is this responsibility. The "divine tripod" of a Christ-centered home, a Bible-believing church, and a kingdom-oriented school, working cooperatively, is necessary to provide the breadth and mutual support required to get the job done.

When one of the legs of the tripod either is missing or is a different length from the others (i.e., not doing its mandated share), the nurturing task becomes much more difficult. Or, stated another way, when creation structures are violated, problems arise. Today, schools are being asked to assume many functions of the home. Two-income families are purchasing services such as daycare (often beginning when the child is six weeks old), before-school care (starting at 6:00 A.M.), after-school care (until 6:00 P.M.), and day camp (for times when schools are not in session). Schools are being asked to feed children, discipline and counsel them, provide recreation and health care, teach sex education and values, and much more. Christian schools are, unhappily, beginning to assume certain responsibilities of the church as well. Some schools have chaplains, thus lessening the need for youth pastors. Early morning Bible studies; daily chapel services; courses in biblical studies, theology, and church history; required service projects; and time- and energy-demanding athletic and performing arts activities all tend to replace the traditional role of the church in the lives of children and youth.

Recently, I attended a Christian education conference in Eastern Europe that included a number of educators who had grown up under communist rule. They described how their former governments systematically sought to replace and destroy both the family and the church. Mothers were forced to work outside of the home. Designated apartments were too small for social activities, so children were provided their socialization through the Young Pioneers. Children were educated by "specialists" in government schools and in daycare, before-school, and after-school programs. The atheistic governments' antagonism toward the church is legendary, a legacy that has left a spiritual void in these countries today. What is so shocking is that the same undermining of the family and church that was forced upon parents in communist countries during the last century is being embraced voluntarily by parents in the free West today. The roles and responsibilities of the home, church, and school are being blurred, a factor that will ultimately damage both the institutions and the children they have been called to serve.

What, then, are the legitimate instructional responsibilities of each of these institutions? The chart below provides an overview based at least in part on issues that have been discussed previously in this book. Although there is much overlap between these institutions in the instruction of God's children, there are certain unique responsibilities as well.

Instructional Agent	HOME	CHURCH	SCHOOL
Command to Obey	Love God	Love your neighbor	Rule over creation
Lesson to Be Learned	Morality	a) Community b) Doctrine	Reclaim and transform culture
Imaging Christ	Reflectively; with integrity	Relationally	Representatively
Office to Be Filled	Prophet	Priest	King
Attribute to Reflect	True knowledge	True holiness	True righteousness

The (Christ-centered) home

God has given the primary responsibility for nurturing children to parents, with the father taking the lead. This has historically been true. God chose Abraham "so that he [would] direct his children and his household after him to keep the way of the LORD by doing what is right and just . . ." (Genesis 18:19). Children are told to honor *both* their father and mother and to obey their parents,[11] but it is the father who has been given the ultimate responsibility for instruction and correction in the Lord.[12] There are exceptions, however. Acknowledgment is given by the Apostle Paul to the nurturing of Timothy by his grandmother Lois and his mother Eunice.[13] In the absence of a (Christian) father, mothers must assume the spiritual leadership of their children, with males from the extended family and the church assisting when appropriate.

The unique nurturing task of the Christian home is to introduce children to their Heavenly Father through his Son Jesus. The children are to be told through actions and words that God loves them and that he wants them responsively to love him back. They are to be shown through modeling how to live moral lives that image the life of Jesus. They are to reflect in their very beings the transforming power of the Spirit of Christ. In doing so, they will be "living" words of truth, proclaiming God's ways as modern-day prophets.

How is God's love revealed through instruction in the home?

The love of the Heavenly Father is best communicated to children through the love of their earthly father and mother. As most of us have experienced, love is more often caught than it is taught. Love is demonstrated and experienced through hugs, time spent together, and random acts of kindness. (Additional ways of communicating love within the family are provided on pp. 56–59.) But God's love must also be taught within Christian homes. The reading of Bible stories before bedtime can begin at a very young age. The family altar (i.e., devotions) should be part of the normal routine, perhaps immediately after dinner. Indeed, children must be told about Jesus and his love for them, early and often.

It is said that the best way for a father to show love to his children is for him to show love to the mother of his children. That statement has lots woven into it, but one strand of truth is the demonstration to children of how a husband loves his wife as Christ loves the church. Modeling a Christlike relationship with one's spouse before one's children is a great gift of love for both the present and the future.

Another gift of love to children is the demonstration and teaching of biblical conflict management. The Bible provides guidelines on how to deal with anger[14] and hurts[15] and on speaking the truth in love.[16] Teaching and experiencing grace and forgiveness within the family setting are powerful precursors to committing one's life to Christ.

But one of the best ways to reflect the love of God is to say "yes" to that which is good and "no" to that which is evil—to be salt and light within one's own home. Parents must be very intentional about this, for the spirits of the times are, indeed, very intentional. Our children are bombarded with secular, humanistic, materialistic, and hedonistic messages seemingly twenty-four hours a day. Spiritual warfare over the hearts and minds of God's children is alive and well. Unless parents actively pursue countermeasures—the best defense being a good offense—there will be no contest. The siren call of today's culture is too strong for many of our children to resist without parental help.

Christ issued a very clear warning that is quite relevant for children and young people today:

> The eye is the lamp of the body. If your eyes are good, your whole body will be full of light. But if your eyes are bad, your whole body will be full of darkness. If then the light within you is darkness, how great is that darkness! (Matthew 6:22–23)

Our children live in an age of image. The "lamp of the body" is very active, and what they ingest, they become. If our children follow the Apostle Paul's admonition to think about that which is true, noble, right, pure, lovely, admirable, excellent, and praiseworthy (Philippians 4:8), their moral character will be molded in Christlikeness. If they watch hours of godless and antinormative video and Internet material, their bodies will be filled "with darkness."

What does this mean, practically speaking? Parents must be aware of what their children read, listen to, and watch, in particular behind closed bedroom doors. Questions need to be asked: Is it edifying? Does it lead toward imaging Christ? If the answers are "yes," be encouraging. If the answers are "no," you must say "no," gently but firmly, providing a biblical rational for your decision. This is an area in which parental example is all-important. Parents need to have God-honoring magazines and books on their coffee tables; parents must rent family-values videos; and parents should think about the stations listened to on their car radios. Unfortunately, this is probably the area in which the Christian family is most vulnerable today. Thousands of children who have been consecrated for holy living by God are being fed a diet of spiritual poison on a daily basis, and many parents appear totally oblivious to the damage being done.

Parents need to understand that it is not simply the filthy or profane words that are at issue; it is the Godless and God-defying way of life being portrayed as the norm for being "cool" in today's world. The underlying worldview of an author of a book or magazine article is as much a teacher of our children as any of their teachers in school. The underlying assumptions of a television program or movie graphically show our children what life should be like according to scriptwriters and producers who may be citizens of the kingdom of darkness. And we invite them into our homes! Parents need both to exercise and to teach biblical discernment in what is heard and watched by their children within their homes, for the greatest dangers are the underlying themes, assumptions, and messages—the worldview—being advanced by the media as normative.

One other source of concern needs to be mentioned: video games. Many video games are pure violence. Often, the goal is to see how many people can be maimed or killed. Battles and warfare are glorified. Some video games dabble in the kingdom of darkness. Not only is such make-believe activity absolutely contrary to the holiness of life in Christ, the hours spent playing these games tend to desensitize children to violence and spiritual darkness. They are a far cry from "nurture in the Lord," and they have no place in homes consecrated to Christ and his lordship.

Let me conclude this section with a personal illustration. I was not allowed to attend movie theaters when I was young. The reasons for this decree were never made clear to me. I think it had something to do with the ungodly lives of Hollywood stars. Anyhow, I did eventually attend my first movie, secretly, at a large theater in downtown Chicago so no one would see me. I saw *The Robe,* a movie that anyone old enough to remember knows is about the life of Christ and might be shown in churches today. Two things are evident from this illustration. One, most of the movies being produced today are much more violent, sexually explicit, and profane than movies of yesteryear. In other words, if there were valid reasons for movies being suspect for Christian families in the past, certainly that is true today. The second thing evident from my illustration is that the mores of society no longer influence what we or our children watch. I had to take a streetcar for an hour to get away from the eyes of people who knew me. Today, movies are welcomed guests in our family rooms, and our children, via the Internet, are able to download pornography in the privacy of their own bedrooms if they to choose to do so. Have things changed? You bet! And not for the better.

What image-bearing response to nurture within the home is desired from children?

Simply stated, the answer is: "Love the Lord, your God, with all your heart and with all your soul and with all your mind, for this is the first and greatest commandment" (Matthew 22:37–38). This is done by personally responding to and reflecting Jesus. It is accepting Jesus the Christ as Savior and committing to him as Lord. It is imaging Christ responsively.

The good news of the Gospel must then be told to the next generation, by our children to their children, for, as noted before,[17] God uses the family as the primary agency for the promulgation of his church.

Imaging Christ as twenty-first-century prophets involves being an embodiment of the truth within contemporary society and culture. To quote a metaphor sometimes used to challenge teens, "You may be the only Bible that some people will read." The lives of our children should exhibit such Christlike integrity that their very presence in a group speaks volumes about the character of God. This is the response to Christian nurture in the home that would be most pleasing to God.

Psychosocial stages of development

Developmental psychologist Erik Erikson has identified a series of what he terms *psychosocial stages* through which children navigate either successfully or unsuccessfully. Although Christian parents may not accept all that Erikson has to say, he appears to have identified a number of truthful nuggets about healthy child development.[18]

Infancy (ages 0–3)

Trust versus mistrust. An infant is almost entirely dependent upon his or her mother for food, sustenance, and comfort. The mother is the primary representative of society to the child. If she discharges her infant-related duties with warmth, regularity, and affection, the infant will develop a feeling of trust toward the world. The infant's trust is a comfortable feeling that someone will always be around to care for his or her needs, even though the mother occasionally "disappears." Alternatively, a sense of mistrust or fearful uncertainty can develop if the mother fails to provide for these needs in the role of primary caregiver. According to Erikson, she is setting up a distrusting attitude that will follow the child through life.

Societal pressures today that call for both parents to work outside of the home as well as the placement of children into daycare after a six-week maternity leave and later into before- and after-school care tend to counter the development of trust in a child. Parenting young children is a full-time job for the primary caregiver, usually the mother. Loving nurture during this first developmental stage of life is critical to producing emotionally healthy ten- and fifteen-year-olds down the road.

Autonomy versus doubt. Opportunities for a child to try out skills at her or his own pace and in her or his own way will help develop the healthy attitude of being capable of independent or autonomous control of one's own actions. Overprotection or lack of encouraging support may lead to doubt about one's ability to control her or his environment or self. The instilling of self-confidence and a sense of being capable, then, should begin during the preschool years, not when negative symptoms show up in kindergarten.

Early childhood (ages 3–6)

Initiative versus guilt. Freedom to engage in activities and the patient answering of questions lead to initiative. Restricting activities and treating questions as a nuisance can lead to a false sense of guilt—of having done something wrong or displeasing when that is not really the case. Obviously, parents sometimes need to restrict the activities of their children and say "no," but explaining the reasons behind these decisions can be very helpful in alleviating the feeling in children that "I was bad" or "It was my fault."

Middle and late childhood (ages 6–12)

Industry versus inferiority. As the child is drawn into the social culture of peers, it is natural to evaluate accomplishments by comparing him- or herself with others. If the child views him- or herself as basically competent in these activities, feelings of productiveness and industriousness will result. On the other hand, if the child views him- or herself to be incompetent, particularly in comparison with peers, then he or she will feel unproductive and inferior. This unhealthy attitude may negatively color the child's approach to life and learning, producing a tendency to withdraw from new and challenging situations rather than meeting them with confidence and enthusiasm.

Appropriate praise and commendation are important in developing a sense of "I can do it!" within children. Negative criticism (e.g., it's never good enough), comparison with others (e.g., siblings) rather than to one's personal growth, and focusing on deficiencies rather than sufficiencies can produce a sense of inferiority that is difficult to overcome in later life. It is vitally important during these formative years to help children uncover *their* unique talents and abilities and to assist them in developing *their* areas of personal interest. The trap for parents to avoid here is seeking to live out their own fantasies and dreams through their children. Each child has been created to be uniquely him- or herself; parents need to help each one uncover and develop that uniqueness.

Adolescence (ages 12–18)

Identity versus identity confusion. A recognition of continuity and sameness in one's personality, even when in different situations and when reacted to by different individuals, leads to identity. An inability to establish stable traits in one's perception of self tends to lead to identity and role confusion.

A healthy sense of identity comes from a stable core knowledge and feeling that "I know who I am" and "I know why I'm here." This sense emerges from the inside out and is not dependent on environmental circumstances. Adolescents may waffle with every new set of circumstances or friends do not possess the inner structure necessary for a healthy sense of identity. Interestingly, a tough, rigid exterior often belies a Jell-O-like interior.

How can parents help their teenage children develop a healthy sense of identity? First, they should pay attention to the four developmental stages. Then they should help their children answer the "Who am I?" and "Why am I here?" questions. This is done both verbally and non-verbally. It is important to say "I love you, and you are of great worth" to adolescents, but they must also *feel* loved and valued through their parents' body language and voice intonation as well as through inclusion in family decisions and activities. Teens need to feel that they are a valued and contributing member of a group that is important to them. That should begin with their family, but it also extends into a group of peers as well. Ideally, because of years of loving and attentive nurture within their family, children will *bring to* their peer group a stable sense of identity, rather than *take from* the group the definition of who they are.

The (Bible-preaching) church

The church is to function as a spiritual extended family for children. Although spiritual development begins in the home, the "care and feeding" of one's spirit continues for a lifetime within the church. This takes place through several "means of grace": the faithful teaching and preaching of the Word; the sacraments of baptism and the Lord's Supper; and, if necessary, the exercise of loving discipline.

Children are a part of the church. Their church family is made up of brothers and sisters in Jesus Christ. It provides the setting within which children can learn about community. It assists them in uncovering and developing their spiritual gifts, and it teaches them how to exercise these gifts for the edification of the entire body.

The church is the place where children learn who their neighbors are and what it means to love them. It is the place where they are equipped to carry out the Great Commission, given by Christ, the head of the church:

> All authority in heaven and on earth has been given to me. Therefore go and make disciples of all nations, baptizing them in the name of the Father and of the Son and of the Holy Spirit, and teaching them to obey everything I have commanded you. And surely I will be with you always, to the very end of the age. (Matthew 28:18–20)

The church is also the "launching pad" and "life-support system" for its members as they are sent out into the world in response to this commission, representing and sharing Christ with the needy. The "world" may be one's neighborhood, school, or job; it could also be a location on the other side of the globe. Either way, the task of the church is to equip and to send its "ministers" out to bring healing to a fragmented world.

The desired outcome of this nurturing by the church is young people who are holy—set-apart persons consecrated by God and sanctified by his Holy Spirit. As modern-day priests who image Christ, God's young people are to serve as advocates and bridges for the marginalized and disenfranchised of the world, bringing healing and restoration to hurting and broken people.

How is God's love revealed through instruction in the church?

The early church made an impact on the world because of the love expressed among the body of believers. It was truly unique in the world of its day. It still is. And children need to experience this love from people who are not blood kin in the usual sense, but who are, indeed, kin in the blood of Christ.

When young children are dedicated or baptized before the church, its members are asked if they will do everything in their power to nurture the children toward a faith commitment to Christ. The fulfillment of such a pledge may include prayers for the children, instruction through church education, or financial assistance for teen mission trips. The body of believers corporately assumes responsibility for the spiritual welfare of the children during their formative years. In a real sense, the church is the back-up and support system for the parents in the nurturing of children in the Lord.

Instruction of children within the church should take them from the "milk" of the Word to the "meat" of the Word—doctrine, if you will (Hebrews 5:11ff). The Apostle Paul's instruction to his spiritual son Timothy still applies to children today:

> . . . continue in what you have learned and have become convinced of, because you know from whom you learned it, and how from infancy you have known the holy Scriptures, which are able to make you wise for salvation through faith in Christ Jesus. All Scripture is God-breathed and is useful for teaching, rebuking, correcting, and training in righteousness, so that the man of God may be thoroughly equipped for every good work. (2 Timothy 3:14–17)

Instruction within the church should focus on at least four areas.

a. Bible study

Children need to hear the stories of the Bible from earliest childhood, but they must gradually be trained to become biblical "scholars" in their own right as well. They are to be provided the tools to find God's answers to the issues of their lives and the world.

b. Biblical doctrine

The truths of Scripture have been organized and systematized in such a way that clarifies much about God, humankind, the world, and our place in it. Many churches have doctrinal confessions, some of which have been written in a form that can be taught to children and young people. In fact, within many Presbyterian churches children memorize the entire *Westminster Shorter Catechism* before they seek to publicly profess their faith in Christ and become believing members of the body.

c. Church history

The church of Jesus Christ has a wonderful history that is replete with examples of God's faithfulness to his people throughout the ages. Many problems within the church today could be avoided if there were a better understanding of church history.

d. The contemporary global church

Again, lots of exciting things are happening today because of the presence and work of the church around the world. But some bad things are happening *to* the church as well: Many Christians are being persecuted because of their faithful witness. Children need to be able to identify with their brothers and sisters from every tribe and nation around the world.

After reading about these four areas of nurture within the church, you may rightly wonder whether churches actually exist that offer such instructional programs. The sad truth is that not many do. Most churches have become centers of entertainment for their youth rather than centers for instruction of their youth, and by so doing have become virtually irrelevant in the equipping of God's children for kingdom service. The biblical illiteracy of the youth of the church today is appalling. A sense of doctrine or an understanding of the status of the church universal is, for the most part, nonexistent.

Peter wrote, "Always be prepared to give an answer to everyone who asks you to give the reason for the hope you have" (1 Peter 3:15). The question is whether our youth today are up to that opportunity. Paul wrote:

> But to each of us grace has been given as Christ apportioned it. . . . It was he who gave some to be apostles, some to be prophets, some to be evangelists, and some to be pastors and teachers, to prepare God's people for works of service, so that the body of Christ may be built up until we all reach unity in the faith and in the knowledge of the Son of God and become mature, attaining to the whole measure of the fullness of Christ.
>
> Then we will no longer be infants, tossed back and forth by the waves, and blown here and there by every wind of teaching and by the cunning and craftiness of men in their deceitful scheming. Instead, speaking the truth in love, we will in all things grow up into him who is the Head, that is, Christ. From him the whole body, joined together by every supporting ligament, grows and builds itself up in love, as each part does its work. (Ephesians 4:7, 11–16)

May our churches today seek to meet this biblical standard as they train God's children to be the leaders of Christ's body for tomorrow.

What image-bearing response to nurture within the church
is desired from children?

The primary response desired of children within the church is, first, a public profession of personal faith in Jesus Christ as Savior and Lord and, second, an expressed need and desire to become active (professing) members of the body of Christ. They are to say, "I love you back" to the God who initiated the relationship many years before and told them, "I love you." This response is to be followed by a willingness to *be* who God wants them to be, to *do* what God wants them to do, and to *go* where God wants them to go. Spiritual gifts are to be identified and exercised; the Great Commission is to be obeyed.

The author of Hebrews admonishes God's people to "not give up meeting together, as some are in the habit of doing, but let us encourage one another . . ." (Hebrews 10:25). When children are young, they are to be taken to church by their parents; when they are older they need to be faithful participants on their own. The church should be their second home and their second family.

Imaging Christ as twenty-first-century priests involves being holy as Christ is holy, separating from all that is profane and joining to all that brings glory and honor to the name of Christ. It is becoming sanctified. It is bringing the *shalom* of God to all people and institutions that are broken and in turmoil, creating unity by building bridges of restoration and relationship.

The (kingdom-oriented) school

The Bible speaks of the family or home as the center for the nurture of God's children. The Bible also speaks of the church, not so much as the nurturer of children, but as the body of Christ that cares for and equips its members. Children are included as part of this body and, thus, are recipients of biblical instruction through this means as well. But the Bible says nothing about schools. They are, in fact, more of a cultural phenomenon than a biblically mandated institution. Two points could be drawn from this. One, parents are ultimately accountable to God for the education of their children, no matter who actually carries it out. Scripture is quite clear that parents have been given this responsibility. Two, parents who homeschool their children appear to be on rather solid biblical ground in doing so.

How, then, can Christian parents justify sending children to schools—Christ-centered schools in particular? There are several possible answers to this question. One, given the complexity of the world today, many parents lack the breadth and/or depth of knowledge required to educate their own children to the degree necessary. They have not been adequately prepared, in a formal sense, to teach. Two, not every parent possesses the spiritual gift of teaching. Scripture indicates that persons without spiritual gifts in particular areas should not seek to claim those tasks within the body.[19] Three, Scripture mandates believers to function in unity and harmony as a body, a very difficult task given the flawed natures of its members. But God places a premium on having his people learn how to work together, iron on iron. It can, at times, be difficult and messy, but such interactivity and interdependence are what God desires. Joining together with other believing parents in a cooperative effort to formally educate God's children is, indeed, in harmony with important tenets of Scripture.

The Christ-centered kingdom school is the nurturing agency that brings the Cultural Mandate and natural talents together for children in a meaningful way. Within a school, an organized curriculum—content, skills, and values—is taught in an intentional manner to equip children and young people for their callings and particular tasks in life.

Accepting the Cultural Mandate. To properly understand the nature of formal education, we must first determine the meaning and purpose of life, because schooling is preparation for the living of life. For the Christian, the purpose of life is to live in a manner that brings glory to God alone (*soli Deo gloria*). Bringing glory to God is not easily definable, but it certainly involves obeying God, praising God, and publicly "lifting up" his name (i.e., his reputation). Only a school with that declared purpose can fully seek to equip children and young people toward that end.

To properly understand how this plays out in actual practice, we must return to the Creation Mandate (Genesis 1:27–28; 2:15) that God gave humankind in the beginning: Have stewardly dominion over creation and its potential as his representatives. The mandate was twofold: first, take care of creation—be environmentalists; and second, subdue and work creation—be developers. The two tasks, which often appear to be in conflict today, must be held in creative tension with each other, neither dominating the other. The original Creation Mandate has since been expanded in two ways.

First, as humankind has moved from a "garden" (Genesis 1 and 2) toward a "city" (Revelation 21 and 22), from a rather simple agrarian economy to a complex and sophisticated urban setting, the mandate has been expanded from ruling over the natural world to caring for and developing all facets of society and culture. Thus, today we use the term *Cultural Mandate* rather than *Creation Mandate*. In fact, the original mandate could have been paraphrased: "Uncover all of the potential I have implanted in creation, and develop and rule over it for my glory." It became plain relatively soon after creation was formed that this potential included the performing arts, as Jubal, the great, great, great, great, great grandson of Adam became "the father of all who play the harp and flute" (Genesis 4:21). Unfortunately, as a descendant of Cain, it is unlikely that Jubal developed music for God's glory. Over the ages, humankind has developed the fine and performing arts, written great literature, and crafted beautiful structures. Today, DNA codes and the intricacies of the Internet are being uncovered and developed. Because the secret things of God are inexhaustible, new frontiers are constantly emerging.

The second way that the Creation Mandate has been expanded is a result of sin. The effects of sin on all of creation have increased the responsibilities of humankind to include such things as evangelism, health care, and social services. Destroying the works of the evil one by shining the light of God's truth on Satan's darkness, indeed, does set people free. This expansion of the original mandate begins with the Light of the World and the Truth Incarnate, Jesus Christ.

Developing natural talents. God's image bearers, as the counterpart of the Cultural Mandate, have been created with all of the resources required to carry out this God-given task. Some abilities are common to all humans, such as reasoning, communication, creativity, and the like. But each person also has been given different measures and combinations of natural talents, for the task at hand is very complex and calls for people who can take responsibility for different facets of it. Each child entering school is distinctive from the next in some very important ways that need to be uncovered and developed to the fullest extent possible. A key responsibility, then, of parents and teachers is to help children recognize and develop the natural talents that God has given them. One role of the school is to assist children in knowing who they are and how and where they fit in God's scheme of things.

How is God's love revealed through instruction in the (kingdom-oriented) school?

To answer this question, one must begin with God, who "*is* love" (1 John 4:16, emphasis mine). God is the embodiment and source of all love. Next, we recognize that God, the fountainhead of love, loves his children. "How great is the love the Father has lavished on us, that we should be called children of God!" (1 John 3:1).

In love, God gives his children life, and he provides for and protects them. The Bible states:

> [Jesus came] that [his sheep] may have life, and have it to the full. (John 10:10b)

> If God is for us, who can be against us? He who did not spare his own Son, but gave him up for us all—how will he not also, along with him, graciously give us all things? (Romans 8:31b–32).

> Who shall separate us from the love of Christ? Shall trouble or hardship or persecution or famine or nakedness or danger or sword? . . . No, in all things we are more than conquerors through him who loved us. For I am convinced that neither death nor life, neither angels nor demons, neither the present nor the future, nor any powers, neither height nor depth, nor anything else in all creation, will be able to separate us from the love of God that is in Christ Jesus our Lord. (Romans 8:35, 37–39)

God's love for his children has been most fully expressed though Jesus Christ, their Creator, Sustainer, and Redeemer.

Love is made known through loving relationships. Schools that nurture such relationships can be channels for experiencing the love of God. Schools that do not nurture loving relationships become "resounding gongs and clanging symbols." Portions of the classic love chapter, 1 Corinthians 13, can be paraphrased to illustrate this. Speaking as a student might:

> *If I know how to converse fluently in twelve different modern languages, with He-brew, Greek, and Latin thrown in, and do not love, my speaking is just a bunch of meaningless noise. If I am so smart and am such a great student that I know every-thing about everything, including the future, and do not love, I've got nothing— zilch. Knowledge is transient, here today, gone tomorrow. But love rejoices in the truth, which lasts forever. When I was a kid, I thought like a kid. But when I be-gan school and learned about God and how he created both me and this wonderful world for me to enjoy, I began to grow in the knowledge of what the love of God is really about. I still have a long way to go in knowing God and how much he loves me, but I can testify that through the loving relationships in my school I can feel the presence and love of God.*

Sadly, the love of God is not always manifested between students in Christian schools. Since all teachers and students walk through the school doors each morning as sinners, a school community can experience a great many hurts each day. The issue is not the absence of sin in a Christ-centered school—there's always enough to go around. The issue becomes: What will the school do about it? Christian schools need to be safe places within which God's *shalom,* his perfect peace, is a dominant presence. Put-downs cannot be tolerated; rather, concern for the welfare of each student is the business of each day. Hurts need to be healed. Conflicts need to be managed biblically. Too ideal? Not really. God's ways of doing things are never too ideal. Such love in action within the school must be intentional, well advertised, bathed in prayer, and empowered by the Holy Spirit, whose presence needs to be invoked each new day. Either Christianity has a distinctive love message, or it's a sham.

This gets us back to the nature of the instruction within a school that claims the name of Christ. Scripture records: "For God so loved the world that he gave his one and only Son . . ." (John 3:16). The embodi-ment of God's love, his Son Jesus, is the *alpha* and *omega,* the beginning and end of education. With Christ as the focal point, let's explore several key facets of an education that brings glory to God alone.

a. Education that is Christian begins with Christ

The introductory words of the Bible "In the beginning God . . ." really point the way. To begin at any other place creates the opportunity for syncretism or secularism to dominate rather than Christ-centeredness.

Syncretism, the unnatural attempt to blend two opposing religions or worldviews, occurs when a curriculum, unit, or lesson begins with a secular position and the Christian message is added after the fact. This happens in Christian schools when state standards or secular textbooks dictate curricular content up front. In contrast, the message for Christian teachers should be: "Don't open your secular textbook until you have thoroughly thought through the affect God and his written Word have on the area under study, for God's Word is a light that illumines and a pair of eyeglasses that transforms what you will teach. God's truth is no add-on. It's the central message!"

Secularism, on the other hand, is taught in schools that believe that the sole addition of Bible reading, prayer, and weekly chapel sessions to the format of the school makes it Christian, leaving the curriculum outside the realm of redemption. This sacred-secular dichotomy or dualism is as insidious as syncretism. There is no part of the Christian school that Christ does not claim as his. Christ is Lord of all—the entire curriculum, every discipline, and every lesson.

b. The purpose of Christian education is the equipping of God's children to unfold and advance Christ's kingdom on earth

Parents send their children to Christian schools for lots of reasons. Some are reactive—for instance, avoiding the evils found in a secular system of education. Other reasons are proactive—for instance, returning the Bible and prayer to the classroom, teaching God's truth, finding friends from Christian families, and the like. While these are all good reasons, each has its limitation, as well.

To properly understand God's purpose for educating his children, one must begin with the earthly ministry and words of Christ:

> From that time on Jesus began to preach, "Repent, for the kingdom of heaven is near." . . . Jesus went throughout Galilee, teaching in their synagogues, preaching the good news of the kingdom, and healing every disease and sickness among the people. (Matthew 4:17, 23)

> "Our Father in heaven, hallowed be your name, your kingdom come, your will be done, on earth as it is in heaven." (Matthew 6:9–10)

> "But seek first his kingdom and his righteousness . . . ." (Matthew 6:33)

The central message of the earthly ministry of Christ was the (re)establish-ment and advancement of God's kingdom on earth. Christ's parting com-mission to his disciples was to continue, as his body, the work that he had begun until he returns. Education that honors Christ prepares children to be kingdom workers. This kingdom, which germinates as a seed of faith within the hearts of individuals, expands to cover the entire world, for Christ is Lord and King of all. There is no area that does not rightly fall un-der the rule and reign of Christ, and God's children have been called to rule in his name until he returns. For this task, special training is required. That training takes place in boot camps called Christian or kingdom schools.

Actually committing to the establishment of a kingdom school re-quires some out-of-the-box and countercultural decision making, not stuff for the weak of heart. Many parents desire a school for their chil-dren that is safe, moral, academically wonderful, and athletically superior. They want a school that is better than other schools, not one that is out of step with other schools. Such parents lose interest in a Christian school that may not have a great campus, that may provide an intramural rather than interscholastic athletic program (one in which *all* students can learn the kingdom skills of operating as a team), or that may insist on holy living as a condition for enrollment. Any school that seriously seeks to follow Christ's Sermon on the Mount will, indeed, become radically distinctive from other schools in the neighborhood, including some schools that claim the name of Christ. There is a price to pay if a school chooses to be obedient to Christ in all things.

c. The heart and soul of Christian education is located in the curriculum[20]

This is a natural follow-up position to the previous two statements. What makes a Christian school primarily Christian? It is the curriculum, for the central task of a school is the teaching and learning of an organ-ized course of study. It is the engine that drives the enterprise.

One of the benefits of being a teacher-educator is the opportunity to visit many different types of schools. One thing that has struck me is that the conduct of the students in a particular school does not necessar-ily correspond with its public image. For instance, the behavior exhibited within religious schools can, at times, be both disgusting and offensive. On the other hand, I have observed students in public schools who behaved in a most courteous and respectful manner. The obvious ques-tion that came to my mind during these observations was: What makes a school Christian? If it is the conduct of the students, some public schools are more "Christian" than some schools that claim the title. As important as I believe holy conduct is within a school setting, however, the answer to the question is found in the content, skills, and values taught—the school's curriculum.

Continuing with my school visit illustration, once while "killing time" in the hallway of a secular school, I observed student artwork that spoke volumes on this issue. One cluster of pieces illustrated Easter bunnies; another featured drawings of rainbows. In the former, a cute and harmless bunny substituted the centrality of a risen Savior and Lord to the message of Easter. In the latter, the central message of the rainbow as a sign of the covenant that God made with Noah was totally missing. In the first set of drawings, truth was falsified. In the second set, truth was truncated—rendered incomplete. These two concepts represent the central problem with secular curricula: Either the content being taught is an outright lie or, more likely, truth is presented in a partial and fragmented manner. Christ as the Truth and as Lord is not recognized.

How can a Christian school "redeem" its curriculum, taking every thought captive "to make it obedient to Christ" (2 Corinthians 10:5)? Several ways could be mentioned, but three that have been personally meaningful will be explained.

(1) Teach the content areas thematically and conceptually. Begin each teaching unit (and lesson, if possible) with a statement of kingdom truth that you want your students to take with them through life. They may forget the facts, but they will never forget the concept, for a good concept can be applied to all sorts of circumstances. For instance, a unit on the American Civil War (or the War between the States, for readers from the South) often deals with interesting but somewhat irrelevant (at least to the lives of the students) information. The strength of the North was found in its industries and numbers, while the strength of the South was in its generals and defense of the homeland. I learned these facts many years ago, and I still remember them, but I can't think of any ways in which I have applied the information to my life, or to living for the Lord, or to advancing God's kingdom on earth. If, however, the central theme of the unit had been "A house divided cannot stand," all sorts of applications come to mind. What a great unit that would be to teach, for "conflict that divides" is in and around each one of us. Every student could provide examples from home, school, church, the workplace, and the daily newspaper. It is a biblical concept; it is a kingdom-advancing concept that extrapolates nicely from the purpose statement of a Christian school. Teachers should always have a kingdom answer for the question: "Why do we have to study this stuff?" If they don't, they

should seriously consider not teaching it. So, in brief, before teaching any lesson, determine the ways in which it "seeks first the kingdom of God" and orient it around a concept that students can carry in their hip pockets with them, out the classroom door and into life.

(2) Place a biblical worldview grid over every unit being taught, particularly in the content areas. When I was a student in a Christian college, I heard a lot about something called a Christian or biblical "world-and-life view." I was told that it was something that every Christian should have. Unhappily, I wasn't too certain what a world-and-life view was, and I surely didn't know what to do with one. At some point, however, I discovered that by rearranging the sequence of the wording world-and-life view, the idea made more sense to me; thus, a world-and-life view became "a view of the world and of my life within it." It was my perspective on life, how I saw things. It was formed by the conceptual eyeglasses that I wore, my belief system. Everything I encountered was interpreted by me through a conceptual framework or grid that I considered to be reality. It was my particular bias on life. Later in life, I was informed that the term *world-and-life view* had become passé and has been replaced by the term *worldview.* I still like the first term (stated in reverse), however, for it holds more meaning for me.

The worldview that was mentioned most often in my circles centered on Creation-Fall-Redemption.[21] Later, the term *consummation* was added as a fourth component. Although I understood and believed each concept, I still didn't know what to do with a worldview. I thought that it was simply the way I saw the world and my life in it. End of conversation! No big deal! But at some point I had an "aha" experience that helped me to see a worldview as a tool for understanding and, subsequently, transforming the world in an obedient and God-glorifying manner. Only then did I become aware of how critical it is for the advancement of the kingdom of God to teach children a biblical worldview and how to use it in real life.

The biblically based Creation-Fall-Redemption-Consummation worldview begins with creation, not with the fall of humankind into sin. That is *really* important to accept, something many Christians do not, at least in practice. It makes all the difference in so many ways. For instance, if we began with humankind being sinful and needing a Savior, once salvation from the punishment of hell had been assured, we would have no further need other than to live a highly moral life and wait for Christ to come and take us to live eternally in a place called heaven. Missing would be the original (i.e., creation) and ultimate (i.e., consummation) vision of the kingdom of God being established on earth, something for which Christ himself prayed—"[may] your kingdom come, your will be done on earth..." (Matthew 6:10). As noted, that kingdom vision began with creation, and it will find consummation at the time of Christ's second coming. It will not be a rescue operation and escape; rather, it will be a fulfillment, a full actualization of the establishment of Christ's kingdom in a renewed heavens and earth. The latter view, indeed, is a radical departure from the former (or vice versa). Yes, one's worldview makes a huge difference!

Omitting creation from one's worldview eliminates God's answers to life's most basic questions: Why are we here? What is the purpose of life? What should we be busy doing? Yes, we should be leading sinners to Jesus. That is *really* important. But the salvation of sinners is a *means* to an end, not an end in itself! The purpose of redemption found in Christ is ultimately restorative—restoration to fellowship with the Father and restoration to our original place and purpose. Adam was mandated, as the federal head of all humankind, to rule over creation as God's vice regent for the purpose of exercising God's rule, his sovereignty, over every aspect of created reality. Creation was the genesis of a kingdom venture, one that will continue throughout all eternity.

A biblical worldview, then, must begin with creation. It seeks to determine how things were meant to be from the beginning. Identifying creation norms, what God would consider "normal" within each sphere of life (e.g., the family, the arts, the workplace, politics), is an important first step in the instruction of God's children. For instance, as parents and teachers instruct children on the nature and functions of the family, the starting place for such lessons is God's revelation. In this case, God's special revelation, the Bible has a great deal to say about the family. Were the lesson on an area of mathematics or physical science, God's general revelation would provide greater detail than his special revelation. Whatever the lesson, however, one must begin with God and what he says about that particular area of study. His norms for that aspect of creation (i.e., creation norms) must be determined up front.

The next step in applying a biblical worldview is to examine the effects of sin on the area being studied. Again, if the focus of instruction were the family, there is a great amount of evidence on how the family of the twenty-first century has departed from the creation norms of God for the family. An honest and realistic look at the "what is" is an important part of Christian nurture. The Bible itself does this over and over, and in that respect, it can be a shocking book to read. But for a doctor to operate on a cancer, the cancer first must be accepted as being a reality and then it must be thoroughly understood if its eradication is to be successful. Recognizing the ugliness and all-pervasiveness of sin is a vital part of applying a biblical worldview. For, since the Fall, the cultural-kingdom task of humankind has had to add a redemptive dimension, that of destroying the darkness of sin with the light of God's truth; it is preserving God's good creation through the ("salting") restraint of evil. Accepting and understanding the concept of sin and its effects on creation norms has a legitimate place in the application of a biblical worldview. Children need to understand the nature of sin and its intrusion into the world.

Redemption is the next component. Because of Christ's atoning death and victorious resurrection, all of life and the world take on redemptive possibilities. The redemptive work of Christ begins in the hearts of individuals, but it grows into a mighty tree that provides shelter and a home for many (Mark 4:30–32). In a like manner, the kingdom of God is redemptive in nature. It counters the effects of sin in every sphere of life. It engages in true *jihad*—holy war. Through spiritual warfare, the enemy is engaged and territory that rightfully belongs to God is regained. Every thought is taken captive in the name of Christ. Every part of creation that has been affected by the parasitic scourge of sin becomes the object of reclamation.[22] And the war will not be over until every square inch of creation has been regained and the enemy, the evil one and his hosts, have been totally defeated and destroyed. This will take place completely when Christ returns to establish his kingdom in fullness. One's biblical worldview, then, is a proactive tool—in this case, an instrument of warfare. For there is a war to be won and work to be done!

Finally, there is the consummation of Christ's kingdom. The second coming of Jesus will mark the full ushering in of his kingdom, a kingdom established on earth in the Garden of Eden many years ago. Much will have happened since the first days of creation, but the goal has remained the same—kingdom establishment, God's rule. The old creation will have become the new creation. In one sense, things will have gone full circle. Paul wrote about the final times: "Then the end will come, when [Christ] hands over the kingdom to God the Father after he has destroyed all dominion, authority and power. For he must reign until he has put all his enemies under his feet" (1 Corinthians 15:24–25). Until Christ returns, however, we are to join him as his body in the active unfolding and advancing of his kingdom. That was the mandate at the time of creation and that was the mandate at the time of the *re*-creation in Christ.

The Creation-Fall-Redemption-Consummation worldview can and should be a part of every unit taught in Christian schools. This can be accomplished by seeking answers to the following questions:

(a) What was God's original intent for the part of creation being studied in the unit? In other words, identify the creation norms, the kingdom purposes undergirding the area of study.

(b) What are the effects of sin and the Fall on the area being studied? What are the (religious) spirits of the times, past and present, that influence the area of study?

(c) What can and should be done redemptively to make the area of study obedient to Christ? What does the "what should be" of the kingdom look like for the area? What can be done to advance Christ's kingdom? Every unit ought to have some tangible kingdom application, such as writing letters to the editor (as prophets), reading to nursing-home residents (as priests), or recycling aluminum cans (as kings).

In summary, a biblical worldview is vitally important for the instruction of God's children. It is a necessary part of instruction in the Lord, for God's children must be taught to think with the mind of Christ if they are to become his responsive disciples.

(3) Except in the area of biblical studies, do not view the Bible as a textbook but as the divine illuminating light and eyeglasses used to see and understand general revelation (the real textbook) clearly. Don't confuse the differing purposes of God's modes of revelation. Strictly speaking, the Bible is not a science or math textbook. Rather, a school's curriculum is abstracted from God's general or natural revelation. The Bible, however, provides interpretive context, insights, and kingdom purposes for the areas under study.

What image-bearing response to nurture within the school is desired from children?

Simply stated, the answers to this question are: first, hearts and minds that are surrendered to Christ as Lord; and second, active obedience in carrying out in society and culture the applicable mandates of God. The children of the King are to acknowledge and accept their royal place and purpose within the kingdom of God on earth. As always, the only acceptable response to godly nurture is "loving God," but within the school setting one learns, in particular, what it means to love God "with all one's mind." Equipping God's children with the mind of Christ is the peculiar foundational responsibility of the kingdom school.

But "there is no Christian mind," wrote Harry Blamires in 1963.[23] More recently, Wheaton College Professor Mark Noll echoed this phase with one of his own that is fast becoming equally famous: "The scandal of the evangelical mind is that there is not much of an evangelical mind."[24] What are these men saying, and why is this important to the instruction of God's children? Let me try to explain through a critique of secular education.

I am opposed to secular education wherever it may exist, whether it is in public schools, nonsectarian private schools, or schools that label themselves as Christian. But it is not the sin of commission within secular education that bothers me most. It is the sin of omission that concerns me—the lie that God is irrelevant to learning and thus is irrelevant to life. Take, for instance, a child from a Christian family and place him or her in a secular school seven hours a day for 180 days each year for thirteen years. For 16,380 hours, this child is taught that God has no relevance to anything that has happened, is happening, or will be happening in the world. For 16,380 hours, the message of marketplace atheism is taught—that the only place God belongs is in one's private devotional life and that he has absolutely no business in the public arena of life. The Creator God becomes Mother Nature, the covenant sign of the rainbow becomes the symbol for multiculturalism or a reading program, the resurrection of Christ becomes an opportunity to draw Easter bunnies in art class, and so on. The ultimate result of this incessant deprivation is a child who will have been neutralized by the evil one without his firing a shot. Spiritual warfare will not even be required. The child's ability to make a difference in God's kingdom will have been severely compromised. And it all happened so innocently, so subtly, so quietly. No one even noticed. Yet a spiritual desensitization took place through that which an education *did not contain.* Education without the living Truth is, indeed, a deadening and deadly education, for it advances a Godless rather than a Christian mind.

What, then, is a Christian mind? It is a mind that is totally absorbed by God's revelation. It is a mind that is guided by the Holy Spirit. It sees the world and one's place and purpose in it through the eyeglasses of Scripture. It acknowledges Jesus Christ as the living Word and Truth through whom the world was created, redeemed, and is held together. The bottom line for the Christian mind is that God is sovereign. There is no room for another, no room for secular—God-absent—thought. There is no dualism, there are no two pathways of truth. There is no dichotomy between a sacred portion of life and a secular portion of life, for all of life is religiously unified and whole. It is seeking to think God's thoughts after him about *every* issue of life. There is no "time-off" in thinking Christianly; it is a 24/7/365 proposition.

The Scripture portion that seems to speak most directly to the idea of a Christian mind is found in Paul's letter to the Romans:

Therefore, I urge you, brothers, in view of God's mercy, to offer your bodies as living sacrifices, holy and pleasing to God—which is your spiritual worship. Do not conform any longer to the pattern of this world, but be transformed by the renewing of your mind. Then you will be able to test and approve what God's will is—his good, pleasing and perfect will. (Romans 12:1–2)

The key words in this passage are "do not conform . . . but be transformed." Paul is telling us not to allow the world—secularism—to shape our thinking, but rather to be transformers of thought within the world. The pathway from conforming to transforming is through a renewed or sanctified mind. How does one gain this holy mind? There are many ways, but the formal education of children is the arena within which ways of thinking and knowing are the intentional business of the enterprise. God's children must be taught how to critique or evaluate what the world offers by using the criteria of truth and normalcy contained in the Bible. God's children need to be made aware of the spirits of the time under study and of how these spirits influence activities within all ages. That type of education can only take place within a home or school committed to that purpose.

The lure of conforming rather than transforming is very inviting for Christian educational institutions. Think for a moment about the many ways that Christian schools come under the influence and pressures of secular organizations. First, which institution has a 90% monopoly on education and, thus, makes the rules? Answer: the government school system. The public school system remains the focal point of reference for many Christian schools. Next, a number of Christian schools seek state or regional accreditation. Accreditation by these bodies is based on a secular set of educational standards, another potential trap. In addition, the many professional organizations that provide materials and training, excellent as they may be, are secular in nature, and the secular universities in which many Christian school teachers and administrators receive their professional preparation teach "conforming" rather than "transforming" viewpoints. Finally, the textbooks and other curricular materials used within Christian schools often are secular in perspective. If one were to add all of these influences together, the likelihood of a transformed Christian mind emerging from such a Christian school would be a sheer miracle. Christian schools and Christian educators who take their cues from the secular educational establishment tend to "sell their birthrights" (Genesis 25:29–34; Hebrews 12:16) before they even teach their first lesson. They base their teaching on the conforming principles of their age. Consequently, transforming young minds into the mind of Christ becomes very improbable.

To better understand this phenomenon, one needs to understand three "levels of change." The first level of change is *cosmetic*—only the outward appearance is altered. For instance, a Christian school may adopt uniforms, put up bulletin boards with Bible verses, and meet in a church educational wing, but change is only in the exterior veneer. The second level of change is *particular*—certain parts or pieces are added or modified. In this case a Christian school may add a morning devotional time, daily or weekly chapel services, a biblical studies component to the curriculum, and a highly moral set of rules and regulations. But change here is only piecemeal, fragmented. The third level of change is *transformational*—the warp and woof of the entire organization is changed because of a fundamental paradigm shift. Within the Christian experience, being born again would constitute such a third-level change. A Christian school that functions within a transformational mode begins with God and with the recognition of his sovereignty over every aspect of life and the world. It allows the light of Scripture to establish the mission of the school and to illumine every aspect of the school. The result is a school that is guided by God's revelation in every part of its operation, from board decisions to teacher in-service programs to the writing of the social studies curriculum. The floodlight of God's truth and his way of doing things transforms all policies and practices. Only when all of this has solidly become fact, when the kingship of Christ has been firmly established, should a Christian school look to secular resources for additional insights—which is, indeed, a valid thing to do. It is a "first things first" issue, not an escape from or ignoring of all things from the secular realm. Sometimes God's truth is made known through the most unlikely sources, and God's truth is God's truth no matter where it is found. But the only way to promote transforming and to avoid conforming is to *begin* on the solid foundation of God's Word and to use it to evaluate everything else. The result will be a school that is unique.

The real issue, in fact, may be the sense of isolation that results from marching to the beat of a different drummer. Lots of Christian parents don't really want their children in a Christian school that truly reflects God's living word, for that would be *too* different. It is more comfortable to conform. And that is sad.

Promoting the development of the Christian mind is no easy task. It will not take place within secular schools, as that is not their purpose. It can take place only within homes and schools that intentionally promote Christian thought within each conversation and subject taught. It is the active and passionate pursuit of God's thoughts, of Christ's mind. Paul wrote:

> . . . though we live in the world, we do not wage war as the world does. The weapons we fight with are not the weapons of the world. On the contrary, they have divine power to demolish strongholds. We demolish arguments and every pretension that sets itself up against the knowledge of God, and we take captive every thought to make it obedient to Christ. (2 Corinthians 10:3–5)

Yes, seeking the Christian mind is serious enough business to call it warfare. The weapons are provided from above. The power is divine. The strategic targets are the viewpoints and thoughts of our day and age. Each is to be brought under the kingship of Christ. Each is obediently to serve his kingdom cause.

Imaging Christ as twenty-first-century kings involves seeking righteousness (i.e., doing right) as Christ is the perfect embodiment of justice, righteousness, and love. It is reflecting Christ representationally in the world over which he is Lord and King. It is faithfully and wholeheatedly obeying the mandates, commands, and commissions that God has decreed—for God's glory.

Chapter Conclusions

Biblical nurture includes two dimensions: instruction in the Lord and correction in the Lord. This chapter dealt with the first of these— instruction. Although these two dimensions of biblical nurture are in constant interplay with each other, instruction must precede correction if children are to understand how to conduct themselves in a manner that is pleasing to God.

The central message to be communicated to children is that God loves them, and God's desire is that his children responsively return that love to him. For loving God is the greatest of all commandments.

To love God, children must know God. But how does one come to "know" God? Knowing for Christians differs from the knowing of this postmodern day and age—or, for that matter, of the modern and premodern eras. For while Christian epistemology encompasses the subjectivity of the postmoderns, the objectivity of the moderns, and the transcendence of the premoderns, it embraces so much more. Biblical knowing is personal, communal, and relational. It is holistic in the sense that one is called to know physically, cognitively, emotionally, and, ultimately, from the heart—with one's whole being.

God's children know through revelation, for God has revealed himself and his truth through several modes: creation, the Bible, and, most fully, through his Son, Jesus Christ. God's truth—that in which we are to be instructing our children—is manifested though each mode, but Jesus has declared himself to be the living Truth. Truth for our children is a person. That perspective differs greatly from the Greek model of dead, passive, and static truth. God's revealed truth *always* calls for a response, for it is alive and relational and seeks interactivity. This has exciting implications for instruction that is in the Lord.

Parents, fathers in particular, are ultimately responsible for the Christian instruction of their children. But a support system for this enterprise is available, for the Christian church and the Christian school stand ready to instruct God's children as well, as part of a "divine tripod." Instruction in the Lord is meant to be seamless rather than fragmented, so all of these institutions have a common task. Yet, in God's economy, the home, church, and school have varied roles and responsibilities as well. Each seeks to focus on a different facet of what it means to be an image bearer of Jesus Christ.

The home takes the lead with instruction on becoming a living embodiment of truth—a prophet of the Lord Jesus Christ in one's own time. Reflecting Christ through true knowledge is not simply a cognitive exercise, although that is part of it. It is living God's truth through one's entire being in every walk of life. It is being the presence of Christ in all situations. The primary way in which parents can teach their children to be living embodiments of truth is by "show and tell"—by example, verbal explanation, and instruction.

The church, on the other hand, has a great deal to do with guiding children into priesthood—reflecting Christ in mediation and healing. The goal is living a life of true holiness, being set apart for godly service in and to the world, in the name of Christ.

Finally, the formal education component of this tripod deals with the kingly task of learning to rule over creation, society, and culture for King Jesus. In that sense, the school needs to be a kingdom institution, preparing God's children for the unfolding and advancing of his kingdom on earth. Preparation is for true righteousness, for doing the right thing in all circumstances. God's rule over all is the operative theme. This kind of education is unique in our world, parting company with education that dismisses God as being irrelevant.

Godly instruction, then, is the sharing of the living truth, as revealed by God, for the purpose of equipping children to love God, to serve humankind, and to develop creation potential for God's glory. The instructional dimension of biblical nurture is quite distinct from that which is considered to be the norm within the world. Christian parents and teachers in particular need to seek out and work at God's ways of doing things. That holds true for the instruction of children; it also is true for their correction, the topic of the next chapter.

Chapter 8: Further Thoughts to Consider

1. Why are the ontological and epistemological questions so important for Christian instruction?

2. Compare and contrast Greek and Hebrew views of truth and knowing. What might each look like in the classroom?

3. How might classrooms that are based on the view that truth has been divinely revealed differ from classrooms based on a modern or postmodern view of truth?

4. Why are biblical studies a vital part of the curriculum in Christian schools?

5. How does a biblically defined wisdom differ from simply being very informed about a topic?

6. In an ideal world, how would the Christian home, church, and school complement each other in the nurture of God's children?

7. Suggest ways that parents could deal with the temptations presented to children through the visual media—television, movies and videos, video games, the Internet.

8. Do you agree that most church youth programs are too much entertainment and not enough education? Why or why not?

9. Can schools be Christian schools and not be kingdom schools? Explain your answer.

10. Do you agree with the statement: "The heart and soul of Christian education is found in the curriculum"? Why or why not?

Chapter 8: Notes and References

1. *New Geneva Study Bible* (Nashville: Thomas Nelson, 1995), 141.
2. *Calvin: Institutes of the Christian Religion*, I, vi (Philadelphia: The Westminster Press, 1960), 1.
3. *Ecumenical Creeds and Reformed Confessions,* (Grand Rapids, MI: CRC Publications, 1988), Article 2.
4. F. A. Schaeffer, *The God Who Is There,* (London: Hodder and Stoughton, 1968), 140.
5. As the church discovered at the time of Galileo, however, the Bible does contain a few inaccurate statements that reflect the state of science at the time it was written. For instance, the earth does not have four corners, and the sun does not rotate around the earth.
6. Acts 8:26–40.

7. For more on this approach to truth, consider Parker Palmer's books *To Know as We Are Known: Education as a Spiritual Journey* (San Francisco: Harper, 1993) and *The Courage to Teach: Exploring the Inner Landscape of a Teacher's Life* (San Francisco: Jossey-Bass, 1998).

8. Hebrews 11 contains a list of heroes of the faith who were doers of the Word. Other portions of Scripture that speak about being both hearers and doers of the Word are: Matthew 7:21, 24, 26; John 14:15, 23–24; James 1:22; 3:13; 1 John 2:3–5.

9. J. Van Dyk, *The Beginning of Wisdom: The Nature and Task of the Christian School,* (Grand Rapids, MI: Christian Schools International, 1985).

10. Deuteronomy 6:4–9; Psalm 78:1–7; Ephesians 6:4.

11. Ephesians 6:1–2.

12. Ephesians 6:4; 1 Timothy 3:4–5.

13. 2 Timothy 1:5.

14. Ephesians 4:26.

15. Matthew 5:23–24, 18:15–16.

16. Ephesians 4:15.

17. Psalm 78:5–7.

18. Much of this information was obtained from *Life-Span Development,* 2nd ed., by John W. Santrock (Dubuque, IA: Wm. C. Brown, 1986), 44–48.

19. 1 Corinthians 12:12–31.

20. The teacher as the "living curriculum" is vitally important as a role model for students. But the nature of a school requires education in the *formal* sense, which calls for a *formal* course of study. The teacher, as instructor and model, needs to "rightly divide" and respond to the truth embodied in the formal curriculum and, in that sense, be a person worthy of imitation.

21. Charles Colson and Nancy Pearcey in *How Now Shall We Live?* (Wheaton: Tyndale, 1999) reflect on this Creation-Fall-Redemption-Restoration worldview.

22. Romans 8:19–22.

23. H. Blamires, *The Christian Mind: How Should a Christian Think?* (London: SPCK, 1963), 4, 7.

24. M. Noll, *The Scandal of the Evangelical Mind* (Grand Rapids, MI: Eerdmans, 1994), 3.

Chapter 9

CORRECTIVE NURTURE

Many years ago, when I was principal of a small Christian school, it was drawn to my attention that there just might be something called a biblically based approach to discipline. To be honest, up until that time, it had never dawned on me that a distinctively "Christian" approach to discipline might even exist. But let me start at the beginning.

The school was in its second year of operation. It had been established the previous year with 23 students in grades seven, eight, and nine. Grade ten had been added after the first year of operation. The entire student body had just returned from a weeklong trip to Washington, D.C., where the students had been housed with families from a host church. Within a few days of our return, it became known that a few of the students had purchased wine before leaving on the trip to be consumed, I suppose, at some point on the trip. I was quite upset over this revelation, primarily because the students had violated the hospitality of their host families by taking alcohol into their homes without their knowledge. As is often true in small schools, the school board wanted to get involved in dealing with this issue and was meeting to discuss how to discipline the offending students. One of the suggestions offered was to suspend the students from extracurricular activities for the remainder of the school year, which still had a number of months to go. It was at this point that a godly, older board member, who also happened to be the father of one of the students being disciplined, stated that, yes, a consequence needed to be imposed but that the consequence should not drag on for the entire year. He said that a lengthy penalty might easily prove to be "discouraging" to the students and, consequently, might be counterproductive to the desired results. Rather, he explained, just as God deals with us cleanly and quickly and then restores us, the punishment for these students should be swift and restorative as well. Then we all had to get on with life, putting the matter behind us, just as God does with us and with our sins. These words translated into an "aha" moment for me, as I suddenly became aware that the Bible did, indeed, contain guidelines for corrective discipline. A few years later, I was able to explore this further through a doctoral dissertation on biblical discipline.

Introduction

A few things need to be said up front about biblical discipline. One is that the discipline that God desires us to carry out with our children is essentially the same discipline that he uses with us. It's not really all that mysterious. For instance, one of the premiere Scripture passages on discipline is found in Hebrews. It is here that we are told that discipline, rightly exercised, is a loving act, "for our good, that we may share in [God's] holiness" (Hebrews 12:10). That brief passage puts an entirely different spin on things. Often, discipline is not done in love but is simply retributive punishment for having done something bad. God's ways differ from ours. Through the proper exercise of biblical discipline, children can be taught an object lesson about God's ways of dealing with our sins through justice, love, and grace.

A second point to be made here is that corrective discipline is a natural and vital part of the nurturing process. Often, discipline is seen as an unhappy interruption in the process or as a counterproductive evil outside of the process. But the Bible views discipline as a vital *part of* the nurturing process. In a real sense, we should perceive misconduct by our children as nurturing opportunities rather than as discipline problems. It may sound rather Pollyannaish to some, but that appears to be what Scripture is saying.

Parents and teachers should not be overly dismayed or discouraged, then, over the presence of misconduct within the home or school. The distinctiveness of a Christian home or school is not in the absence of wrongdoing, for all children sin. It is, rather, in the manner in which sin is dealt with. Disobedience provides a wonderful opportunity for several biblical principles to be activated: conflict resolution via the Matthew 18 (15-17) principle, repentance, forgiveness, and restoration, just to name a few. The biblical approach to resolving conflicts and problems is quite different from that found in the world. Prayerfully, our children will experience "the better way."

A third point emerges from the second. As stated in Chapter 7, the Greek word for nurture in the New Testament, *paideia,* has two connotations. In some contexts, the word means "instruction." In other contexts, the word is translated as "correction." Thus, the biblical definition for the nurture of children includes both instruction and correction. Taking this definition a step further, the Bible also tells us that this nurture should be "of the Lord" (Ephesians 6:4). This means that parents and teachers must search Scripture for God's approaches to both instruction and correction.

The previous chapter sought to do that for the area of instruction. This chapter continues searching the scriptures, this time for godly insights into correction, or what might more commonly be called discipline.

The chapter is divided into two sections: preventive discipline and corrective discipline. First, preventive discipline, which actually continues to fall under the instructional dimension of nurture, deals with both the nonverbal or "caught" instruction and the verbal or "taught" instruction about appropriate conduct. The second section of this chapter provides several response options for the occasions when children either fail to live up to their responsibilities or cross over the line and get into territory where they shouldn't be.

Preventive Discipline

Simply stated, preventive discipline is everything parents and teachers do up front to promote right conduct and to "prevent" wrong conduct by children. It is being anticipatory and insightful, thinking smarter and wiser than children. It reflects an understanding of children—how they think and why they act.

Most discipline problems can be avoided by thinking through situations in advance. Another way of stating this is that the majority of misconduct by children can be traced back to adults who didn't do their homework or weren't exercising their authority or responsibilities in a proper manner. Yes, there are exceptions. Some children will act out, no matter how much anticipation and planning took place. But, with proper planning, 90% or more of all behavior problems need never take place.[1]

Much of preventive discipline is nonverbal in nature. It is more caught than taught. This is examined first, for it provides the context for preventive discipline that is more verbally instructive in nature.

Preventive discipline that is caught

The vast majority of communication is nonverbal. Parents and teachers know that children "hear" and imitate their actions much more precisely than they follow their words. Within schools, the process of education—the way things are done—sometimes teaches more than the product, or the written curriculum. It provides the unspoken "hidden" curriculum of what is *really* valued by those in charge. Some things in life are caught more than they are taught. The same is true for the prevention of conduct that requires discipline. Nonverbal demeanor and actions speak volumes to children.

Four ways in which nonverbal communication can promote preventive discipline are examined here. They are: 1) creating a conducive environment; 2) acting authoritatively; 3) understanding what motivates children's behavior; and 4) carrying out God's agenda God's way.

Creating a conducive environment

Everyone needs space—personal space, inviting space, and safe space. That is true for children, both at home and at school.

a. Creating personal space

Within the school setting, how and where students are seated is an important factor in promoting cooperative behavior, for most misconduct involves other children.

(1) Establishing a sense of community. The seating arrangement in a classroom tells students a lot about the goals and values of the teacher. There should not be a clear demarcation between teacher-space and student-space. At the elementary level, tables or study clusters work well. There doesn't need to be a "front" to the classroom. At the secondary level, a seating arrangement with students facing each other on two or three sides of the room and a walkway for the teacher in the middle provides easy access for the teacher to all parts of the room (and to all of the students). Seating secondary students around tables rather than at desks is an acceptable option as well and sends an unspoken message to students about the teacher's relational and participatory approach to education. All of these arrangements promote communication, relationship, and a sense of community by allowing students to look at the faces of other students rather than to sit in rows and stare at the back of heads. The arrangement of classroom furniture can, indeed, be a key contributor to a positive, interactive learning environment.

(2) Providing for separation needs. Sometimes students enjoy community a bit too much and need to be moved from the source of their temptation and, possibly, closer to the teacher's work station. Separating students from each other (and, sometimes, from *all* others) is probably the most effective preventive discipline measure a teacher can take. Assigned seating continues to have merit.

b. Creating inviting space

Unkempt environments breeds disrespect; sterile environments invite disengagement. Aesthetically pleasing surroundings stimulate positive attitudes. I'll never forget the elementary school I visited that looked more like an children's museum than a school—with easy chairs and sofas, reading lofts, student projects and artwork everywhere, study centers, books and more books, and classical music playing in the background. You get the idea. Look around your home, school, or classroom and think about what changes in the physical surroundings could be made to promote attitudes and behavior that are positive, engaging, and respectful.

c. Creating safe space

Both the home and the school must be places in which the basic needs of children can be met. One of these needs is safety. A number of years ago, Abraham Maslow devised a hierarchy of needs that has been helpful to parents and teachers as they seek to care for their children. The model below illustrates this hierarchy.

(5) Need for self-actualization   (Higher-being need)

---

(4) Esteem needs
(3) Love and belonging needs   (Deficiency needs)
(2) Safety needs
(1) Physical needs

According to Maslow, all persons begin with the first level, physical needs, and then move toward the higher-level need of self-actualization. Needs must be met at each level before one can move to the next. Thus, if children feel threatened, unloved, or worthless, they will not be able to reach self-actualization. The first four levels are called deficiency needs because a person is dependent on others to have these met. The higher-being need of self-actualization, according to Maslow, can be met by one's self.

At the physical level, children need shelter, nutritious food and drink, enough sleep, and proper health care. Although these needs should be met within the home, they sometimes are not. Rather than ignoring them, schools may have to intervene and provide meals and health care. Christ did much the same thing during his earthly ministry—feeding the hungry and healing the sick.

Safety needs have always existed, but in recent years neither the home nor the school has been a safe place for some children. Harassment,[2] abuse, and the use of deadly weapons have become commonplace within settings that should be safe havens. Fear for personal safety is taking its toll on too many children today, and this is totally contrary to the desires of Christ, who blessed children while holding them securely in his arms.

The other deficiency needs, those of being loved, belonging to a community, and feeling good about oneself do, indeed, need to be met by others as well. Every child deserves to feel the love of God, evidenced through parents, teachers, and other significant people in their lives. This love is manifested and reinforced through membership in and contributing to broader communities—the family, the church, and the school. Children who feel unconditional love and acceptance by others will also feel centered—inwardly stable, secure, and capable, confident that they will be able to meet the challenges of life that come their way.

Homes and schools need to be safe places in which love and inclusion are practiced, for these are biblical principles.

Adults acting authoritatively

We have all been in the presence of adults who could not properly deal with out-of-control children. It may have been in a restaurant or a supermarket, or it may have been in a classroom. It's not pretty, and it elicits from us all sorts of emotions. In the majority of cases, the children have a problem because the adults have a problem with acting in an authoritative manner. As described in Chapter 7, acting authoritatively with children involves the proper balance of three things: *power, insight,* and *service*. Let's examine each of these more closely as part of the preventive discipline process.

a. Power

If exercised by itself, power may produce compliant children, but the goals of biblical nurture cannot be met through the use of power alone. A dictatorial, authoritarian approach will simply produce angry children who probably will become dictatorial, authoritarian adults. But power, or the authority to act, is a good and necessary component of child rearing and classroom management. Usually, the adult does, in fact, possess the right to act. After all, he or she is the parent or the teacher. So what is the problem? There are probably many answers to this question, but one is that the adult may not *feel* in control. The adult may be young, inexperienced, insecure, or fearful of being disliked or failing. A person may see him- or herself as being inadequate as a parent or teacher or even as a human being. Children can detect insecurities intuitively, and they tend to take control when they sense that they have more power than the adult. One of the causes and results of the Fall is wanting to be in control, and children, just like anyone else, move into power vacuums when the opportunities arise.

What can one do about having Jell-O-like feelings when dealing with children? The problem has probably been long in the making, so the solution may be long-term as well, possibly involving counseling or therapy. But the least that must be accepted in one's heart of hearts is the conviction that parents and teachers are indeed the ones in charge, not the children, because God has declared it so.

b. Insight

By itself, insight may simply be wishful thinking when dealing with children. But insight, too, is an important part of the nurturing process. At least three foci of insight are necessary when dealing with children. One, the adult must have self-understanding. That may relate to the issues mentioned above under "power." Two, the adult must have insight into children, their nature, development, needs, motivation, and the like. That's the primary reason developmental and educational psychology courses are required in teacher education programs. Insight into children helps adults determine reasonable expectations under varying circumstances. For example, McDonald's with its Playland is no doubt a better environment to take a five-year-old than is a five-star restaurant. Three, insight into the particular setting is necessary as well. Much behavior is not morally right or wrong, but it may be inappropriate for the time or place. It is important for adults to learn to discriminate when and where particular behaviors are appropriate and inappropriate and then to teach these insights to their children.

c. Service

By itself, service may lead to the doormat approach to nurturing children. Some adults take pleasure in having children walk all over them, taking advantage of their inability to say no. That approach is ultimately not helpful to either party. Again, one's self-concept may come into play here. But service is a vital part of being authoritative, for children must feel that the adult in charge genuinely has their best interest in mind. Self-centered adult behavior does not foster cooperative attitudes in children.

Research has determined that there are several behaviors by teachers that help keep students on task. Each reflects an authoritative approach to adult-child relationships.

(1) With-it-ness. Teachers communicate to students that they know what is going on in the classroom. This is done nonverbally, by their actions rather than by their words. They seem to have "eyes in the back of their head." They are aware, using their senses at all times, no matter what they are doing or where they are in the classroom. In that sense, they are "with it."

(2) Overlapping. Teachers are able to handle more than one situation at a time. They do not become so immersed in one issue or one student that they lose contact with the other activities or students in the classroom.

(3) Movement management. Teachers are able to begin, maintain, and end lessons in a manner that is smooth and has momentum. The opposite actions would be jerkiness or slowdowns.

Jerkiness

(a) Goal-directedness may be contrasted with stimulus-boundness. Teachers who are goal-directed always know where they are heading and keep the classroom activity moving in that particular direction. Teachers who are stimulus-bound seem to have little self-will and react to unplanned and irrelevant events within the classroom.

(b) A thrust is a teacher's sudden "bursting in" or interruption of the students' activities with an order, statement, or question in a selfishly spontaneous manner. In other words, the message was not worth the disruption in learning that it caused.

(c) A dangle is an activity begun by a teacher and then left "hanging in midair" by going off to some other activity. Later, the activity is resumed. In *truncation,* the activity is not resumed.

(d) In *a flip-flop,* the teacher terminates one activity, begins another, and then returns to the terminated activity.

Slowdowns

(a) Overdwelling occurs when a teacher dwells on an issue or activity beyond what is necessary for understanding to take place. Overdwelling would produce a reaction on the part of most children of, "All right, all right, that's enough already!" There are various kinds of overdwelling: nagging over behavior patterns; overinstructing on where to sit, how to stand, or how to hold a pencil; or overemphasizing materials so that the focus of the activity is lost.

(b) Fragmentations are slowdowns produced by a teacher's breaking an activity down into subparts when the activity could be performed as a single unit.

- Group fragmentation occurs when a teacher has members of a group do singly and separately what a whole group could be doing as a unit at one time. This tends to produce waiting periods for individuals and thus slow down the movement.

- Activity fragmentation occurs when a teacher fragments a meaningful activity into smaller components and focuses upon their separate subparts when the activity could have been performed as a single, uninterrupted sequence.

Understanding what motivates children's behavior

Why do children act the way they do? Why do they obey? Why do they disobey? Answers to these questions contribute to the insight that authoritative teachers need in the nurturing process. Wise parents and teachers seek to understand the motivation of their children.

Having said that, where does one begin? The list of things that motivate children appears endless. To begin, for persons of all ages, but younger children in particular, pleasure-pain motivators are important. Young children tend to do things that feel good or are pleasurable, and they tend to avoid doing things that feel bad or are painful. As noted previously, Abraham Maslow has listed basic needs as motivators for certain types of behavior. In Chapter 5, the various facets of one's self-image were discussed. Self-perception, indeed, is also a strong motivator of behavior. Anyone working with young adolescents would immediately cite puberty (and raging hormones) as a motivator that needs to be reckoned with. At times, it appears that nothing else is on the mind of a thirteen-year-old. The list goes on. Given the nature of this book, however, only a half dozen or so motivators that appear to have some scriptural foundation or connection will be considered.

a. The spiritual connection

Since the heart is the primary source of motivation for all people, the heart direction of children tells a lot about the choices that they make. From conception until regeneration, human hearts are guided by a sinful nature that sets themselves up as idols. Children who are directed by sin-inclined hearts tend to be self-serving in their behavior, and they tend to rebel against someone telling them what to do. A regenerated heart, on the other hand, is guided by the Holy Spirit and desires to do that which is pleasing to God. One's former sinful nature continues to lurk in the wings, though, and can still motivate bad choices. These choices, however, are usually spontaneous or habitual rather than premeditated. They are the residue and remnants of earlier sin bondage, and everyone seems to have some area of vulnerability of this type.

While some of the behavior of children may originate from their own sinful natures, their conduct could also be in response to being sinned against by others. Such sin could range from being bullied on the way to school to one of several forms of abuse within the home, or it could be related to alcohol, drugs, or pornography. There are many forms of threats and temptations outside of themselves that can afflict children and adolescents and motivate them to act the way they do.

b. Moral development

Secular psychologists have developed their own set of theories for why children choose certain moral actions. Since their theories do not begin with children's hearts, they are fundamentally flawed, but they do contain certain insights that can be helpful. Jean Piaget described the choices made by young children, ages two through seven or eight, as being based on either seeking rewards and approval or avoiding punishment. Right actions are seen as those that satisfy personal needs. Deference is paid to those in positions of power for the purpose of staying out of trouble. Children from seven or eight through eleven or twelve see actions two-dimensionally, as right or wrong, black or white, good or bad. There are no middle, gray areas. The letter of the law is followed, with no exceptions. The rightness or wrongness of the actions outweighs the intent or results of the actions or any special set of circumstances. Older adolescents, on the other hand, deal more with the intent of the actions than with the actions themselves. Motives and circumstances are taken into account. The spirit of the law is followed. They are becoming aware that other people may have different points of view and that some issues do fall in middle, gray areas.

c. Environmental perception

The manner in which children perceive their environment affects their behavior. A distinction must be made, however, between the physical environment of children and their psychological environment. They can be and often are the same, but they also can be different. That is a reason parents and teachers sometimes have difficulty determining the motivation behind a particular act. For instance, the physical environment of a young person may be a typical classroom with other students seated at desks with textbooks in front of them. The psychological environment, however, may include only the student and his girlfriend parked in a car on the edge of a lake the evening before. Obviously, the conduct of the student in the classroom will not reflect his physical environment, for his mind has transported him to a different psychological environment. A younger student may be thinking about the smells coming from the school lunchroom, especially if she has had no breakfast. Or she could be viewing the classroom as a threatening environment, especially if she does not know her memory work and is scheduled to recite next.

One example of a student functioning in a psychological environment that still haunts me took place during my first year of teaching. During that year, both parents of one of my fifth-graders died, one in the fall and the other in the spring. They were ill with respiratory problems and had moved to Arizona for that reason. This student, as an only child who was in the process of losing both parents, functioned in a very different world the entire year, and I had to continually call him back from his psychological environment to the physical environment of the classroom.

The eyes through which children see and interpret their world have a lot to do with how they respond to it. Reality is, indeed, interpreted through the mind's eye of the beholder. Children are not miniature adults; they have their own form of logic that makes sense to them. It is, consequently, important for adults to enter the world of children when possible. Is their world viewed as a scary place or a friendly place? Are teachers or other children seen as helpful or harmful? Inviting children into conversation through open-ended questions and doing a lot of listening both to verbal and body language can provide windows through which to enter a child's perception of reality.

(The self-perception of children greatly influences their behavior as well. This topic has been dealt with on pp. 99–103.)

d. The three Cs behind choices

Psychologist Rudolf Dreikurs[3] concluded that the ultimate goal that directs the behavior of children is fulfilling the need to belong—to feel significant and important to others. Dreikurs encapsulated his theory of child behavior into three Cs: *connecting* with others, *contributing* to the group, and feeling personally *capable*. These three Cs comport well with Scripture.

First, in connecting with others, the ultimate connection is God and his love for us. It is this relationship that makes all other relationships possible. Children need to be loved, especially when they are the most unlovable. Unconditional love practiced regularly and sacrificially is a very powerful "connecting" motivator.

The next "C"—contributing—is very powerful as well. It is participating, giving of oneself to the larger group or cause. Preachers from the Apostle Paul to Billy Graham have emphasized the importance of becoming an active member of and contributor to the broader body of Christ. We are told to use our unique spiritual gifts for the edification of the saints. The result will be a sense of dignity, that we are making a significant contribution to the cause, that we are good for something.

The third need, according to Dreikurs, feeling capable, can be met through uncovering and developing an area of interest and/or ability in which a child can experience some measure of success. Every child needs to have one foot in a "safety circle" of competency before she or he will dip the other foot into uncharted and, therefore, riskier waters.

All three Cs should be in place for all children, both at home and at school. If they are, the likelihood of seeking to belong through deviant behavior will be minimized.

e. Competence and achievement motivation—the push

Children were created to be creators. As image bearers of God, they intuitively seek to emulate the divine Potter who has formed them from the clay of the ground. In doing this, they quite naturally seek to develop a level of competence in the process of creating and forming their own "original" works and products. This is called competence motivation and relates closely to Driekurs' third C above—capability. Enjoyment is gained from the process of creating. But a sense of fulfillment is also gained from forming and completing a product. This is called achievement motivation. Both competence and achievement motivation allow children to be obedient, responsive culture formers in the name of Christ.

Competence (process) motivation and achievement (product) motivation have important implications for parents and teachers as they seek to guide children in the way they should go. At the beginning of time—the push, if you will—humankind was given the mandate to develop creation (i.e., culture) for God's glory. People were told to create and to form in a manner that reflects God and brings honor to his name, and parents and teachers have been instructed to teach these things to their children.

Humankind was also created to be inquisitive, as people who possess an innate desire "to know." We have been created with a need to explore and uncover. Along this line, it has been said (kiddingly) that teachers have eternal job security, for only God is omniscient and both teachers and students will be able to spend eternity exploring the mind of God without ever exhausting the process. It was, however, this "desire to know" that served as the basis for the fall of humankind into sin. Genesis records Satan's tempting lie: "'You will not surely die,' the serpent said to the woman. 'For God knows that when you eat of it your eyes will be opened, and you will be like God, knowing good and evil'" (Genesis 3:4–5). Eve wanted to know but for the wrong reason. Her seeking after knowledge was not for the purpose of subduing and having dominion for God's glory but, rather, for the purpose of becoming like God.

Both of these characteristics of humankind, that of being a creator with competence and achievement motivation and that of being a knower with an innate desire to uncover truth are attributes that all children possess as image bearers of God. Parents and teachers need to validate these attributes as they nurture their children.

f. Teleological motivation—the pull

The Apostle Paul writes about a dynamic, forward-looking motivation based on establishing and working toward goals: "Forgetting what is behind and straining toward what is ahead, I press on toward the goal to win the prize for which God has called me heavenward in Christ Jesus" (Philippians 3:13b–14). This goalistic motivation is in contrast to the deterministic motivation of Freud and the causistic motivation of Skinner, both of which are backward looking and do not recognize personal responsibility or purpose in behavior. Goalistic motivation is teleological in nature, for it is based on future purpose. For followers of Christ, that purpose is contained in Christ's second coming and the consummation of his kingdom in a new heavens and earth. Motivation in this setting is anticipatory, with one eye on the present evil age in which we live and the other eye on the age to come.

g. Faith trumps the other f-words

Fear is a primary motivator. Anger, in fact, is usually based on fear; consequently, a healthy way to deal with anger is to try to determine what or who is the source of the fear. A person tends to respond to fear through either the fight or the flight response. The Bible states, however, "There is no fear in love. But perfect love drives out fear" (1 John 4:18). Earlier (v. 16), it states, "God is love." To fear, then, in the "being afraid" or "in terror" sense, should not be a motivator for God's children. In fact, Scripture shows that the words "fear not" often are the greeting expressed in personal encounters with God or his messengers.[4]

Fear or being afraid is probably the number one deterrent to kingdom service. People do not do what is right (or righteous) because they fear the opinion of others more than the opinion of God. They fear failure and looking foolish in front of others. Because of fear, they refuse to rid themselves of their visible and tangible crutches and trust dependently on God. The chief antidote to fear is faith. The classic definition of faith is found in Hebrews: "Now faith is being sure of what we hope for and certain of what we do not see" (Hebrews 11:1). Stepping out in faith is doing what's right no matter what the consequences, trusting that God will provide the resources needed and be pleased with the trust placed in him. In God's economy, faith, indeed, trumps fear, fight, or flight as motivators. That's an object lesson that needs to be lived out in front of children.

Carrying out God's agenda God's way

All families have agendas, most of which are unspoken and may go unrecognized by the family members themselves. But these agendas teach children about the roles, rules, and relationships of family life.

A family agenda may include enmeshment (one for all and all for one) or disengagement (functioning under one roof as "ships in the night"). Both extremes can create problems. For example, the "no boundaries" of enmeshment—boundaries reflecting the degree of separateness between family members—can lead to anorexia as a daughter tries to take control of her own life in a quest for separate identity. On the other side, the "rigid boundaries" of disengagement—each family member functioning in her or his own world—can foster a lack of concern or awareness by parents toward what is going on in the lives of their children. The children may have too much freedom and too little accountability. The desired balance lies somewhere between the two extremes—a blending of togetherness and separateness, with boundaries that exist but are permeable and flexible.

Another family agenda item is the values that are taught, mostly nonverbally. What is being read, listened to, or watched within the home? How do people speak to each other, especially children to their parents? Do conversations exist? Do people listen to each other? Do common family mealtimes exist? Is there a family devotional time? Is the home chaotic or orderly? Is it noisy or quiet? Are roles and responsibilities of family members clearly defined, or are they confused? How are conflicts resolved? What is valued the most, experiences or things? Does the entire family attend church together regularly? Are visitors welcome within the home? Is alcoholism present? Is there abuse of any kind? The answers to these and similar questions begin to establish a picture of the lessons being taught to the children within the home. The values that are actively embraced by the parents contribute directly to the values that are embraced by their children and to the actions that are motivated by them.

Sin has taken its toll on the family as it has on other areas of life. The Bible describes God's desires for the family very clearly, and those desires have been dealt with earlier in this book. What is said next is not meant to produce a guilt trip over any particular mode of parenting, for only God knows individual needs, circumstances, and the reasons people do what they do. But it becomes quite obvious after taking a quick look at our society that God's norms for marriage and the family are in disarray. There is separation and divorce, which create single-parent and blended families. Many children have stepsiblings and half siblings, plus two places they call home. With both parents working outside the home, there are more children in daycare and before- and after-care as well as latchkey children. All of this has affected children profoundly; just ask any teacher who has been working with children for more than twenty years. Many of the lessons being caught by children about family life are truly frightening. Yes, families have agendas that affect the behavior of children.

But the agendas or curriculums of schools also affect the way in which children conduct themselves. And schools, too, have unspoken, hidden curricula in addition to the official written versions. The former deal more with the pedagogy, the teaching-learning process; the latter describe or list the content and skills that are to be learned—the product, if you will. Much could be written about how both the process and the product of a school contribute to the behavior of students, but only two concepts will be explored here, those of *integrity* and of *connectedness*.

First, when considering pedagogy, teachers must exercise integrity, for classroom practices need to reflect the nature of their students and how they learn. The first portion of this book explored the nature of children. There was a reason for that: The nurture of children—their instruction and correction, to be done God's way, must be based on their God-given natures. The nature of children has everything to do with the nurture of children. Chapter 2 described how created attributes—dependence, finiteness, and accountability—relate to behavior. Chapter 3 explored the various modes of expression with which children have been endowed: rational, culture-forming, lingual, social, values, creative, moral, loving, and faithful. Chapter 4 described how sin has affected children and the world in which they live. Chapter 5 outlined what it means to be a renewed image bearer of God and to actively image Christ. Reflecting Christ as prophets, priests, and kings has much to say about classroom activities. Finally, Chapter 6 explained the necessity for and way of redemption, perhaps the most important component of biblical nurture. The more that teachers understand and act upon the nature of children as defined by God, the more effective they will be in the instruction and correction of their students. It's a matter of integrity.

Second, while teaching the written curriculum, teachers must demonstrate connectedness. The central thread that defines a godly curriculum is connectedness. There are reasons for this. First, the source of most of a school's curriculum is the created reality found in God's general revelation, and the dominant feature of creation is its unity, its connectedness. This relationality allows the world to be known. Second, the way students learn is based on the seeing and making of connections. One's "mental map of the world" is a complex web of interrelated cognitions or schemes that are constantly connecting with both old and new information. Third, given their disconnected world of sound bites, video clips, and lack of contextualization, students today are crying out for relationship, whether they can verbalize it or not. A primary need of postmodern children is wholeness, relationship, and stability. Fragmentation and change have frazzled many a psyche today. Children need to be presented with a world that has connectedness and one in which the sovereign God is acknowledged as being in charge.

Several types of connections that help children make sense of their world need to exist in classrooms. Lessons should begin with context, answering the "Where are we?" question. Contextualization—the setting, the backdrop, and the field—must be established. Next, goals and objectives are to be developed, answering the "Where are we going?" question. Following that, the "How will we get there?" question needs to be explored. It is at this point that worldview enters, for a worldview offers a conceptual template that helps to make sense of the portion of created reality being examined. Assessment follows. Teachers and students must be able to determine when they have successfully arrived at the goal or destination. All of these steps help create a sense of connectedness. But there is more. To accurately reflect created reality, unit and lesson plans need to be integrated, at least to some degree. Lessons need to relate to other lessons, disciplines need to relate to other disciplines. The world in which we live has a unified structure that teaching and learning should respect and reflect. But lessons must also connect to things that students have learned previously. New material needs to be attached or connected to things the students already know, for without such connections learning lacks personal meaning. Finally, unless students can see how a lesson applies or relates to their lives personally, there is a good likelihood that any connections made initially will quickly fade.

Two additional ways to promote connectedness in the curriculum are to teach authentically and to teach conceptually. Authentic teaching is teaching that comes as close to real life as possible. Real-life problems are explored, real-life activities are experienced, real-life products or performances are the outcomes. Conceptual teaching, on the other hand, deals with related concepts and big ideas rather than with unrelated facts. A concept has been defined as "a mental construct that is timeless, universal, and abstract."[5] Conceptual teaching allows connections to be made throughout history, between cultures, and within one's own mental schema. Concepts function "across the curriculum" and allow for direct application to the lives of students. Combining concepts can lead to the big ideas of generalizations and principles. These, in turn, form conceptual frameworks or worldviews, the stuff Christ-centered education thrives on.

Unconnected lessons are breeding grounds for behavior problems, for they promote boredom and frustration. Teaching with integrity and connectedness, on the other hand, provides students with a sense of respect, dignity, and personal meaning. Instruction that is connected goes a long way toward achieving responsible behavior.

In summary, preventive discipline—the actions that parents and teachers can take to increase appropriate behavior and decrease inappropriate behavior—begins with a number of nonverbal measures. They include creating an environment that is conducive to responsible behavior. One such focus is on space, the need for both personal space and inviting space. In addition, the space must meet both the physical and safety needs of children. Next, parents and teachers need to act in an authoritative manner when dealing with children. That involves possessing and acting with insight into the nature of children and understanding what constitutes godly nurture. It also includes the exercise of legitimate power that seeks the welfare of the children involved. Another nonverbal contributor toward proper conduct is the understanding of motivation. The things that motivate holy conduct need to be encouraged, and the things that motivate disruptive behavior need to be eliminated. Finally, the "programs" found within homes and schools need to implement God's agenda God's way—with integrity and connectedness. All of these measures together tend to create a sense of *shalom*—God's presence and peace—that fosters harmony and consonance rather than disharmony and dissonance. And "an ounce of prevention (still) is worth a pound of cure."

Preventive discipline that is taught

God has created a world that operates within certain laws or norms. The same is true for children. They have been created to function within a certain framework or structure. The strands of that structure are composed of laws, rules, or guidelines that are necessary for children to find freedom in the fullest sense. This is one of the paradoxical aspects of the Christian life—one must lose one's life to find it (Matthew 16:25). Children must learn to submit to the laws of God to become truly free. Any attempt to operate outside of that structure leads to frustration and defeat. The analogy can be made of a train "submitting" to running on tracks so that a goal or destination can be reached. Musicians, too, must "submit" to the music and to the conductor so that harmonious sound can be produced.

Children, of all people, should have little difficulty with this concept, because they often voluntarily create their own structure within which to find freedom to function. Each time they begin to play a game, they intuitively first establish the rules by which to play. If there are not enough ball players to provide for a right fielder, any player hitting the ball into right field is automatically out. One can only run within the boundaries of the playground while playing tag. The first person to miss while jumping rope must take a turn at the end of the rope. Life is full of such rules, such structure, which become an important part of each child's experience at an early age. The simple fact is that ground rules or guidelines are necessary for people to function together as they work toward a particular goal. One must "learn to play by the rules."

The law of God affects all children

Expectations and guidelines for conduct need to be understood by all parties involved—up front. In that way parents, teachers, *and* the children are able to evaluate whether a particular behavior is appropriate. Evaluation always demands criteria for judging, and evaluating the behavior of children requires stated criteria as well. The Bible calls these criteria mandates, commandments, commissions, admonitions, or laws. They are standards for proper conduct that are to be followed. For children, these standards are called rules, but they still function as God's law for them.

The law of God is designed to serve several purposes. Depending on the stage of one's spiritual development or measure of spiritual health, the law can serve as a restraint, as a mirror, or as a guide.

First, children who have not yet been regenerated will often view rules or laws as restraints on their freedom. They tend not to like rules or boundaries that keep them from doing what they want to do. In this case, sinful natures are dictating the direction of their hearts, and external guidance or intervention by parents or teachers may be required to countermand this sinful leading.

Second, at an age of understanding that only the Holy Spirit knows, the law can serve as a mirror that clearly shows children and young people their need for a Savior. In this case, the law reveals how inadequate they are in their own power to live lives that are pleasing to God. But for one to submit to Christ as Lord, one must first accept Jesus as Savior. To begin this process, the Spirit of God uses the law—the standard of God for moral perfection—as a mirror to reflect our need for someone outside of ourselves to save us from ourselves. The law used in this manner provides the bridge between the law as restraint and the law as guide and, thus, can be a powerful instrument in the corrective nurture process.

Third, for children and young people who have consciously committed their lives to the lordship of Jesus Christ, the law has become a friend and a guide, for it shows the way to please the Heavenly Father. The Spirit resides in their hearts, directing them toward seeking and doing the will of the God. The psalmist describes this new way of seeing the law of God.

> Oh, how I love your law!
>   I meditate on it all day long.
> Your commands make me wiser than my enemies,
>   for they are ever with me.
> I have more insight than all my teachers,
>   for I meditate on your statutes.
> I have more understanding than the elders,
>   for I obey your precepts.
> I have kept my feet from every evil path
>   so that I might obey your word.
> I have not departed from your laws,
>   for you yourself have taught me.
> How sweet are your promises to my taste,
>   sweeter than honey to my mouth!
> I gain understanding from your precepts;
>   therefore I hate every wrong path. (Psalm 119:97–104)

While it may be a bit much to expect regenerated children to respond with such exuberance, they should, indeed, view God's guidelines for their lives as positive and helpful aids for Christian living.

Rules are about relationships

Without relationships there would be no need for rules. Working and playing in community require rules. The real issue when rules are broken is the damage caused to relationships. To be in proper relationship with God, children need to love God—the first of the love commands—and in so doing obey his laws or rules.[6] Disobedience to God's commands creates a breech between children and God, a breech that can be healed only through Jesus. Not showing an interest in others or offending them in some way damages relationships and breaks the second of the love commands. Breaking rules always damages relationships, whether with one's parents, with one's teachers, or with one's friends, for it is really breaking troth or covenantal trust with them. Children need to understand this.

Because rules have everything to do with relationships, rules should be created in ways that reflect relationships. The basic four relationships of life—those that we have with God, others, creation, and ourselves—are a good place to begin. Children are to:

- Love God, which means, within this context, obey his commands;
- Love others, which means demonstrating a sacrificial concern for the welfare of people with whom they work, play, or just "happen" to meet;
- Be faithful stewards of time, opportunities, resources, and property; and
- Respect and take care of themselves.[7]

Note that these rules are broad principles and few in number. The summary of the law spoken by Christ is a great model: Love God and love your neighbor. That really says it all. In addition to being broadly applicable and brief, the summary of the law is also positive—a third guideline. Tell children what they are to do, not what they are not to do. Rules are to be expectations of conduct. Finally, rules must be enforceable. Usually, this means that the rule should speak to behavior that is observable. Thus, the principles listed above need to be fleshed out with practical examples, an activity that could well be done cooperatively.

There are several biblically and educationally sound reasons for having only a few rules, stated as broad principles. First, there are too many different situations within homes and schools to create a rule for each one of them. In fact, whether a certain behavior is appropriate often depends on the situation. For instance, running is a wonderful activity, but not through the kitchen or in a school hallway. Thus, a widely applicable principle can be designed to cover many differing circumstances. Second, the more rules that are established, the more there is a tendency for legalism to creep in. The spirit of the law is to be the guiding force rather than the letter of the law. Third, a law for every circumstance takes away children's freedom to choose and that, in turn, takes away their opportunities for responsible action. The more latitude within which children can respond as unique beings, the better able they are to function as responsive image bearers.

In keeping with the concepts of "rules serving relationship," focusing on the spirit of the law, and involving the children as responsible image bearers, Scripture includes an interesting set of principles for the manner in which we are to conduct ourselves in relationships.

a. The principle of liberty

Many actions in and of themselves are neither good nor bad. Whether they are biblically acceptable or unacceptable depends on one's heart intent and on the circumstances within which they take place. Scripture states:

> As one who is in the Lord Jesus, I am fully convinced that no food is unclean in itself. But if anyone regards something as unclean, then for him it is unclean. (Romans 14:14)

> Eat anything sold in the meat market without raising questions of conscience, for, "The earth is the Lord's, and everything in it." (1 Corinthians 10:25–26)

> For everything God created is good, and nothing is to be rejected if it is received with thanksgiving, because it is consecrated by the word of God and prayer. (1 Timothy 4:4–5)

This principle states that people have the freedom to do that which the Bible has not specifically forbidden. It speaks to the Christian life as being one of freedom and celebration rather than one of legalistic bondage, and it advances the reality that God's good creation is to be engaged and enjoyed. But even here, there are two secondary principles that must be taken into consideration.

b. The principle of edification or helpfulness

1 Corinthians 10:23 states that "'Everything is permissible'—but not everything is beneficial. 'Everything is permissible'—but not everything is constructive." Although people may have the freedom to engage in certain activities, unless they are edifying both personally and to the body of Christ and/or helpful in imaging Christ and bringing glory to God, they should refrain from engaging in the activities.

c. The principle of love and consideration

Again, people may be free to engage in certain activities, but if, however unintentionally, they harm the Christian walk of others or are viewed to be offensive activities by others, out of a love for these people and for the cause of Christ the activities should be avoided. The following scriptures speak to this:

> If your brother is distressed because of what you eat, you are no longer acting in love. Do not by your eating destroy your brother for whom Christ died. . . . Let us therefore make every effort to do what leads to peace and to mutual edification. (Romans 14:15, 19)

> Be careful, however, that the exercise of your freedom does not become a stumbling block to the weak. For if anyone with a weak conscience sees you who have this knowledge eating in an idol's temple, won't he be emboldened

to eat what has been sacrificed to idols? So this weak brother, for whom Christ died, is destroyed by your knowledge. When you sin against your brothers in this way and wound their weak conscience, you sin against Christ. Therefore, if what I eat causes my brother to fall into sin, I will never eat meat again, so that I will not cause him to fall. (1 Corinthians 8:9–13)

Rules and the breaking of rules are all about relationships. Yes, we have the freedom to enjoy all aspects of God's good creation. But Christ's laws of love supersede our freedom. It's not all about us. It's about the glory of God, the welfare of others, and the advancement of Christ's kingdom.

Who makes the rules?

Based on the well-accepted idea that persons affected by decisions (e.g., rules) should be able to provide input into the formation of those decisions, the ideal rule-making scenario is that of a cooperative venture between all parties involved.[8] In that sense, the home, the school, and the classroom should "belong" to all who live, work, or study there. These places and spaces should not be the domains of just the people in authority. A sense of empowerment and of ownership goes a long way toward a cooperative relationship between adults and children. It is good preventive discipline.

Having said that, however, the answer to the rule-making question depends on the cognitive, emotional, social, and spiritual development of the children involved. When dealing with very young children, it is the parent or teacher who must establish the rules. As children mature, however, they can be invited into the process, but parents and teachers, as persons placed in positions of authority by God, always have the final approval or veto. One way to approach this broader involvement is to pose a situation or potential problem that needs a guideline or rule and brainstorm together over possible solutions. For instance, parents or teachers, at times, may desire a quiet context within which to work. The children could be asked to suggest guidelines that would be a win-win, a solution acceptable to everyone.[9]

Before implementing rule making, it is important to establish a base or source for the values that give birth to rules. Rules should not be based on someone's personal biases or whims, including those of the parent or teacher. God warns parents (fathers, in particular) against that in Ephesians 6:4 when he states that disciplining children *their way* rather than *God's way* will create anger and resentment in children. A cardinal tenet of servant leadership is to make decisions that serve the well-being of the persons under authority. Children can easily see through rules that primarily serve those in charge, the ones with power. Thus, criteria for rules should be in harmony with scriptural principles. These include justice, righteousness (doing what's right), love, and mercy, to name a few.

True community involves conflict management and cooperative decision making

Just as failure can be an effective part of the learning process, conflict, another perceived "negative," can have great value in community building. Given the fallen nature and diversity of humankind, differences of opinion will continue to exist in every home and school until the Lord returns. Unhappily, many Christians believe conflict is always a sin and is either to be avoided or not to be acknowledged at all cost. Few members of the body of Christ have received training in conflict management or resolution.[10] As mentioned above, there is no way to establish a rule in advance for every situation that might arise. At times, good people simply need to sit down with each other and "reason together." In the end, they may not always agree, but they do need to come to an agreement about how to live and work with each other in a civil and, hopefully, loving manner.

One program that has found some success in middle and high schools is that of peer counseling and mediation. Based on the Matthew 18 principle,[11] an objective third party, in this case another student who has received training in mediation, is invited by the two students with the conflict to help find a solution agreeable to both of them. The Bible contains some wonderful guidelines for conflict management and resolution that need to be learned and practiced by children and young people.

Any community, whether it is a family at home or a class at school, will need to have family or class meetings on occasion to discuss unanticipated problems. Again, every situation cannot be anticipated by a set of previously agreed-upon rules. A mechanism needs to be in place for these times. Mutual respect and cooperation are the tools required for such meetings. Put-downs, competition, or power plays have no place. If the issue involves only the children, they should be the ones directing the meeting, with adult guidance and encouragement available as needed. Family and class meetings can have a powerful, long-term nurturing effect, for open discussion of issues that matter to children combined with a sense of ownership and empowerment are very motivating and meaningful to them.

Obedience is a matter of the heart

A proper heart attitude must be the motivating force behind any behavior, or God deems the behavior unacceptable. This principle was applied at the dawn of history, when Cain and Abel offered sacrifices to God. One was acceptable, the other was unacceptable, solely because of heart attitude.[12] God's laws do not deal first of all with outward behavior, for obedience is fundamentally a matter of the heart. When one's heart is in loving submission, the actions that follow will be acceptable to God. It is possible for a person outwardly to be keeping all of the Ten Commandments, but inwardly be committing murder or adultery.[13] Christ condemns this, not because of the outward behavior, but because of the absence of a heart that is willing to do the will of the Father.[14]

A key danger in attempting to change or modify the behavior of another person is to focus solely on the external. The authoritarian approach to behavior change is through power and fear; the behavioral approach is through reinforcement (i.e., manipulation) and punishment. Both deal solely with the outward symptoms of behavior rather than with their inner causes. David, in his prayer of confession, approached behavior change in a radically different way. He acknowledged a sinful heart as being the cause, and he sought help from the only true agent of change, God himself: "Create in me a pure heart, O God, and renew a steadfast spirit within me" (Psalm 51:10).

The establishment and proliferation of rules *per se* effect little change. The outward following of rules or guidelines without having a corresponding heart commitment is the same form of legalism that Christ condemned during his earthly ministry. All behavior begins with one's heart.

In summary, children gain a sense of security when they operate within a framework of guidelines, a set of rules. This is a normal part of God's economy, his way of doing things. Heart submission to God's laws is more the goal of biblical discipline than a modifying of outward behavior through power or manipulation. Rules should not be arbitrary; they should have purpose and reflect the place for which they are designed.

Rules are to be few, broad, and positive. They are to be justifiable and fair. They are not to be legalistic ends in themselves, but means to an end. The Bible is the source of guidelines both for the rules and the heart responses to the rules.

Jim Fay, in *Discipline with Love and Logic*,[15] suggests the use of "choices" as a way of getting children to behave in a positive and appropriate manner. His suggestions probably fall more within preventive than corrective discipline, since all choices provided are designed to lead to acceptable behavior. First, he lists reasons for the use of choices:

1. Choices create situations in which children are forced to think.
2. Choices provide opportunities for children to make mistakes and learn from the consequences.
3. Choices help us avoid getting into control battles with youngsters.
4. Choices provide opportunities for children to hear that we trust their thinking abilities.

Fay then provides rules for giving choices:

1. Always be sure to select choices that *you* like. Never provide one you like and one you don't because the child will usually select the one you don't like. The following are examples of choices that parents could live with, either way:
   - Would you rather clean your room on Saturday or Sunday?
   - Do you think you will be spending your allowance on fun things this week or paying someone to do your chores?
   - Do you guys want to settle the problem yourselves or draw straws to see who sits by the window?
   - Would it be best for you to do your homework today or while the rest of us are at the amusement park tomorrow?
2. Never give a choice unless you are willing to allow the child to experience the consequences of that choice.
3. Never give choices when the child is in danger.
4. Never give choices unless you are willing to make the choice for the child in the event he/she does not choose.
5. Your delivery is important. Try to start your sentence with:
   You're welcome to _____ or _____.
   Feel free to _____ or _____.
   Would you rather _____ or _____?
   What would be best for you, _____ or _____?

Corrective Discipline

Every child messes up sometime, just like adults. The reason, of course, is that all children are sinners, even those who love Jesus. Some of these infractions are sins of omission—something is not done that should have been done. There was failure to measure up. But sometimes children will go "over the line" and commit sins of commission. They do something wrong. They break the rules. In both cases, preventive discipline was not enough. No matter how hard parents and teachers try to avoid them, there are times when corrective discipline is needed. Children, on occasion, do need to be redirected in the way they should go.

What to do? This next section of the chapter explores the corrective side of discipline, or nurture. First, a foundation is laid by contrasting correction with punishment. This is followed by guidelines and principles for corrective procedures. Finally, corrective suggestions are offered for both minor and major incidents.

Use correction rather than punishment

Instruction is one part of biblical nurture or discipline (i.e., *paideuo/paideia*—the Greek word used in the New Testament); correction is the other part. To correct means to redirect. The emphasis is on future actions, not on past misdeeds. Parents and teachers are not to ignore past misdeeds, for they certainly can provide insight in choosing a proper response, but the focus is on producing acceptable and appropriate conduct in the future. That is a difficult concept for many to accept, because most people have been reared in a climate in which retribution—punishment for past misdeeds—was the norm when misbehavior occurred. But Scripture is quite plain that corrective discipline *differs from* punishment.

Correction has already been defined as a word or action that redirects a person along the pathway on which she or he should be traveling. It is reformative and has personal growth as a goal. It is a means of nurturing a person. It is done in love and focuses on the future. Punishment, on the other hand, is a penalty inflicted upon an offender as retribution or payment for misdeeds. It focuses on the past and reflects anger, being an end in itself rather than a means to an end. Penology (which means punishment) has to do with retribution. Hell itself is punitive and not reformative.

Scripture explains the differences between *correction* and *punishment*.

Correction

> Blessed is the man you *discipline*, O LORD;
> the man you teach from your law . . . . (Psalm 94:12, emphasis mine)

> I have surely heard Ephraim's moaning:
> "You *disciplined* me like an unruly calf, and I have been *disciplined*.
> Restore me, and I will return, because you are the LORD my God.
> After I strayed, I repented;
> after I came to understand, I beat my breast.
> I was ashamed and humiliated
> because I bore the disgrace of my youth."
> (Jeremiah 31:18–19, emphases mine)

> When we are judged by the Lord, we are being *disciplined* so that we will not be condemned with the world. (1 Corinthians 11:32, emphasis mine)

> Those whom I love I rebuke and *discipline*. So be earnest, and repent.
> (Revelation 3:19, emphasis mine)

Punishment

See, the day of the LORD is coming
   —a cruel day, with wrath and fierce anger—
to make the land desolate and destroy the sinners within it.
The stars of heaven and their constellations
   will not show their light.
The rising sun will be darkened
   and the moon will not give its light.
I will *punish* the world for its evil,
   the wicked for their sins.
I will put an end to the arrogance of the haughty
   and will humble the pride of the ruthless. (Isaiah 13:9–11)

Then they will go away to eternal *punishment,* but the righteous to eternal life. (Matthew 25:46)

This will happen when the Lord Jesus is revealed from heaven in blazing fire with his powerful angels. He will *punish* those who do not know God and do not obey the gospel of our Lord Jesus. They will be *punished* with everlasting destruction and shut out from the presence of the Lord and from the majesty of his power . . . . (2 Thessalonians 1:7–9, emphases mine)

Scripture is quite plain in distinguishing between correction and punishment. The characteristics of each as carried out by parents and teachers can be described in the following manner.

	Correction	Punishment
Purpose	Redirects towards acceptable and appropriate conduct. A means to an end.	Inflicts a penalty for an offence. And end in itself.
Focus	On future, acceptable conduct.	On past, unacceptable conduct. Also on the child's person.
Attitude	Reflects love and concern on the part of the adult.	Reflects hostility, frustration, and, at times, sadism.
Resulting emotion in the child	Security	Fear, guilt, resentment, the possibility of rejection

Correction is *reformative;* punishment is *retributive.* The life and death of Jesus Christ were intended to satisfy divine justice on two counts. Not only did Jesus fulfill God's demand for perfect obedience, but through his death he also paid the penalty for humankind's failure to render that obedience. When persons acknowledge Christ as Savior, they are no longer liable for punishment. This is reserved for those who have not accepted Christ's payment for sin. Scripture bears this out:

> But he was pierced for our transgressions,
>   he was crushed for our iniquities;
> the punishment that brought us peace was upon him,
>   and by his wounds we are healed. (Isaiah 53:5)

> But God demonstrates his own love for us in this: While we were still sinners, Christ died for us.
>   Since we have now been justified by his blood, how much more shall we be saved from God's wrath through him! (Romans 5:8–9)

Since God does not inflict avenging punishment upon his children, Scripture seems to indicate that adults should not punish theirs. Punishment, as righteous vengeance, is to be within the jurisdiction of a holy and omniscient God.

> "It is mine to avenge; I will repay.
>   In due time their foot will slip;
> their day of disaster is near
>   and their doom rushes upon them."
> The LORD will judge his people
>   and have compassion on his servants
> when he sees their strength is gone
>   and no one is left, slave or free. (Deuteronomy 32:35–36)

> Do not take revenge, my friends, but leave room for God's wrath, for it is written: "It is mine to avenge; I will repay," says the Lord. (Romans 12:19)

Scripture quite explicitly points out that people are prohibited from exacting vengeance (i.e., judgmental punishment) precisely because only God can judge right and wrong. God alone can judge and exact vengeance; humankind can only love and exercise corrective discipline.[16]

God does not motivate his children by fear of punishment. In fact, God removes the threat of punishment; then he asks for the grateful response of obedience. This is the whole point of justification by grace.

> Therefore, there is now no condemnation for those who are in Christ Jesus . . . for God's gifts and his call are irrevocable. . . . Therefore, I urge you, brothers, in view of God's mercy, to offer your bodies as living sacrifices, holy and pleasing to God—which is your spiritual worship. (Romans 8:1; 11:29; 12:1)

> There is no fear in love. But perfect love drives out fear, because fear has to do with punishment. The [one] who fears is not made perfect in love. (1 John 4:18)

Parents and teachers who use punitive control techniques often defend their position by saying that it may not agree with modern psychology, but it certainly works! There are several problems with this line of thinking. First, followers of Christ are to look to Scripture and not to themselves for direction on the nurture of children. Second, doing something simply because it works is pragmatism. The Bible instructs us to do what is right or righteous. Third, punishment does not teach correct conduct. And fourth, fear can motivate one to great activity, but this outward conformity is biblically unacceptable. Love based on heart commitment produces actions that are acceptable to God.

In summary, the Bible directs parents and teachers to correct and redirect their children in love, to guide them in the direction that is acceptable to God. The Bible also directs that vengeance or punishment is to be left to God.

Follow the principles of clarity, consistency, and fairness

All corrective procedures should take place within a framework of firmness and kindness. Corrective measures that are firm demonstrate respect for one's position of authority. Measures that are kind demonstrate respect for others. Within this framework of firmness and kindness are found three principles that should be followed for effective correction. They are clarity, consistency, and fairness.

Be clear

The expectations or rules must be clear up front. Children cannot be held accountable for that which they have not been told or do not understand. When irresponsible behavior is exhibited, children should be informed quite precisely of the nature of the problem. It is possible that they either were not aware of their behavior or did not consider it to be inappropriate. Children often view things differently than adults. When adults explain the reasons for their concerns, children are provided with opportunities for insight into their behavior. Clarity of expectations is an important prerequisite for engendering self-discipline.

Be consistent

Parents and teachers must be consistent in the exercise of corrective procedures. They must say what they mean (i.e., provide clear instruction), and they must mean what they say (i.e., provide consistent correction). They should be directed by predetermined guidelines rather than by personal moods. An act of disobedience is wrong at any time, no matter what the mood of the person in authority. God has provided guidelines by which to live. Whenever these guidelines are ignored, consequences occur—consistently. Consistency means dealing with small, seemingly insignificant infractions. This will often deter larger, more serious problems. Consistency also means that adults are to follow up on their requests or commands. Sometimes adults become preoccupied or sidetracked and fail to determine whether children have complied with a request or order. Children tend to respond in direct proportion to the consistency of the adults.

Be fair

Another principle for effective correction is fairness. The correction should not be of greater severity than the misdeed warrants, since that could produce a feeling of unfairness in the child that might exacerbate the problem. Both the seriousness of the misconduct and the attitude behind the act, as best as can be determined, should have a bearing on the corrective measures taken.

The corrective measures must also fit the person. Some children need a greater amount of corrective influence or a more distinctive form than others. Corrective measures that do not reflect the uniqueness of the individual often will be ineffective. On the other hand, personalized discipline can be a vehicle for communicating love and concern and for fostering effective redirection.

Teachers ought to be aware of something called the "ripple effect." This occurs within a classroom immediately after correction has taken place. The effects spread out like concentric wavelets from the child who was corrected to those classmates who witnessed the episode. The ripple can reflect a positive, exemplary effect, but the ripple can also be negative. The use of highly emotional threats by teachers can cause children to lower their estimation of the teachers' helpfulness, likeability, and fairness. They tend to produce a great amount of distracting behavior and can easily impair the learning process. Viewing oneself though the eyes of the children and understanding the effects on the children of one's actions can help teachers in the corrective discipline process.

Finally, when inappropriate behavior occurs, parents and teachers ought to consider certain things before responding. For the more experienced, these types of considerations may have already become second nature.

a. Determine whether the incident is worth responding to

Is it simply a personal annoyance, or is there more to it? Within a classroom, assess whether the student's activity is hindering progress toward meeting the educational goals of the student or of the class.

b. Try not to "lose" everyone while correcting one

Within the classroom, try to resolve the issue without missing a beat in the lesson. Put out the immediate fire so that the class can continue functioning. Follow-up, if required, can take place at a more appropriate time. Not allowing one student to take control of the classroom through disruption is a proper exercise of authoritative insight.

c. Use quiet, firm, decisive action rather than threats
Some children test to see whether the adult means business or not, and words don't count with them.

d. Remain cool and objective—or at least try to!
Most misconduct is not meant to be personal, as much as it may, at times, feel like it. The child (or the other children) should, therefore, be able to view the handling of a problem as a logical response rather than as a personal vendetta.

e. If the situation calls for humor or laughter, try it.

Minor incidents call for minimal corrective response
It has been said that one should not try to kill a flea with a cannon. That principle applies to corrective discipline as well. The majority of misconduct is minor and calls for a correspondingly minimal response from the person in charge. But it cannot be emphasized strongly enough that minor infractions soon become major problems if they are not dealt with in a timely and appropriate manner. Either ignoring problems or hoping that they will disappear of their own accord seldom works. When a minor infraction takes place, pay attention and progressively "turn up the heat" until the misbehavior stops. Move from the nonverbal to the verbal to action.

Send nonverbal messages
Within a classroom setting, begin with nonverbal signals or messages, because they tend to be the least disruptive. They may be used individually or in combination.

a. Use silence
Stop speaking until the person or persons who are not on task become conscious of their behavior and begin paying attention.

b. Stare (or glare) at the student until you have her or his attention
Eye contact is a very effective corrective device.

c. Use head or hand signals
(1) Shake your head, "No."
(2) Place your finger to your lips, indicating "Stop talking."
(3) Point your finger to the student's work, indicating "Get busy."

d. Use bodily position
  (1) Walk toward the student.
  (2) Stand close to the student. Teach from that position.

Send verbal messages

a. Simply call the child's name
  (1) Within a classroom setting, follow this with a nonverbal cue for direction.
  (2) If the child is doing something wrong, tell her or him what to stop doing. If the child is not doing something she or he should be doing, tell her or him what to begin doing. When verbally correcting a child, a lower voice and a deliberate rate of speech can be effective.

b. Send the message that compliance precedes discussion
  Children often choose to argue or "discuss" the issue at this point. This is generally unacceptable because it is an act of disobedience, no matter how sweetly it may done. The message must be communicated that compliance precedes discussion. Diffuse potential confrontations by sending the message that you "hear what she or he is saying" and that you will discuss the matter at a later time—after compliance (i.e., obedience) has taken place. This allows emotions to calm down, gives you both the time required to adequately discuss the issue, and you will have had more time to think about how to respond.

c. Assume compliance
  The older the children are, the more important it is not to embarrass them—especially the males—in front of their peers or girlfriends. Students will view a one-on-one private conversation ("Let's step out into the hall a second") that explains what conduct you want from them as being respectful. Then say "thank you" and return to class. This assumption of compliance avoids the potential confrontation of a forced compliance, allowing the student to save face and to "choose" to comply.

Take appropriate action

a. Remove temptation and/or reinforcement
  The simplest and most effective action response to misconduct, whether it takes place at home or in school, is either to move the child or to remove the temptation. Relocating or separating a child away from the source of temptation, often another child, also removes the temptation, the source of fun, stimulation, attention, reinforcement, or whatever other word may be appropriate.

b. Remove privileges

This is commonly referred to as a "time-out." At home, that may be sitting quietly in the living room or some other place free from distractions. (Sending children to their rooms can be counterproductive, since most children love being in their rooms.) At school, the assigned location may be a particular seat in the classroom, a desk in the hallway, or some designated place elsewhere in the school. Children should remain there until the parent or teacher either chooses or has the opportunity to discuss the matter with them. Children should be restored to their previous position when they voice a willingness to cooperate, be nice, or do whatever they should be doing. Allowing them to return after a preset period of time is simply having them "serve time" and does not deal with a changed heart or attitude.

(1) Some children may be responsible enough to go voluntarily to the time-out area when they sense a loss of control coming on. They also should be allowed to return at will.

(2) Sadly, within a school setting, some students are unwilling to pledge cooperation. If this happens, progressive separation may be required. An in-school suspension and a conference with the parent(s) may be the next step. If cooperation is still not forthcoming, additional steps such as expulsion and/or a transfer to another school may be necessary.

When a parent or teacher *does* take time to discuss the issue with a child, a question such as "Why do you think I sent you out?" can establish a nonthreatening rapport. It allows children to explain their actions from their perspective, and it provides them with the opportunity to evaluate their actions and to show remorse. In addition, the adult can gain insight into the perceptions, attitude, and actions of the child so that appropriate corrective measures can be devised.

One other important point needs to be made here. In many schools, students are sent to the vice principal (or some other person in authority), who is expected to resolve teacher-student conflicts even though one member of the conflict, namely the teacher, is not present. Often, this person assumes the student is at fault. This is grossly unfair and unbiblical. According to Scripture, the two parties in any conflict are first to attempt to resolve their differences *between the two of them.* As the adult, the teacher needs to take the initiative in this. The Matthew 18 principle applies here: "If your brother sins against you, go and show him his fault, just between the two of you. If he listens to you, you have won your brother over" (Matthew 18:15). If a one-to-one conference does not resolve the matter to the satisfaction of both parties (i.e., produce a "win-win"), then the second part of this principle must be put into effect: "But if he will not listen, take one or two others along, so that 'every matter may be established by the testimony of two or three witnesses'" (v. 16). At this point, the vice principal or some other appropriate third party should serve as advisor, arbitrator, and/or witness. But the issue, ideally, remains for the teacher and student to resolve between them. If that proves to be impossible, a solution will have to be imposed by the third party, but through the teacher, so that her or his position of authority can be maintained. This approach is not only biblical, it has certain practical benefits as well. If a teacher and a student are to function effectively together in the classroom, genuine healing must take place. Also, it is possible that the teacher may have been the one in the wrong. Assuming the student is always guilty is both disrespectful and unrealistic. Healing cannot take place within an atmosphere that lacks a sense of justice.

Before moving on to suggestions for correcting more serious behavior problems, one other dimension of corrective discipline should be discussed: Care must be taken to focus on solutions to problems rather than on who's to blame. The question to be asked is: "What can be done to redirect this child so that he or she can begin acting in a more responsible way in the future?" Emphasis is to be placed more on future actions than on past misdeeds. Adults and children can become so bogged down by attempts to determine blame that they lose sight of how to promote more responsible behavior, which is the goal of biblical discipline. This should not be surprising, since the second recorded sin of humankind was that of Adam blaming Eve for his disobedience, and then Eve blaming the serpent for hers. People have been seeking deterministic and causistic excuses for their misbehavior ever since, for it frees them from personal accountability. But that does not truthfully reflect the nature of humankind, for people have been created as responsible and accountable beings, with the freedom to choose. People's actions are direct results of their own choices, and, thus, they are personally accountable. Personal blame must be accepted for one's irresponsible conduct. Only then can plans be made for acting in a more responsible manner in the future.

Major behavioral problems require greater intervention

Major behavioral problems are those that repeat themselves (i.e., there's a pattern of misbehavior) and/or produce significant harm to oneself, others, or property. They are often premeditated. Sometimes, the person is simply "out of control." The infractions are not incidental in nature; rather, they are serious enough to warrant outside intervention by others. This section offers corrective discipline suggestions for more serious behavioral problems.

All choices have consequences

Two biblical truths converge at this point to form one of the cardinal principles for corrective discipline. First, humankind was created with the ability to choose. Image bearers were created as responsible *and* accountable agents. Conscious choices can be made, and humankind can be held accountable for those choices, for they are made freely. (See Jim Fay's use of choices listed on pp. 228–229.) Second, consequences for those choices are a built-in part of God's economy—his way of doing things. All choices have consequences, both good and bad. This truth emerges from the biblical principle of "sowing and reaping" cited in Galatians:

> Do not be deceived: God cannot be mocked. A man reaps what he sows. The one who sows to please his sinful nature, from that nature will reap destruction; the one who sows to please the Spirit, from the Spirit will reap eternal life. Let us not become weary in doing good, for at the proper time we will reap a harvest if we do not give up. (Galatians 6:7–9)

The principles that humankind possesses the freedom to choose and that all choices have consequences were built into the human experience by God from the very beginning. Adam and Eve were given a command, a choice, and a consequence: "You are free to eat from any tree in the garden; but you must not eat from the tree of the knowledge of good and evil, for when you eat of it you will surely die" (Genesis 2:16–17). Failure to choose to obey this command did, in fact, lead to death. But the gracious intervention of Jesus Christ reintroduced this eternal choice and consequences for humankind:

> This day I call heaven and earth as witnesses against you that I have set before you life and death, blessings and curses. Now choose life, so that you and your children may live and that you may love the LORD your God, listen to his voice, and hold fast to him. (Deuteronomy 30:19–20a)

The Apostle Paul captures this eternal choice-consequence rhythm with the words: "For the wages of sin is death, but the gift of God is eternal life in Christ Jesus our Lord" (Romans 6:23). This particular choice of eternal life, however, must originate with the Spirit of Christ in our hearts, who makes the choice irresistible. For we love God only because he loved us first (1 John 4:19).

The entire premise of biblical discipline is that there are laws or rules to obey and that the choice to obey will produce positive consequences and the choice to disobey will produce negative consequences. The consequences, however, are not meant to be retributive but reformative. The purpose of consequences is to get our attention, often through pain, and redirect us onto the pathway that leads to God and his righteous kingdom.

The next several sections will describe the ways in which consequences, both natural and imposed, can be used to redirect children and young people back to the "way they should go."

Natural consequences should sometimes be allowed

At times, it is best to let "nature to take its course" and to allow children to suffer the natural consequences of their choices. These consequences are based on the natural flow of events and are those that take place without adult interference. Parents and teachers could ask themselves: "What would happen if I didn't interfere?" (Obviously, there are some circumstances in which a child's safety would be endangered and allowing natural consequences would not be an option.)

Sometimes, then, consequences are built naturally into an experience, and experience can be "the best teacher." This means that parents and teachers may purposely choose to allow children to experience the consequences that are naturally built into their choices. Providing children with choices is an appropriate nurturing tool, and allowing children to learn from the consequences of their choices, even if that means failing at a task or experiencing minor pain, is powerful instruction. It is evident in Scripture that God sometimes allows people to learn from their mistakes.

> He who is pregnant with evil
> and conceives trouble gives birth to disillusionment.
> He who digs a hole and scoops it out
> falls into the pit he has made.
> The trouble he causes recoils on himself;
> his violence comes down on his own head. (Psalm 7:14–16)

> Therefore God gave them over in the sinful desires of their hearts to sexual impurity for the degrading of their bodies with one another. They exchanged the truth of God for a lie, and worshiped and served created things rather than the Creator . . . . (Romans 1:24–25)[17]

The parable of the prodigal son recorded in Luke 15:11–24 provides a redemptive and restorative example of natural consequences being used as a teaching device for one's choices. Sometimes, with older children in particular, when all else has failed, "tough love" dictates that we "let our children go" to suffer the consequences of their actions. Bathed in prayer, Lord willing, they will return to us with chastened hearts.

One of the most difficult experiences for parents is seeing their children in pain. But it is often true that with no pain there is no gain. God allows his children to "walk through the valley," for, oftentimes, the only way to the mountain is through the valley. Many of us can point to growth in our Christian walks that emerged from experiences that were exceedingly painful. The same is true for our children. At times, no matter how difficult it may be, we must allow our children to experience the painful consequences of their choices. Sometimes, protecting children from experiencing pain is not being helpful to them.

The behavioristic principle of *satiation* is similar in some ways to natural consequences. Most of us have experienced getting sick from overindulgence at some point in our lives and thus sick of that food or activity. That is satiation. It's too much of a "good" thing. The satiation principle states that to stop children from acting in a particular way, parents and teachers may allow them to continue performing the undesired act until they tire of it. The hope is that children will become satiated by the consequences of their behavior because of boredom or fatigue. This view of natural consequences, however, appears to depart a bit from the biblical model that seeks to have the individual gain insight into the misconduct as evaluated against biblical norms. Satiation carries with it implications of stimulus-response, which does not necessarily include insight.

One other behavioristic principle that calls for no action is *extinction*. The concept of extinction states that to stop children from acting in a particular way, parents and teachers can arrange conditions so that the children receive no rewards or reinforcement following undesirable actions. This, too, can be dealt with on a purely stimulus-response level that does not do justice to a biblical view of children. But extinction has certain applications that appear to be consistent with scriptural teaching. It may be appropriate for parents and teachers to ignore certain behaviors that are meant to bait them (such as foot tapping or gum popping) and to deal with the attitudes and actions at a later time. Perhaps certain obnoxious behavior, especially the type that may emerge during adolescence, should be ignored with the hope that it will soon run its course. If it is not a moral or eternal issue, it may not be worth losing the relationship over. But priestly image bearers of Christ cannot ignore others who by their actions are crying out: "Help me. I need someone to pay attention to me, to care about me, to love me."

Most times, consequences need to be imposed

The distinction between biblical nurture and what is commonly referred to as discipline or punishment comes into play very clearly at this point. At least three variables need to be added to consequences imposed by parents and teachers to align them with biblical nurture: First, consequences should be logical; second, consequences should be accompanied by instruction; and, third, consequences should be reformative and restorative. All three of these seek to provide children with insight into their conduct and how it relates to the path of righteousness on which they should be walking.

a. Consequences should be logical

The "sowing and reaping" principle described above states that every choice, every action, is followed by a consequence, either positive or negative (depending on one's viewpoint). Logic suggests, then, that parents and teachers should select consequences for their children's choices that are in harmony with the norms of Scripture, norms that may differ from societal norms. Thus, an object lesson on the types of behavior God views as right or wrong can be provided. The second logical aspect to consequences is that they need to relate to the choice in a way that can easily be seen by the children. This ties in to natural consequences, for choices do often naturally relate to outcomes. Imposed consequences should provide children with the same type of insight through connection, so that in the future they can make choices with outcomes in mind. Punishment, on the other hand, often does not relate to the choice; it usually is arbitrary. By relating to the choice rather than to the person, logical consequences promote rather than denigrate a child's sense of worth and dignity.

The imposition of logical consequences for one's choices can help to avoid power struggles because they teach personal responsibility and, thus, tend to eliminate unnecessary warnings and nagging. But logical consequences have their limitations as well. Unless children can gain insight into their choices and develop a heartfelt commitment toward redirection, logical consequences become nothing more than external devices for modifying another's behavior. And any form of correction that is based on power alone, logical or not, is viewed by the child as punishment.

b. Consequences should be accompanied by instruction

Previously, it was mentioned that biblical nurture is very much show and tell. Parents and teachers are to do something or take an action that is in harmony with God's Word and simultaneously or shortly thereafter explain the reasons for the action. Instruction is to accompany correction for proper nurture to take place. There should be no mysteries about what is going on. For the day is coming that these same children will be on their own, making decisions for themselves and others. They need to understand the rationale underlying right choices.

c. Consequences should be reformative and restorative

Logical consequences and punishment may appear to be quite similar to the outside observer. Connecting the consequence to the choice and explaining the rationale for it help. But the ultimate difference between corrective discipline and punishment is the purpose that guides each. The former is reformative and restorative, whereas the latter is retributive. The former seeks future righteous conduct, the latter deals with the past and is often an angry "getting back" at the child, a giving of "what they deserve." Grace is absent. Which, once again, reminds us of the Scripture verse that begins: ". . . the wages of sin is death. . ." What the child deserves and has earned is punishment. That's true. But the remainder of the verse reads: ". . . but the gift of God is eternal life in Christ Jesus our Lord" (Romans 6:23). The goal for biblical discipline is always a positive, future-oriented, redirecting, loving, gracious seeking of the path of righteousness that leads to God. And that's a reformative and restorative "gift of God."

Biblical discipline, then, is more than simply a smarter game plan. It has been designed to show children God's ways of dealing with them. It's an object lesson of sin, salvation, and service. It deals with the big picture of this life and beyond. It is part of biblical nurture.

Consequences for right (or righteous) behavior

Thankfully, our children often—and perhaps usually—do things right according to God's standards. These actions need to be acknowledged as part of direction-giving nurture. So often the words we speak to our children are of the "you need to be fixed" type rather than the "you did that really well" variety. Encouragement is a part of God's way to strengthen resolve and behavior patterns that are pleasing to him. Parents and teachers need to show and tell their children how pleased they are when right choices are made and when God-glorifying actions are taken. This positive nurture can take two forms: a positive consequence can be added (+ +) to children's lives and a related negative "consequence" can be removed (- -) from their lives. Both serve to encourage them to continue walking the pathway on which they are already walking.

a. Encourage right behavior through adding positives (+ +) to children's lives

Just as we crave to please our Heavenly Father, so children desire to please their parents and teachers. A good amount of that pleasure should be evidenced through simply loving and enjoying children for who they are rather than for what they do. Love is to be unconditional and unending, no matter what. But when they behave in a manner that "makes us proud," we need to let them know that we are pleased with their choices and conduct, for this will provide nurturing encouragement for them to continue in that same direction. We can do that by adding a positive to their lives—a plus-plus, if you will, as an affirmation of "well done." This lets them know that we think they are on the right track.

(1) Pay attention to them. Notice children—what they do, what they wear. Comment on these things—like, "Wow! Cool shoes!" Pay attention to each child and to the details in their lives. Adolescents, in particular, are egocentric, perceiving that they are on the stage of life and that everyone notices everything about them. Noticing (in a positive or at least a neutral way) clothing, hair, jewelry and the like is very relationship building for them. In that simple way, you can acknowledge them as unique persons, which contributes to their sense of identity and self-respect. To them, that's a big deal. Saying "Hi, Jeremy (or whatever her or his name is)" when you see them in the hall at school, at church, in the mall, again, tells children that you view them as real people. As the old song says, "Little things mean a lot!"

> *I'll never forget being present at a family birthday celebration while visiting relatives in the Netherlands. There were nine children in the family, and it was the five-year-old's turn to receive special attention. He stood on his chair after dinner, and everyone sang "Happy Birthday" to him. Then came the presents, which were opened one at a time with great fanfare. The entire event took about forty-five minutes. It was a big deal! And the little boy was obviously pleased as punch at being treated as a VIP.*

(2) Be there for them. Children of all ages really value the presence of parents and/or teachers in their lives and activities. For parents, that may mean attending programs, recitals, athletic events, and the like. Attendance at these events is an endorsement of the event as being a good, worthwhile activity. Activities done together as a family, such as camping or eating out, also contribute to this "being there" feeling. For teachers, attending school activities in which students are involved is very noticed and appreciated by them. They really like this creation of relationship within "their" world. What trumps even that is attending a nonschool activity, such as a church or community event, in which the student is participating.

(3) Commend them. When children do something right or well, they should receive commendation for it, for positive words tend to encour-

age them to repeat what they have done or to increase their effort the next time. Commendation differs from praise, however, in that commendation makes it very clear as to what was being done well. Praise can be indiscriminate (e.g., "Great job!"), whereas commendation specifically describes what made the job so great. Because praise doesn't specify the criteria by which an action was judged, it can tend to create dependency, for even though children know that their actions were pleasing, they don't know the reason. So they randomly try to please again, until they hit the jackpot once more. Commendation, on the other hand, can help children move toward self-evaluation, which is a goal of nurture.

(4) Reward outstanding effort. Rewards should not be the reason children do a job or do it well. Scripture tells us to do all *to the glory of God* (1 Corinthians 10:31), not for our own well-being or advancement. In that sense, rewards should probably be more after-the-fact surprises than things promised or anticipated. Recognition in the form of payments, rewards, or awards is a normal part of life, however, that will continue even into eternity. People get paid for work they do, and the more responsible jobs usually command higher salaries. Efforts made beyond the call of duty often result in bonuses or gifts. There is nothing wrong with these things, for "Scripture says, 'Do not muzzle the ox while it is treading out the grain,' and 'The worker deserves his wages'" (1 Timothy 5:18). In school, students may receive happy faces and/or positive written comments for work that is outstanding. But this is where a few distinctions need to be made.

Following the 1 Timothy principle cited above, those who contribute their efforts ought to have a share in the profits, and those who work should receive some form of compensation. Applying this to children within a family, it appears that an allowance could be viewed as being legitimate, not as a reward or even as pay for doing household chores (because those are communal, nonpaying responsibilities), but as a sharing of the family income. A case could also be made, perhaps, that since children's primary "work" is being a student, monetary awards might be viewed as recognition of this as well. Allowances could be provided for tithe, discretionary spending, clothing and other personal supplies, and savings. In this light, only efforts that go far beyond one's normal performance or the call of duty should be recognized by a "bonus." Within a school setting, grades should be viewed as assessments not as rewards or punishments. Teachers (early elementary, in particular) should not use rewards as motivation for work or conduct that is expected of students. This teaches the wrong lesson. Award ceremonies may have their place, but in keeping with the spiritual gifts and body passages of Romans 12:3–8 and 1 Corinthians 12, *everyone* needs to be recognized for the contributions he or she has made, not just the favored few. Again, to summarize, rewards are not to be used as motivation for anticipated behavior but as recognition of outstanding performances.

The "work before play" dictum may apply here. This has been called "Grandma's Rule," that "once you have finished your veggies you may have dessert." There are many legitimate applications of this for both the home and the school. Hard work can be rewarded by a break or some fun activity. But, again, concern needs to be taken for the reasons we do things. *Solo Deo gloria!*

b. Encourage right behavior through removing "negatives" (– –) from children's lives

Parents and teachers can also encourage children by taking away burdens and barriers that produce discouragement in their lives—a minus-minus, if you will. Christ spoke of this form of encouragement:

> "Come unto me, all you who are weary and burdened, and I will give you rest. Take my yoke upon you and learn from me, for I am gentle and humble in heart, and you will find rest for your souls. For my yoke is easy and my burden is light." (Matthew 11:28–30)

One of the common characteristics of the children of this new millennium is that they feel overwhelmed by a world that they cannot control. They are a stressed-out generation. There are probably many reasons for this, but the one common denominator is *disconnect*. Children today experience a constant disconnect within their worlds. It may begin with a divorce and a single-parent or blended family. It continues through the media with its sound bites and video clips. Television shows have six themes running at once. Threat seems ever-present in their world. No horror is unimaginable, from school killings to planes flying into tall buildings. No place is safe, no relationship is permanent, and no plan is forever. Children desperately need context, stability, relationships, and connectedness. It is within this fragmentation and dissonance that children need parents and teachers who are there for them no matter what and who will walk side by side with them through the scariness of their worlds. They need adults who can encourage them by removing some of the bad things from their world. They need adults who will get next to them and offer to help, to walk through the valleys with them.

The removal of burdens and barriers is a very priestly thing, for those who are too weak to fend for themselves—the marginalized and disenfranchised—need someone to smooth the pathway for them and to give them hope. They need to be shown that there is light at the end of their tunnel. This type of "minus-minus" help can take many forms. At home, it may be working together on a task that feels too big for a small child to do. It may be doing the dishes for a teen who feels totally overwhelmed by work- school- or friend-related pressures. At school, it's helping a student work through a math problem or cutting some slack for a high-schooler who has been sick and fallen behind—or who is alcoholic and in rehab for a month.

So encouragement can come in several forms. Yes, there is the verbal commendation and the reward or award for a job well done—the plus-plus. But there is also the lightening of a load into something more manageable, the shortening of an agenda that is too packed, and the pitching in to get the too-big job completed—the minus-minus. That is encouragement, too; encouragement not to give up, but to "keep on truckin.'"

Consequences for wrong behavior

All children sin, for they are born with sinful natures. Even following regeneration, the former sinful self continues to be present, albeit in a less visible and dominant form. This means that all children at some time will either not do what they should be doing or will do what they should not be doing. They will commit sins of either omission or commission.

The vast majority of these acts of disobedience can be dealt with as minor infractions, using some of the approaches previously cited. But the more serious misdeeds may need additional thought and planning. There are two basic approaches to corrective discipline that seek to redirect children: first, positives in the lives of children can be removed—a minus-plus (– +); and second, negatives can be added to the lives of children—a plus-minus (+ –). Both interventions are meant to get the attention of children and to create a level of discomfort that will help them make different and better choices in the future. Again, the consequences imposed should be logically related to the misdeeds and include instruction.

Before describing these two approaches to corrective discipline, however, an additional, more foundational "correction" should be explained: *restitution*.

a. Seeking restoration of relationship through restitution

The act of restitution is, perhaps, the most biblical and logical of all corrective consequences. For that reason, it needs to be considered *before* other corrective consequences are employed. Restitution is "making things right." If disobedience is a sin first and foremost as a breech in relationship, then restitution is a primary means to restore relationship.

Restitution carries with it the potential for restored relationships with God, with others, perhaps with "creation," and, ultimately, with oneself.

Restitution was a vital form of Old Testament Hebrew law and tradition. Exodus 22 deals with the topics of protection of property and social responsibility, and the solutions to damaged property or damaged relationships often were restitution or (re)payment. That law was obeyed by Zacchaeus the tax collector after he came to know Christ: "Look, Lord! Here and now I give half of my possessions to the poor, and if I have cheated anybody out of anything, I will pay back four times the amount" (Luke 19:8).

Jesus Christ accomplished the ultimate act of restitution through his life, death, and resurrection. Every sin that we commit hurts God and our relationship with him. For that relationship to be restored, the restitution found in Jesus must be appropriated.

Restitution should take place when a misdeed negatively affects a person or property. The former may relate, in extreme cases, to the breaking of criminal law and the latter to the breaking of civil law. The former is usually more difficult to "restore" than the latter.

Diane Chelsom Gossen, in her book *Restitution: Structuring School Discipline,*[18] lists the philosophical tenets and characteristics of restitution:

1. Everyone makes mistakes. Mistakes are normal; to err is part of the human condition.

2. People know when they have done wrong.

3. Even a child understands when he has broken something or hurt someone.

4. Guilt and criticism contribute to defensive behavior. People put up walls and use a lot of energy rationalizing past wrongs to preserve their self-esteem while under attack.

5. People can learn a better way if we can keep them on the success side. If we can view them as capable, responsible, and willing to change even in the face of their mistakes, they have incentive to move forward.

6. People are strengthened by the opportunity to make restitution. Because everyone makes mistakes, an important life skill is learning to repair them.

7. People won't lie or hide their mistakes if they believe they are capable of making restitution and will be given an opportunity.

8. The process of making restitution is a creative one, which builds problem-solving skills in the offender. People who have been allowed to make restitution are generous with others who made mistakes. They are nonpunitive themselves as adults.[19]

A good restitution will have the following characteristics. They can serve as an evaluative checklist for any restitution suggested by the child or adult.

1. It will be seen by the victim as adequate compensation.
2. It will require effort.
3. It does not in any way encourage repetition.
4. It will be relevant to the general area of the mistake.
5. It will be tied to a higher value or mission statement so that a child doesn't see the restitution as an isolated event, but part of a larger picture of how people treat each other.
6. It strengthens the child.[20]

Restitution has a number of practical applications both within the home and school:

- An act of disobedience must be corrected by obeying the request that was made.
- If children speak to adults (or other children) in a manner that is unacceptable, they should repeat themselves in a more acceptable manner.
- An act of disrespect can be corrected through an apology or repeating the act in a more courteous manner.
- Hurting another person calls for at least an apology.
- If children steal or damage another's property, they should return or restore it.
- If children do an unacceptable job on a task, they should do it over in an acceptable manner.
- If time is misused, it should be used properly at some other time in a make-up session.

Restitution of these types requires children, as part of the corrective or redirective process, to undo or make right what they have done wrong.

One of the best results of an act of restitution is what it does to the offender. Yes, one could seek and receive forgiveness. That is very important in the restoration of relationships. But greater healing can and often needs to take place. This is not "works redemption"; it is an act of justice and righteousness. The offender needs to be able to undo or make right that which has been harmed. It's a matter of penance, yes, but more of reparation and restitution that is cathartic and inwardly cleansing. This "self-restitution," however, is not ultimately dependent on the victim's acceptance. A proposed restitution that is rejected still contributes to inner healing and restoration.

Finally, restitution will not work with every child. Generally speaking, restitution works best with persons who have reached puberty and/or Jean Piaget's cognitive stage of formal operations. Very young children have difficulty understanding the pain others feel from hurtful actions, for they tend to be egocentric. Middle-school-age children also have difficulty getting into the minds and feelings of others, for to them their actions are right or wrong based on some code of conduct, not on how the actions affect others. And there will be some children who do not want to make restitution for whatever the reason. Restitution, then, is to be invited, not demanded. If children "cannot" or "do not want to" make restitution, other corrective consequences can be imposed.

b. Redirecting toward better choices through the removal of a positive (– +)

Certain forms of misbehavior call for logical consequences that remove things that a child values. These could include a privilege or a possession. It is important that whatever is taken away is something valued by the particular child, or the intervention will not be effective.

> *Sadly, I was not a very cooperative student during much of my high school experience. I had not yet surrendered my life to Jesus, and it showed. I was "kicked out" of more classes than I care to recount. I was even removed from the lunchroom. We normally ate around picnic tables in the lunchroom with our homerooms. My friend and I always sat on one end of a table, opposite each other; our homeroom teacher sat on the other end. When my friend and I were finished with our (glass) pop bottles, we would roll them down the table toward the other end. Obviously, someone would have to catch them or they would roll off the table, crash onto the cement floor, and splatter. That "someone" was the homeroom teacher, and he was not happy about this additional responsibility. After several warnings to stop and after continued persistence on my part (we loved watching him react), he exiled me to the school office to eat my lunch each day. The intent was to remove the privilege of eating lunch with my friend. But I soon discovered that I had become a school hero (at least in my own eyes) as other students who came into the office inquired why I was eating lunch there. Every time I told the story, I received all sorts of reinforcement, since most of the students thought the story was very funny. In this case, the removal of a privilege backfired, since I received more positive (I saw it as positive) attention through eating in the office than I did eating in the lunchroom.*

Several examples come to mind when thinking of removing a positive in the lives of children. At home, children may have to miss a family activity so that they can do or redo (if it was done poorly) some chore or task. Adolescents may have to keep the door to their room open if it becomes evident that they aren't doing their homework behind the closed door. At school, students who do not stay on task during the regular class time may have to stay in during recess or lunchtime or after school to complete their work. High school students who do wheelies with their cars in the school parking lot may lose the privilege of using the school parking lot. You get the idea. The tricky part is logically connecting the lost privilege to the infraction. If nothing comes to mind immediately, it may be necessary to make an appointment with the child to discuss the matter later. That will provide additional time to think of a logical consequence, and it will allow the child to contemplate a bit longer the "horrible" things that may be in store.

The Bible provides two broad uses of plus-minus logical consequences that could be applied to many situations, both at home and at school: progressive separation and the loss of privileges.

(1) The *progressive separation* intervention was mentioned before as an appropriate response to minor infractions. It can be applied very effectively to more serious situations as well. Within Scripture, this approach is seen in the withdrawal or isolation by God from his people. When the people of Israel did not honor their covenantal relationship with God, God would withdraw his (full) presence from them until such a time as they would repent. Deuteronomy records one such event. Here, God is speaking to Moses:

> ". . . these people will soon prostitute themselves to the foreign gods of the land they are entering. They will forsake me and break the covenant I made with them. On that day I will become angry with them and forsake them; I will hide my face from them, and they will be destroyed. Many disasters and difficulties will come upon them, and on that day they will ask, 'Have not these disasters come upon us because our God is not with us?' And I will certainly hide my face on that day because of all their wickedness in turning to other gods." (Deuteronomy 31:16–18)

The central theme described here is relationship—*broken* relationship. God had initiated a covenantal relationship with his chosen people. They responded with unfaithfulness and broke covenantal troth with him. God's response was to separate himself from his people, withdrawing his presence and his blessings, until they would repent and seek to return to a covenantal love relationship with him.

It was mentioned previously that virtually all discipline problems are breeches in (covenantal) relationships. Discipline problems are not unconnected, isolated events. Other people are always affected by our misdeeds. Relationships are damaged or broken because of them. A logical consequence for this breech in trust and relationship is progressive separation. If one cannot properly tend to relationships, that privilege must be withdrawn until such a time as the person is willing to become a contributing partner in the relationship. This action also protects the other person or persons involved. Christ taught this, and later Paul advised the church at Corinth in this same way.

> "If your brother sins against you, go and show him his fault, just between the two of you. If he listens to you, you have won your brother over. But if he will not listen, take one or two others along, so that 'every matter may be established by the testimony of two or three witnesses.' If he refuses to listen to them, tell it to the church; and if he refuses to listen even to the church, treat him as you would a pagan or a tax collector." (Matthew 18:15–17)

> I have written you in my letter not to associate with sexually immoral people—not at all meaning the people of this world who are immoral, or the greedy and swindlers, or idolaters. In that case you would have to leave this world. But now I am writing you that you must not associate with anyone who calls himself a brother but is sexually immoral or greedy, an idolater . . . or a swindler. With such a man do not even eat.
>   What business is it of mine to judge those outside the church? Are you not to judge those inside? God will judge those outside. "Expel the wicked man from among you." (1 Corinthians 5:9–13)[21]

Several things become clear from these passages. First, separation is progressive, one step at a time, with the hope that the person will repent and seek to reverse course. Restoration is always the goal of biblical discipline. Second, the "judge not" portion of Scripture that some persons like to refer to does not apply to the body of believers. We are told to hold believers accountable. Thirdly, the last passage adds another reason for separation in addition to that of acknowledgment of broken relationship: one expels an immoral brother to maintain purity and holiness within the body. Paul stated earlier in this same passage: "Don't you know that a little yeast works through the whole batch of dough? Get rid of the old yeast that you may be a new batch . . ." (1 Corinthians 5:6). A fourth reason for separating the unrepentant sinner from the body is the name or reputation of Jesus in the marketplace. That holy Name, at which every knee shall ultimately bow, is to be held high in honor.

Separation within the home is more difficult than within the school. Usually, it will be of the time-out variety. In extreme cases, however, when the child (usually an adolescent) refuses to live by the rules within the home and insists on living an ungodly life, tough love may dictate that the child either find or be placed in another living arrangement. That is both a sad and scary scenario for parents, but in the cases of which I am aware, God did a spiritual number on those kids and led them back home, ready for a renewed relationship. God is faithful to his children.

(2) The *loss of privileges* intervention is seen in Scripture as well. God denied Adam and Eve access to the Garden of Eden after they were irresponsible with their freedom.[22] He refused to allow Eli's sons to become priests when they misused the trust placed in them.[23] King David was denied the son born to Bathsheba and him because of their sin.[24]

At home, the "grounding" of children or "placing them on restriction" is probably the most notorious usage of privilege loss. Television or computer privileges may be curtailed because of irresponsible usage. Late-night activities outside the home may be curtailed because of broken curfew. Driving privileges may be lost after receiving a speeding ticket or not filling the gas tank (for the tenth time) after draining it. The list is endless. At school, the improper use of equipment, whether in P.E. or the science lab, may call for a temporary ban on using the equipment. Breaking team rules means you don't play. Coming drunk or high to the school dance means you don't get in. Breaking pop bottles (if there still were such things) in the school lunchroom means you no longer eat there. This list, too, is endless.

A behavioristic principle that may loosely fall under the category of removing a positive is that of incompatible alternatives. This principle states that to stop children from behaving in a particular way, parents or teachers may reward or reinforce an alternative action that is inconsistent with or cannot be performed at the same time as the undesired behavior. Examples of this principle being applied within a school could include the appointment of a litterbug as the leader of an anti-litter committee or the appointment of a playground bully as a member of the safety patrol. Once again, if insight and commitment to change are absent, the change in behavior may be superficial. However, this technique could be used with the foreknowledge of the student who has the problem. A student who has difficulty listening to others during small-group sessions might be appointed chair, with the responsibility to see to it that all opinions are heard. A disruptive student might be invited to teach a lesson so as to experience the difficulty of teaching, especially if students are misbehaving. And to counter the adage that "idle hands are the devil's playthings," the teacher could provide those idle hands with plenty of worthwhile things to do—which is also good pedagogy!

b. Redirecting toward better choices through the addition of a negative (+ −)

The adding of a negative to children's lives could very easily be seen as punishment, so it is important to apply negatives in as wise a manner as possible. Crassly stated, negatives are intended to increase the pain associated with a particular behavior or pattern of behavior until the person cries "uncle" and becomes willing to reverse his or her course of action and begin making better choices. Yes, accompanying instruction and insight will, hopefully, lead to heartfelt redirection, but there are no guarantees. This is where corrective discipline can become hard for everyone, for parents and teachers don't like to see their children in pain, and they certainly don't like being the cause of the pain. The old adage that "This is hurting me more than it's hurting you" has some truth to it. Adding a negative is truly a case of "no pain, no gain," however, and Scripture speaks of God disciplining his children in this way.

> "My son, do not make light of the Lord's discipline,
>   and do not lose heart when he rebukes you,
> Because the Lord disciplines those he loves,
>   and he punishes[25] everyone he accepts as a son."
> Endure hardship as discipline; God is treating you as sons. For what son is not disciplined by his father? If you are not disciplined (and everyone undergoes discipline), then you are illegitimate children and not true sons. Moreover, we have all had human fathers who disciplined us and we respected them for it. How much more should we submit to the Father of our spirits and live! Our fathers disciplined us for a little while as they thought best; but God disciplines us for our good, that we may share in his holiness. No discipline seems pleasant at the time, but painful. Later on, however, it produces a harvest of righteousness and peace for those who have been trained by it. (Hebrews 12:5–11)

Indeed, corrective discipline by its very nature and purpose is painful.

Within the home, two common forms of plus-minus corrective discipline are verbal reprimands and spankings. Children may actually hate the former more than the latter. In either case, it is best to let tempers cool before proceeding, or correction may become abuse. A calm administration of negative consequences definitely helps them to sink in more and last longer. Children listen better when we are calm and deliberate.

(1) A *verbal reprimand* should include several components. Parents should begin by explaining what is upsetting to them about the child's choices and actions. A "We message" may be appropriate: "We are (name a feeling—sad, disappointed, angry, upset) over (cite the choice and/or action) because (cite the rule that was broken, the trust that was misused, the relationship that was damaged). In other words, lay out the problem as you see or have experienced it, focusing on the issue rather than on the child, as much as possible.

A reprimand should never become an attack on one's person. The goal, again, is a redirection of behavior; thus, the focus must be primarily on the behavior. Obviously, attitudes, values, motivation, and the like quickly involve the person as well, but calling a child names or telling them how stupid they are does more harm than good. Choices and actions may be stupid, but children aren't.

The next step is really critical. Allow the child to explain her or his side of the story from beginning to end, and listen carefully without interruption, except for clarification. Discussion can follow, citing the standard that was either not met or was broken, probing reasons for the disobedience, seeking and granting forgiveness, and developing a game plan for the future.

Throughout the entire process, parents must keep their eye on the ball and constantly remind themselves that the goal is not punishment (no matter how upset you feel) but, rather, on reconciliation, restoration, and better choices in the future. Certain restrictions may be imposed but more as reminders during a probationary period than as retribution for the misdeed.

(2) Spankings are the second common approach within the home for adding a negative consequence in the quest for behavior change. Can spanking be justified through Scripture? A study of the Bible reveals that there may be a place for spanking within the family context. Practically all references, however, to the use of the rod to correct a child occur in Proverbs:

> He who spares the rod hates his son,
>> but he who loves him is careful to discipline him. (Proverbs 13:24)

> Folly is bound up in the heart of a child,
>> but the rod of discipline will drive it far from him. (Proverbs 22:15)

> Do not withhold discipline from a child;
>> if you punish him with the rod, he will not die.
> Punish him with the rod
>> and save his soul from death. (Proverbs 23:13–14)

> The rod of correction imparts wisdom,
>> but a child left to itself disgraces his mother. (Proverbs 29:15)

There is no doubt that these references support the directive stated many times in Scripture, that parents are to correct their children from wrongdoing. The use of the word *rod* certainly indicates that nurture and discipline are to take place. But whether the use of the word *rod* indicates the form of correction to be a spanking is more problematic. There are a few cautionary notes one should make before establishing that as a rigid conclusion.

First, the book of Proverbs is written in the form of Hebrew poetry, a form that often uses vivid imagery. In other Old Testament books, there are uses of *shebet,* the Hebrew word for "rod," which obviously call for a symbolic interpretation of rod:

> "Woe to the Assyrian, the rod of my anger,
> in whose hand is the club of my wrath!" (Isaiah 10:5)

> He will strike the earth with the rod of his mouth;
> with the breath of his lips he will slay the wicked. (Isaiah 11:4b)

> I am the man who has seen affliction
> by the rod of his wrath. (Lamentations 3:1)

Usually one would look to the context for a clearer understanding of a word, but the book of Proverbs provides no such context for the use of the word *rod.* For the most part, the individual proverbs stand alone, unrelated to those that precede and follow. One must be cautious, then, about translating these references to the word *rod* as commands to physically correct children. They are, indeed, commands to correct or redirect them, but to be more specific than that is to read into the texts that which is not necessarily there.

Secondly, all references to using the rod on children are found in the Old Testament. The Greek word for rod, *rhabdos,* is used eleven times in the New Testament and never to command the physical correction or spanking of children. Indeed, *rhabdos* is used very meaningfully in 1 Corinthians 4:21, where it obviously symbolizes correction as a general directive to follow rather than as a specific endorsement of spanking: "What do you want? Shall I come to you with a rod, or in love and a spirit of gentleness?" (NKJV).

While Proverbs does instruct, then, that correction must be exercised, it gives no clear command as to *how* it should be done. On the whole, the Bible teaches that genuine correction is that which attempts to return the person to the proper way of life. That is what parents and teachers have the responsibility to do, and, with the guidance of the Holy Spirit, they can use whatever means will effectively and lovingly accomplish that end.

Scripture often encourages actions of moderation. The moderate and wise use of spanking is certainly within biblical freedom. It is the misuse of physical correction that is biblically unacceptable. Adults who are unable to restrain their anger when spanking their children should ban it totally from their options.

For those parents who believe that moderate and wise use of spanking is acceptable and can be rightly handled by them, the following guidelines are meant to be helpful:

(a) Be certain that spanking is the most appropriate means of correction available. In most cases, it should be near the bottom of the list of options—"when all else fails!"

(b) Be certain that the spanking is being used as a means to "redirect the child in the way she or he should go" and not as a punishment for past misdeeds.

(c) Be sensitive to the effects of a spanking on particular children. For some children, a spanking may instill an unhealthy fear of the person administering the spanking.

(d) Don't spank when you are out of control. If a spanking, in your best judgment, is warranted, it will be just as warranted when you calm down.

(e) Physical correction is better "understood" by younger children than is reasoning; thus spankings may be viewed as acceptable until somewhere in the age range of six to eight years old.

(f) Use your hand rather than an instrument, so that you, too, can feel the power of your strength.

(g) Strike only the child's bottom. Striking a child elsewhere can easily cause bodily harm. Striking a child on the face can cause psychological damage.

(h) Be certain that both you and your child feel the love that must be present within biblical discipline.

Finally, what about spankings within the school? While corporal punishment is legal in a number of school districts and locales in the United States, I advise against using it for two reasons: First, only the same hands that hold the child in loving nurture, those of the parents, should be allowed to strike a child in a spanking;[26] and second, in today's litigious society, the potential legal hassles are not worth whatever benefit there might be to the educational process.

Within a school setting, there do not appear to be a great number of legitimate options for adding negatives to the lives of children as a means of redirecting their behavior. Most corrective measures in schools fall under progressive separation or the withholding of privileges. The infamous and mindless writing of lines comes closer to punishment than correction. Teachers have also used satiation at times: "If you want to throw spitballs, how about making a thousand before going home today!" or "If you like to spit, how about filling a glass before returning to class!" Satiation smacks of punishment as well. The truth of the matter is that in today's society, the humiliating negatives from the past (e.g., wearing a dunce cap, sitting facing the corner, holding one's nose in a circle on the chalkboard) rightly have disappeared from schools.

Rudolf Dreikurs, in his book *Psychology in the Classroom,*[27] outlined an approach to corrective discipline that aligns itself relatively well with scriptural principles. According to Dreikurs, "man is recognized as a social being, his actions as purposive and directed toward a goal, his personality as a unique and indivisible entity." Based on this premise, Dreikurs' belief is that the basic goal of the student is social acceptance, having a place in the group. If this goal is perceived by the student as being unattainable through socially acceptable behavior, however, the student will choose to reach the goal of social acceptance through deviant behavior.

While the goal remains social acceptance, the student will likely choose one of four deviant behaviors through which to achieve this acceptance. They are:

A. Seeking attention
 1. *Active form:* Being a nuisance. The student does all kinds of behaviors that distract the teacher and classmates.
 2. *Passive form:* Being lazy. The student exhibits one-pea-at-a-time behavior and operates on slow, slower, and slowest.
B. Seeking power
 1. *Active form:* Being rebellious. The student is disruptive and confrontational and exhibits temper and verbal tantrums.
 2. *Passive form:* Being stubborn through quiet noncompliance. The student does his or her own thing, yet is (often) pleasant and even agreeable.
C. Seeking revenge
 1. *Active form:* Being vicious by physical and psychological attacks. The student is hurtful to the teacher, classmates, or both.
 2. *Passive form:* Being passive. The student is sullen and withdrawn, refusing overtures of friendship.
D. Fear/acceptance of personal inadequacy
 1. *Active form:* Exhibiting frustration through tantrums. The student loses control when the pressure to succeed becomes too intense.
 2. *Passive form:* Exhibiting hopelessness. The student procrastinates, fails to complete projects, develops temporary incapacity, or assumes behaviors that resemble a learning disability.

These behaviors are substituted for more acceptable ways to gain membership in the group, ways that students feel do not work for them, for whatever reason. Students act on the logic that one of these forms of misbehavior will provide them with the acceptance by the group that they desire. They have come to believe that status and a sense of personal value are more easily attained through deviant behavior than through more appropriate and acceptable actions.

All children need to be loved and accepted by a community, for they have been created that way. Yet too many children feel unloved and unaccepted by their peers. This, apparently, is one of the primary reasons for the rage that sometimes erupts into killings within schools. Students who have been incessantly harassed and picked on can't or won't take it anymore and seek to gain respect from or get back at their tormentors through violence.

Christian schools, unhappily, too often are places of intolerance. Teasing, harassment, hazing, and shunning are present in schools in which a sense of community and loving acceptance should be the norm. All schools should put into place a zero-tolerance policy on harassment. Such practices should be totally unacceptable. Schools need to be psychologically and physically safe havens for children.

Before intervening, teachers need to identify and verify the motivation behind a particular behavior. This can be done in three ways:

A. Observe the child's behavior and try to match it with those described above.
B. Analyze your spontaneous reaction to the child's misconduct.
  1. Attention seeking
    a. *Feelings:* Irritation, annoyance
    b. *Action impulse:* Verbal
  2. Power seeking
    a. *Feelings:* Anger, frustration, or fear
    b. *Action impulse:* Physical
  3. Revenge seeking
    a. *Feelings:* Dislike, hurt, devastation in addition to anger, frustration, fear
    b. *Action impulse:* Fight or flight
  4. Inadequacy
    a. *Feelings:* Professional concern, helplessness
    b. *Action impulse:* Prescriptive or resigned to failure

Acting on these feelings and impulses will usually simply reinforce the behavior. It is the way the child expects and wants you to respond. She or he can gain control. It is usually best to do the opposite of what you feel like doing. That, in fact, is a worthwhile approach to many discipline problems.

C. Help the child self-disclose reasons behind the misbehavior. Simply telling children to behave is often futile; they already know they should behave. Rather, the teacher should ask students if they know why they misbehaved. Usually, the answer will be, "No." In response, the teacher can then ask the following questions:
  1. Could it be that you want attention?
  2. Could it be that you want your own way and would like to be boss?

3. Could it be that you want to hurt others as much as they have hurt you?

4. Could it be that you want to be left alone?

Children may not answer these questions with a verbal "yes" or "no," but they will usually demonstrate a recognition reflex, for example, a slight smile, when the question accurately reflects their motivation. Once this bit of honesty is shared between the student and the teacher, they can get on with seeking a solution to the problem.

Before devising an intervention for misconduct, it is wise to gain some insight into possible origins of the behavior. Perhaps by adding or deleting a variable in the formula, the "need" to act a certain way can be removed. Several potential reasons are offered for each of the four behavior patterns:

A. Attention seeking:
1. Children may be deprived of sufficient personal attention.
2. Parents and teachers may be providing more attention to misbehavior than to appropriate behavior.
3. Children may be valued more by what they do than who they are; consequently, they seek praise and recognition.
4. Children haven't been taught how to ask for attention appropriately.

B. Power seeking:
1. Children may be having high standards or expectations placed on them. The pressure is always on to achieve.
2. Parents may nag, criticize; the children's performance never measures up.
3. Parent(s) may be dominant; the children have no voice, no empowerment.

C. Revenge seeking:
1. Children may be teased, humiliated, harassed, and/or abused.
2. Children may have experienced rejection or abandonment.
3. Children may not feel included; they feel on the outside looking in.

D. Inadequacy:
1. Too many negatives (putdowns, criticisms, attacks on one's person) and too few positives (successes, commendations, recognitions).
2. Children have not been trained to do things for themselves.
3. Children have not had mentoring, a support system, or someone to help.
4. Fear of failure (if effort is made) and of disappointing others or self.
5. A belief that only perfection is acceptable.

Finally, teachers need to develop a plan that will allow and encourage children to make better choices. This could begin with insight by students into the nature of their actions. They may truly not understand what is happening. Plus, the "games people play" aren't as much fun when others have the games figured out. Next, teachers could explore some of the possible origins of the behavior to determine whether a motivator needs to be added or deleted. Is there too much of something present, or too little of something? Finally, the pattern of misbehavior needs to be broken. Even young children have been practicing their behavior for years, and many other adults have tried during that time to "help" them, long before you came along. They did what came naturally, and the children's behavior was reinforced, one more time. Again, doing the opposite of what comes naturally is a refusal to get sucked into the games children plan. Remain the wise adult who sees the big picture and can guide the problem (versus being guided by the problem) into a solution. The following are a few suggested ways to respond to each of the four behavior patterns.

A. Attention seeking
  1. Do not provide attention on demand. Ignore obvious attention-seeking behavior.
  2. Provide attention randomly at other times.
  3. Base your attention more on who children are than on what they do.
  4. Instruct children on appropriate times, places, and ways to gain attention.
  5. Try to move children from passive to active attention seeking, and then from destructive to constructive.

B. Power seeking
  1. Don't fight back; don't give in. Remain calm; stand firm.
  2. Commend the student; do not criticize.
  3. Empower students by providing choices.
  4. Find ways for students to exercise legitimate power/leadership.

C. Revenge seeking
  1. Do not communicate hurt, either verbally or nonverbally. Turn the other cheek.
  2. Convince students by your actions that they are liked and lovable.
  3. Actively listen; recognize and acknowledge feelings. Demonstrate that "you hear them."
  4. Seek an end to the hurt/abuse in students' lives.
  5. Develop true community through cooperative learning rather than competition.

D. Inadequacy
  1. Admit that you can't *make* a student do something.
  2. Provide a place in the group and a manageable (bite-sized) task.
  3. Commend. Teach for success. Give credit for and build upon that which is done well and/or correctly.
  4. Work alongside students when obstacles might overwhelm them.
  5. Believe in and see good in students as they are, not as they could or should be.

In conclusion, Driekurs believed that every misbehaving student is a discouraged student; therefore, the key tools needed by both parents and teachers are sincerity and encouragement.

Chapter Conclusions

Biblical nurture or discipline begins with instruction, but it also includes correction, the focus of this chapter. Preventive discipline should help eliminate the majority of discipline problems before they occur. Included in this prevention is discipline that is caught—the creation of an environment conducive to learning and adults acting authoritatively, understanding the motivation of children, and carrying out God's agenda God's way. Discipline that is taught includes understanding and acting on appropriate rules, relationships, and roles.

Biblically based corrective discipline differs from punishment in several important ways, not the least being that punishment is retributive whereas correction is reformative and restorative. Correction should be exercised clearly, consistently, and fairly. Minor incidents call for nonverbal and verbal communication, and, if required, action on the part of parents and teachers.

Resolution of major problems calls for consequences that match the choices made. Some consequences are natural, other need to be imposed. All consequences should be logically related to the misdeeds so that insight can take place. Right behavior needs to be encouraged by the adding of positives and the removal of negatives in the lives of children. Restitution may be the most biblical and logical approach to misbehavior. If the offender does not choose restitution, consequences need to be imposed, either by the removal of positives or the adding of negatives. Physical correction has a legitimate but limited place.

Instruction and correction together form the essence of biblical nurture. The goal is to guide children in the way they should go, along the path of righteousness that leads to God and his eternal kingdom. Sometimes, however, children and young people who, indeed, have given their hearts and lives to God experience struggles that distance them from God. Their behavior does not reflect the holiness of God. God is faithful, however, and has provided biblical admonition to be exercised by other members of the body. That is the topic of the next chapter.

Chapter 9: Further Thoughts to Consider

1. Describe the relationship between a show-and-tell approach to nurture and an instruction-and-correction approach to discipline.

2. Explain how adults can be the primary cause for discipline problems.

3. Provide examples from home and school for each step on Maslow's hierarchy of needs.

4. Explain how Driekurs' three Cs behind choices "comport well with Scripture."

5. Provide examples of how fear "is probably the number one deterrent to kingdom service."

6. Explain how all discipline problems affect relationships. Provide examples.

7. Explain the differences between correction and punishment. Can you support these differences from Scripture?

8. In what ways do behavioral approaches to discipline differ from a biblical approach? Are any behavioral approaches in harmony with scriptural principles? Explain.

9. Provide examples from Scripture of
- restitution
- progressive separation
- loss of privileges

as consequences for misdeeds.

10. In what ways does Dreikurs' approach to discipline "align itself relatively well with scriptural principles?" In what ways does it not?

Chapter 9: Notes and References

1. Richard L. Curwin and Allen N. Mendler in *Discipline with Dignity* cite the 80-15-5 Principle, that 80% of students rarely break rules or violate principles, 15% of students break rules on a somewhat regular basis, and 5% of students are chronic rule breakers and generally out of control most of the time (Alexandria, VA: Association for Supervision and Curriculum Development, 1988, 27–28).
2. *Reviving Ophelia: Saving the Selves of Adolescent Girls* by Mary Pipher (New York: Ballantine Books, 1994) is an excellent source on the harassment of adolescent girls.
3. R. Dreikurs, *Psychology in the Classroom*, 2nd ed. (New York: Harper & Row, 1968).
4. I once heard a pastor state in a sermon that the words "Fear not!" or their equivalents were spoken 366 times in the Bible. If that is true, we have a message for every day of the year, including leap year.
5. H. L. Erickson, *Concept-Based Curriculum and Instruction: Teaching Beyond the Facts* (Thousand Oaks, CA: Corwin, 1998), 25.
6. John 14:15; 1 John 5:3.
7. Forrest Gathercoal in *Judicious Discipline*, 4th ed., has come to similar conclusions about rules (San Francisco: Caddo Gap Press, 1997, 86ff).
8. The four relational rules listed previously are a good place to begin a cooperative effort as practical examples are provided.
9. T. Gordon, T. *Parent Effectiveness Training/Teacher Effectiveness Training* (New York: Wyden, 1970/1974)..
10. Peacemaker Ministries in Billings, Montana, provides both resources and training in reconciliation involving a third party.

11. Matthew 18:15–17; also consider Matthew 5:23–24.
12. Genesis 4:3–7.
13. Matthew 5:21–22, 27–28.
14. Matthew 12:34; 15:18–20; 23:27–28. Also read Samuel's words to Saul in 1 Samuel 15:22. The difference between Saul and David was the matter of a proud heart versus a submissive heart. Psalm 51 reflects where David's heart was.
15. J. Fay, and F. W. Cline, *Discipline with Love and Logic* (Study Guide), (Golden, CO: The Love and Logic Press, (1994), 117–18.
16. See Romans 12:9–21.
17. Also see Proverbs 22:8; Matthew 26:52; 2 Thessalonians 3:10.
18. D. C. Gossen, *Restitution: Restructuring School Discipline,* 2nd ed. (Chapel Hill, NC: New View Publications, 1997).
19. Gossen, 128–29.
20. Gossen, 49–50.
21. Also see Romans 16:17; 2 Thessalonians 3:6, 14–15.
22. Genesis 2:23–24.
23. 1 Samuel 2:31–36.
24. 2 Samuel 12:15–23.
25. The word *punishes* in verse 6 is *mastigoo* in Greek, which, indeed, means "punishes" and not "corrects." Its uses elsewhere in the New Testament all refer to the scourging (i.e., flogging; whipping) of Jesus or his followers by Jewish or Roman authorities (Matthew 10:17; 20:19; 23:34; Mark 10:34; Luke 18:33; John 19:1). Hebrews 12:5b–6 is, however, a quotation from the Old Testament—Proverbs 3:11–12. The preacher of this sermon in Hebrews 12:5b–11 follows this quotation with an exposition of what this Old Testament passage means. He equates "punishment" with "discipline" (*paideia/paideuo*) no fewer than seven times. This interpretation actually begins in verse 6, where "because the Lord disciplines those he loves" is parallel to "and he punishes everyone he accepts as a son."
26. I came to this conclusion after a mother of one of my students (and a board member of the Christian school in which I was serving), in a conversation not even relating to her own children, expressed these sentiments. For some reason, I had never thought about this viewpoint before, but as soon as she spoke the words, they resonated with me as being truthful. Thanks, Marilyn.
27. Driekurs, *Psychology in the Classroom,* 2nd ed. (New York: Harper & Row, 1968).

Chapter 10

RESTORATIVE ADMONITION

"... fathers ... bring up [your children] in the nurture and admonition of the Lord." (Ephesians 6:4, KJV)

Introduction

The responsibility of parents and teachers for the conduct of their children is threefold. The word *nurture* (*paideuo/paideia*) in Ephesians 6:4 has two connotations within Scripture: instruction and correction, directives that were dealt with in the preceding two chapters. The third directive is admonition, the topic of this chapter.

The word *admonition* in Ephesians 6:4 is a translation of the Greek word *noutheteo/nouthesia*. This word can also be translated as "a warning or gentle, friendly reproof," "teaching or instruction," or "counsel." The Living Bible translation of this word is helpful: it reads "suggestions and godly advice." The biblical use of admonition implies that godly (i.e., scriptural) direction is being given. Several other Scripture passages that use the word *noutheteo/nouthesia* can shed further light on its meaning:

> I myself am convinced, my brothers, that you yourselves are full of goodness, complete in knowledge and competent to *instruct* one another. (Romans 15:14, emphasis mine)

> These things happened to them as examples and were written down as *warnings* for us, on whom the fulfillment of the ages has come. (1 Corinthians 10:11, emphasis mine)

> Let the word of Christ dwell in you richly as you teach and *admonish* one another with all wisdom, and as you sing psalms, hymns and spiritual songs with gratitude in your hearts to God. (Colossians 3:1, emphasis mine)

> Now we ask you, brothers, to respect those who work hard among you, who are over you in the Lord and who *admonish* you. (1 Thessalonians 5:12, emphasis mine)

> Yet do not regard him as an enemy, but *warn* him as a brother. (2 Thessalonians 3:15, emphasis mine)

> *Warn* a divisive person once, and then *warn* him a second time. After that, have nothing to do with him. (Titus 3:10, emphasis mine)

As noted before, *noutheteo* or admonition is a word used to address a different set of people than *paideuo* or nurture. This word appeals more to the reasoning ability and understanding of a mature Christian. Thus, the admonition of *noutheteo/nouthesia* becomes more applicable as children mature in the faith and become more accountable for their actions. It seems to speak to older people rather than to younger children.

The recipients of admonition: Regenerate children

The Bible tells fathers to rear their children in the nurture *and* admonition of the Lord. The father's responsibility is not limited to either nurture or admonition; rather, both nurture and admonition are commanded. It is at this point, however, that an important distinction must be made. All children, no matter what their spiritual status before God, can benefit from biblical nurture—godly instruction and correction. But only persons who have been regenerated—born again—can benefit from biblical admonition. For unless the Holy Spirit resides in the hearts of individuals, the "things of the Spirit" that are essential to biblical admonition will not be understood by them. The Apostle Paul wrote:

> We have not received the spirit of the world but the Spirit who is from God, that we may understand what God has freely given us. This is what we speak, not in words taught us by human wisdom but in words taught by the Spirit, expressing spiritual truths in spiritual words. The man without the Spirit does not accept the things that come from the Spirit of God, for they are foolishness to him, and he cannot understand them, because they are spiritually discerned. (1 Corinthians 2:12–14)

The "man without the Spirit" is described in Jude 19 as one who follows "mere natural instincts." Persons not directed by the Holy Spirit are still guided by the sinful nature with which they were born. They have not been equipped to receive truth that comes from the Spirit. They need the new birth[1] for their minds and hearts to be opened to understand the things of God. Children who have not yet experienced regeneration, who do not yet enjoy "the full riches of complete understanding," should not receive admonition in the "the mystery of God," that have not yet been revealed to them—"namely, Christ, in whom are hidden all the treasures of wisdom and knowledge" (Colossians 2:2–3).

The goal of admonition: Restoration

It is within this context that the restorative function of admonition needs to be understood; for to be restored, one needs to have been at a particular place before—a place from which one has fallen. The place of restoration sought by admonition is that of "being in right relationship with God." Only the regenerate individual has experienced being in that right relationship.

Children either are regenerated or they are not. This act of the Holy Spirit is instantaneous; there is no middle ground or third option. Only God knows whether a child has been regenerated, but outward evidences that regeneration has occurred can, indeed, be manifested. There should be a sincere desire to "please Jesus." And the fruit of the Holy Spirit—love, joy, peace, patience, kindness, goodness, faithfulness, gentleness, and self-control (Galatians 5:22–23)—should be evidenced in the child's life. Parents and teachers have to make judgment calls on whether they believe regeneration has or has not taken place and, consequently, whether to begin the discipline process with correction or admonition or a mix of both.

While it is true that the ultimate purpose for biblical instruction, correction, and admonition is for one to "love God" wholeheartedly, each process can take place at different points on one's spiritual journey. Biblical nurture—instruction and correction—is meant to lead toward initial commitment to Christ. Admonition, on the other hand, is designed toward recommitment, or restoration after backsliding.[2] Nurture is primarily for not-yet-believers or for those who are spiritual babies;[3] admonition is for those who have professed faith in Christ but are back under the bondage of sin. Instruction is a vital part of both correction and admonition. And correction and admonition have many similarities. But they are applied at different places in one's spiritual walk and for different reasons.

The context of admonition

Admonition is intended for believers who have fallen under the bondage of sin
When persons experience spiritual rebirth and profess saving faith in Jesus Christ as Savior and Lord, their heart's desire is to please God and to not sin. In fact, premeditated sin should be virtually nonexistent for believers. But believers still sin, nonetheless, for the old person, the old sinful nature, has not totally disappeared. Old habits, cravings, and bondages continue to linger. And the evil one knows just how to exploit these weaknesses if one's spiritual armor is not in place. Usually, regressions into sin of this type are one-time episodes. One's guard is down, and a person gets blindsided and falls into sin before he or she is aware

of what's going on. Sometimes, old habits die hard. When these sins take place, believers are usually so horrified at having displeased and dishonored God that they immediately "seek God's face" for forgiveness. Typically, admonition by others is not needed in these instances, for restoration to right relationship with God is sought by the person.

Sometimes, however, believers fall under the bondage of sin to such a degree that they become trapped by their own sin cravings. Their personal needs and desires outweigh their desire to please God. An inner drive or passion exists that burns more intensely than their love for or fear of God. A pattern has developed; the sin has control. One has fallen into the deep pit of bondage with, seemingly, no way out. A terrible battle often rages between the cravings of the temptation and feelings of guilt and shame. This is the time for admonition.

Sins that come to mind that fit this scenario include addictions to drugs, alcohol, pornography, illicit and/or deviant sexual relations, lying, cheating, stealing, abuse, and profanity.[4] Obviously, these types of sins are not typically committed by young children, which is one more reason that correction is for the young and admonition is for the more mature.

My Uncle John on my mother's side was an alcoholic. The misuse of alcohol ruined his marriage. It hurt people around him. It made a shambles out of his life. He eventually ended up on skid row in Chicago—West Madison Avenue. He became one of the homeless who are all too familiar to us. When his brothers discovered where he was, they picked him up and placed him in rehab to dry out. Then my Uncle Walt took him in, gave him a bed in the attic of his home (many of us slept in attics in those days!), and found a job for him at a local laundry. Uncle John walked home from work every day at about 4:00 P.M. My mother knew that he had to walk past a bar on his way, so she promised him a cold glass of ginger ale if he would stop by and visit with her. He did that every day. On weekends he would come by and watch the Cubs games on TV with us. He was a great baseball fan. Only once, of which I am aware, did he go "off the wagon" during those final years of his life. One Saturday, he went back "to visit his friends" on West Madison.

I believe my Uncle John committed his heart to Jesus when he was a young man. I also believe that he went to be with Jesus when he died. But, he backslid over and over during his lifetime. He was a man in bondage to alcohol. On the other hand, two of his brothers were home missionaries. They, too, went to be with Jesus when they died. It's grace, either way.

Admonition begins with a one-to-one

When parents or teachers become aware of this type of sin within the lives of children or students who have professed the name of Jesus as

Lord, the parent or teacher must go to the individual personally, one to one. The Matthew 18 principle (Matthew 18:15) and other Scripture passages (Leviticus 19:17; Luke 17:3; Galatians 6:1; James 5:19–20) appear to call for privacy and containment in the initial confronting of a brother or sister enmeshed in sin. The natural inclination is to discuss the matter with others first, either out of fear of going to the person directly or for other self-centered reasons. Fear is never an excuse for not doing what is right, and keeping the matter between the two individuals protects the other person and is an act of love and concern. Yes, this is difficult, but it's the most efficient and effective approach to take.

Admonition is done in loving concern

Admonition takes place between one brother or sister in Christ and another brother or sister in Christ. It is approached from loving concern for the welfare of another member of the body. It is done humbly, with a "there but for the grace of God go I" attitude.

> *He was one of the most mild-mannered older men I had ever met. He told me that he had been a farmer most of his life, but that he had also driven trucks on occasion. One time when he returned unexpectedly from a trip he found his wife in bed with another man. He got his gun and killed them both. Now he is serving the final years of his life behind prison walls. For sixty-five years he was just like you and me; now, he's a convicted murderer. But he's still very much like you and me.*
>
> *One thing I have learned during my lifetime is to never say "It couldn't happen to me" or "I would never do that." For it has and I did. The Bible verse that states "Pride goes before destruction, and a haughty spirit before a fall" (Proverbs 16:18) is very true. Never say "Never."*
>
> *Through Prison Ministries weekends and Man-to-Man programs, I have befriended a number of wonderful men and brothers in Christ who are serving time, some of whom will die in prison. Many of them did one really stupid thing while under the influence of alcohol, drugs, or anger, and they are paying the price. I think of the many stupid things I have done or could have done, given the proper circumstances. There but for the grace of God. . . .*

Speaking the truth in love is to know what must be said and what can be left unsaid. Including nonessential information can confuse the issue and can, in fact, further weaken relationships. Persons should not have a burden placed on them that they are not equipped to handle. As truthful as certain messages are, they may tend to overwhelm or shatter persons, and such sharing or confrontation may have selfish connotations. The person doing the sharing may feel relieved, but the recipient may have unnecessarily been given a problem that hinders rather than helps the act of healing. Truthfulness is essential in a healthy relationship, but love must always remain "the greatest" (1 Corinthians 13:13).

Admonishing a person in love includes a willingness to walk side by side with the person through the admonition process. This is a declaration of unconditional love and unending commitment. All sinners need advocates, and we must be willing to serve as advocates for others, through thick and thin. That is the kind of love expression that is felt and believed by them.

Admonition is based on Scripture

Previously in this book, it was stated that the law of God is designed to serve several purposes and, depending on the stage of one's spiritual development or measure of spiritual health, that the law can serve as a restraint, a mirror, or a guide. For children who are receiving nurture— instruction and correction—the law serves as a restraint. Hopefully and prayerfully, the law can also serve as a mirror that convicts them of their need for a Savior. For persons receiving admonition, however, the law serves as a guide to bring them back to where they should be. The Apostle Paul wrote of this use of the law:

> All Scripture is God-breathed and is useful for teaching, rebuking, correcting and training in righteousness . . . . Preach the Word; be prepared in season and out of season; correct, rebuke and encourage—with great patience and careful instruction. (2 Timothy 3:16; 4:2)

Admonition, by its very nature, is evaluative. One person helps another to understand and evaluate what's going on. The act of evaluation always requires criteria against which to make a judgment. The criteria or standards used to evaluate in the admonition process are found in the Bible. The plumb line of God's standards is used as the objective set of measures for biblical admonition, for admonition must be "of the Lord." It cannot be based on our personal agenda or "what people might be saying or thinking." One's conduct needs, gently but firmly, to be placed next to the line drawn in Scripture to determine whether it measures up to or has crossed over that line.

Several years ago I came across a little booklet titled *The Secret to Constructive Discipline*[5] that contained ideas that made a great deal of sense to me. I don't know if the ideas work because I have never tried them. But I pass them on to the readers of this book because the ideas appear to be very much in harmony with what I believe the Bible says about admonition.

The approach is centered on three questions that are asked of the child being disciplined, to be followed by a concluding statement.

> The first question is, "What did you do wrong?" Ask it in a tender way, not accusing. This allows the child to admit personal sin. It's important for the child to take responsibility for part of the problem and demonstrate sorrow for it.[6]

> A second question, "Why was that wrong?" should be used to address heart issues directly. Point out the character qualities like pride, selfishness, anger, or disrespect. Help the child learn that behavior is only a symptom of something deeper.[7]

> Once a child realizes why the behavior is wrong, the third question helps clarify what should be done instead. "What are you going to do differently next time?" focuses on a better way to respond.[8]

> Finally, always end with an affirmation. A helpful statement is, "Okay, go ahead and try again." This says "I believe in you. Yes, you're going to make mistakes, and there are consequences, but we can debrief and learn together." Give children the encouragement to try again. Everyone makes mistakes, and the best response is to stop, think about it, and then try again.[9]

> A positive conclusion is important every time you discipline. It is the secret to making your discipline times constructive experiences. . . . After the positive conclusion, the child may need to complete restitution or reconciliation, enabling the child to establish a clear conscience.[10]

This approach may appear a bit idealistic and, perhaps, not very practical, but there is something in it that rings true. Basically, it reflects pure grace. And if we can teach our children about grace by having them experience it personally within a family or school setting, I think we need to try. I am reminded of the biblical account of the woman caught in adultery:

> Then Jesus stood up and said to her, "Where are your accusers? Didn't even one of them condemn you?"
> "No, sir," she said.
> And Jesus said, "Neither do I. Go and sin no more."
> (John 8:10-11, *The Living Bible*)

Those words of Jesus must have felt wonderful to this woman. She had been given a fresh start. The old was forgiven and forgotten. Future actions were now the important thing. That's grace. We need to utilize opportunities for children to personally experience grace in their lives.

The stages of admonition

The approaches taken in the process of admonition should not be rote formulas that are applied to sinful situations in some boilerplate fashion. Every situation is unique and should be treated that way. Pray about how to proceed. Remain open to the guidance of the Holy Spirit.

The following steps may prove helpful as you consider how to proceed with your particular person and issue.

a. Confrontation

The word *confrontation* doesn't have a nice gentle ring to it, yet it is the proper place to begin admonition. To confront is to take initiative, to take action, to care enough to risk. It's the opposite of avoiding or ignoring. It's "biting the bullet" and doing what's right for the sake of the kingdom of God. It's going to the person instead of talking about the person.[11] It is making persons aware of the fact that they are sinning and that this sin is hurting them and hurting others.

The illustration from the Bible that may best demonstrate confrontation took place between Nathan the prophet and King David, following David's sin with Bathsheba. The account, recorded in 2 Samuel 12, comes to a peak with the words of Nathan: "You are the man!" Nathan had everything to lose by confronting the king with his sin, yet he did it because God told him to, and it was the right thing to do.

Confrontation need not be confronting. Truth can be shared gently. Do so calmly. Come in sadness, not judgment. Do not accuse; do not preach. Simply share what you have observed or have heard. And share genuine concern for the person because of what you have observed or heard.

b. Clarification

Until we speak one to one with a person, we can't know their side of the story. Thus, it is important that we invite the person to add information and to refute or clarify what they believe to be incorrect or incomplete information. We need to listen, to try to understand the facts and the context. Allow the person to speak without interruption. When she or he is finished, ask questions for clarification.

If a person denies all and/or admits to nothing, one of several options needs to be taken. First, if there is proof of wrongdoing and/or witnesses who are willing to come forward, the Matthew 18 principle indicates that that may be the necessary next step to take.

I was serving as principal of a Christian middle and high school. One day, two eighth-grade girls asked to talk to me in my office. They shared that a ninth-grade boy had bragged about having alcohol in his locker and that he often appeared to be drugged or intoxicated. I excused the girls and called the boy to my office. He had transferred into the school that fall, and I really didn't know much about him except that he was friendly any time we had met in the hallways. I shared with him what I had heard, and he denied everything. But when I asked him if it would be okay to check out his locker, he became unglued and broke down crying. The story was that he had a problem with alcohol. After his parents left for work each morning, he would raid their liquor cabinet, drinking some then and taking some to school with him. Because of that confrontation and ultimate clarification, we were able to work with this student and his parents to provide the help that they needed.

Second, if a person will not admit to wrongdoing, even after conclusive evidence has been presented, the admonition process should be curtailed and corrective consequences imposed.

c. Confession

This stage of admonition seeks to deal with the sin and whatever damages it has caused. If the person is unwilling to take any of the following steps, the process needs to revert to corrective discipline with the imposition of logical consequences.

(1) The assumption of responsibility. The person essentially needs to say, "Yes, I did it. No one else made me. I accept responsibility for my choices and actions."

(2) The admission of guilt. Here, the person agrees that what was done was sinful, and she or he can explain the reason it was a sin, based on the Bible. While a sense of shame (e.g., embarrassment) may be felt, an acknowledgment of guilt is called for. The person must state how God's law was violated.

(3) The confession of sin, the expression of sorrow, and the seeking of forgiveness. God has provided a way for persons to rid themselves of guilt. The Apostle John wrote:

> If we claim to be without sin, we deceive ourselves and the truth is not in us. If we confess our sins, [God] is faithful and just and will forgive us our sins and purify us from all unrighteousness. (1 John 1:8–9)

Sin damages relationships. The primary relationship that sin affects is one's relationship with God. Thus, God is the first person to talk to. But only someone who claims Jesus as Savior can come to the Father in this way, for the gift of forgiveness is based on Jesus having taken that sin personally upon himself. The sin must be confessed, admitted to, in specific language so nothing is glossed over. Sorrow must be felt and expressed. Then the words "Please forgive me" need to be said. This is simple, yet profound, for as the verse written above states, forgiveness is provided by God immediately. The person's slate is wiped clean. A new beginning is provided. This prayer is uttered in the name of Jesus, for he serves as Savior, Mediator, and Advocate at the right hand of the Father.

Sin often damages other relationships as well. They, too, must be dealt with. Confession extends as broadly as the sin. If one other person was sinned against, that one other person must be approached in confession and a seeking of forgiveness. If there were ten persons, ten must be sought out. And so on. All of the people who were hurt need to be provided with this opportunity for healing

The forgiveness that is sought must be more than "I'm sorry," for this allows the offender to remain in control. True sorrow and repentance places one in the debt of the other. The words "Will you forgive me for sinning against you?" must be said, for they call for a response of forgiveness from the other. Both persons need that opportunity. Even if the offended party does not grant forgiveness, the one who has sinned knows that he or she has been forgiven by God and has obediently followed God's instructions for seeking reconciliation. What could be done was done.

It has been said that "confession is good for the soul," and it probably is. It has a cathartic or healing quality to it. It is cleansing. James alluded to this when he wrote: ". . . confess your sins to each other and pray for each other so that you may be healed" (James 5:16). It is experiencing grace—an undeserved gift. Confession is a vital part of the restorative nature of admonition.

At times, the admonition process can get stuck at this point if true sorrow for wrongdoing is not expressed. It is one thing to admit guilt, but it is quite another thing to be sorry for it. This is a difficult factor to deal with. A parent or teacher cannot force children to be sorry for what they have done. They either are or they are not. The author of Hebrews spoke of Esau who was sorry not for his actions but for the consequences of his actions (Hebrews 12:16–17). That, too, is unacceptable. If this happens, a switch will have to be made from the admonition process to that of corrective discipline.

The act of forgiveness can be another stuck point. What if the sin is repeated many times? There are, perhaps, two responses to this dilemma. One, the offender may not have been serious about his or her expression of sorrow for the misdeed, for as Proverbs 28:13 states, true repentance involves a turning away from the sin: ". . . whoever confesses and renounces [his sins] finds mercy." In that case, logical consequences may be needed. The second response is to forgive again and again as Christ commanded.[12] There is no limit on forgiveness if repentance is sincere.

(4) The provision of restitution. The expression of guilt and sorrow and the seeking of forgiveness is "one shoe" of the restorative process. The "other shoe" that must yet drop is that of restitution. Every effort must be made to make things as right as they were before the sin was committed. In a real sense, restitution may be viewed as a logical consequence for one's sinful choices and actions. What was hurt must be healed; what

was damaged must be restored. Again, it's a matter of justice and righteousness. And it's God's way.

Much was written about restoration in the previous chapter that need not be repeated here. Rather, a few examples (and dilemmas) of restoration will be examined.

(a) The restoration of God's holy name. Any time a child, a young person, or an adult who claims the name of Christ commits a sin that is made public, the name or reputation of God is sullied. This becomes magnified when the person is a pastor, a Christian school principal or teacher, or a student within a Christian school. There are always people who will use these occasions to reinforce their unwillingness to consider Christ and his kingdom, "for those Christians are no better than anyone else. They just think they are!" David faced this issue following his sin with Bathsheba:

> Nathan replied, "The LORD has taken away your sin. You are not going to die. But because by doing this you have made the enemies of the LORD show utter contempt, the son born to you will die." (2 Samuel 12:13–14)

The fact is, these "enemies of God" are partly right. We *are* no better. It is not the absence of sin that marks the Christian family or church or school, for every person in these institutions is a sinner and will continue to sin their entire lives. Yes, we work and pray toward a testimony that will lift up the name of Christ, but failure to do this is not uncommon. The Christ-honoring testimony rests more on how sins are dealt with within the community of faith than with their absence. They need to be confronted and confessed. The restorative process must be put into place. And that includes restitution.

How does one restore the name of Christ to the place of honor and holiness that is prayed for in the Lord's Prayer? As in the case of David, the public must know that standards of conduct are high within Christian institutions and that the breeching of these standards is taken very seriously. Even though the sins of the sinner may have been forgiven by God and others and the subsequent spiritual and relational restoration may have taken place, consequences may still need to be imposed, more for public consumption than for any other reason. For example, suppose the members of a Christian school's sports team have broken school or team rules and the incident hit the newspapers. These team members could, theoretically, confess their sin, express genuine sorrow for the act, and seek forgiveness from God, other team members, and the entire student body. Before God and humankind, they are forgiven and, thus, need to be restored to full fellowship in the body. *But*—and that "but" is a big one—the name of the Lord needs restoration in public as well. One way to do that would be to have these team members sit out the next game. For the public "understands" that type of consequence for wrongdoing. If the public knows about the sin, the public needs to be made aware, forthrightly, of how the sin has been dealt with—for the sake of Christ's name.

A case could also be made, perhaps, for the team members to sit out a game as a painful reminder for the future. Such a consequence may be helpful if temptation comes their way once again. But to consider this to be a penalty for their wrongdoing after they had repented would be punishment and not correction (which had already taken place). It would be retributive and biblically unacceptable.[13]

(b) The restoration of others' persons, reputations, and/or possessions. Damage to one's person or to one's reputation is difficult, if not impossible, to restore fully. Words, in particular, can never be retracted once they have been uttered. Obviously, restitution for physical damage to another person can include payment for medical expenses, help with tasks that can no longer be done because of the injuries, and help with getting back on one's feet (sometimes literally). Slander to one's person or reputation can only be countered by the truth. In both cases, it would be best to work with the other person to determine the most acceptable way to do this.

The restoration of property or possessions is, perhaps, the easiest form of restitution, for the least that one must do is to restore or replace the property to its original form and value. Stolen property needs to be returned or repurchased. Damaged property must be fixed to the satisfaction of the owner. Ideally, this can be accomplished though the personal efforts of the offender. It would be similar to a slow motion reversing of the destruction that took place, and the "undoing and/or renewing" process can be quite cathartic.

(c) The restoration of lost trust. A young child takes money from his mother's purse and lies about it, but then confesses. A teenager admits to having sex with his girlfriend or being addicted to drugs, alcohol, or pornography. A student admits to cheating or plagiarism. A student leader has misused the trust placed in him and is exposed by the school paper. A teacher or principal or the pastor of a church confesses to committing adultery. A wife cheats on her husband and is found out. (These last two illustrations are included to provide additional perspective on the fact that the principles of admonition apply to believers of all ages and walks of life.) How, then, does one restore lost trust?

At this point, it is important to remind ourselves, for the sake of this illustration, that all of these people are born-again believers who have processed through the previous stages and steps of admonition. Should trust simply be granted to them as an act of restoration? After all, wouldn't that be the Christlike thing to do? I think not. Trust is not something that is given by fiat; it must be earned. For that reason, the same pathway that was walked to earn trust the first time must be re-walked the second time. And it will be more difficult the second time.

In each of these cases, a restriction of some type may be imposed so that the individual can be removed from the source of temptation and have the opportunity to work back into a trust relationship. In the cases of the child and teenager, their freedom of movement may be reversed to that of a younger age or stage. The student may be provided additional supervision and be required to document work more thoroughly. The wife may have to place some restrictions on herself and be willing to live an openly accountable life. The various leaders need to remove themselves from their positions of leadership until trust can be earned once again. In each case, forgiveness can take place and restoration, in that sense, can also take place. But the person or persons sinned against will have lost trust in the other person, and lost trust cannot be regained through words. Trust comes through trustworthy behavior. And that takes time. In the leadership cases, the time must be provided by a temporary removal from office with the trust factor to be reexamined periodically.

d. Covenanting

The final stage in the admonition process is that of covenanting. Confession dealt with the past and the present. Covenanting, essentially, is a coming together and developing a game plan for the future. It's answering the question: "Where do I go from here, and how can I make certain that I don't succumb to the same sin another time?" This could be parents covenanting with a child or a teacher, guidance counselor, or principal covenanting with a student. It likely may be the person who initiated the admonition process in the beginning. Covenanting always involves two parties. In this case, the adult may want to take the initiative at each step, but the more the other person can contribute to the game plan, the more likely it will work.

(1) Identify future actions and describe what they should look like. Paint a picture of what the person's conduct in this particular area should be. Go to Scripture for the norms and principles by which to live. Establish and understand right standards. Focus on the future; do not dwell on the

past except to better understand the future. The past is done and can't be undone. Since the person is beginning with a clean slate and has done her or his best to make past misdeeds right, the attention and energy have to be directed toward future godly living.

(2) Jointly develop a plan of action. This step may relate to the "restoration of trust" suggestions listed above. For some form of imposed limitations or self-restriction may need to be a part of the plan. Avoiding the persons and places of temptation should be a requirement. The Bible instructs us to "flee from" sin (1 Corinthians 6:18; 10:14; 2 Timothy 2:22) and to "resist the devil" (James 4:7). If we have been burned by a particular temptation in the past, we have no business playing with the same fire in the future. The question could be asked: "What other restrictions or help will you need to be able to walk the 'straight and narrow' in the future?"

This is the time for brainstorming ideas. No idea should be immediately ruled out for consideration. The parts of the plan need to be win-win—both parties need to feel good about them. A sense of ownership on the part of the person seeking restoration needs to be felt.

(3) Create built-in accountability. An answer to "How can we both know when this agreement or covenant has been broken?" must be developed. Accountability can include scheduled meetings; daily journals; testimonies by others, such as teachers or church youth workers; telephone calls; e-mails; or the like. There is no perfect means of accountability other than totally restricting freedom. So a measure of trust has to be established once again. But that is probably a good thing. We need to learn to trust those entrusted to us.

(4) Consequences of a default should be determined at the time of need. There are different opinions about whether to establish and advertise consequences ahead of time for the breaking of rules. Advertised consequences may smack of punishment. They can't adequately deal in advance with the person or the unique circumstances of the default. They tend to box us in and force us to act even when we think it might not be wise. And the child or student may weigh the consequences ahead of time and decide the sin might be worth the consequences. Wise consequences take time to put together, and only when the covenant agreement has been broken will the need be present and the facts known.

Chapter Conclusions

Parents, fathers in particular, are mandated in Scripture to include admonition in the rearing of their children. Admonition is to follow the previous two nurturing mandates, those of instruction and correction, for the goal of nurture is for children to love God with every part of their beings. Admonition builds off of this commitment, for to understand and be able to participate in the process of admonition, one must possess the Holy Spirit in one's heart through regeneration. Admonition is for brothers and sisters in Jesus, no matter what their ages.

Admonition is restorative by its very nature. A daughter or son of God has become enmeshed in sin and, seemingly, has been overpowered by it. They are truly in bondage. An outside intervention is required. God needs to intervene, and he usually does so though people. The intervention must be bathed in prayer, in love, and in genuine concern. The standards of Scripture serve as the focal point, the plumb line, against which conduct is evaluated.

Admonition begins with firm but gentle confrontation. A sister or brother shares what is being observed and the need to face the issue. Time is taken to clarify the issue, to hear the other side, to lay out all of the pertinent information. The individual is then urged to make confession, to seek forgiveness, to provide restitution. The final stage of admonition is covenanting. This is a coming together to develop a plan for the future that will help the person walk the pathway of righteousness once more. Restrictions and accountability are built in as aids.

Biblical instruction is a vital part of both correction and admonition. When the process of admonition breaks down for whatever the reason, applying corrective discipline with its imposed logical consequences is usually appropriate. Either way, the goal remains the same—children who love God and seek to walk in his ways.

Chapter 10: Further Thoughts to Consider

1. Why would it make sense to deal with the sinful actions of regenerated, or born-again, persons differently from those of not-yet-regenerated, or unregenerate, persons?

2. Basing your answer on information provided earlier in the book, how young could a person be for regeneration to have taken place? What evidences might there be that regeneration has occurred?

3. Do you agree that there are some things that a person who has not (yet) been regenerated cannot understand? If yes, what might they be? Can you cite Scripture for your answer?

4. How do the goals for biblical admonition differ from the goals for biblical nurture?

5. What is the motivation for or source of sin in an unregenerate person? In a regenerate person?

6. Is there ever merit in simply telling a person to "Go and sin no more" without also administering a consequence for a misdeed? Why or why not?

7. Why is each of the four stages of admonition—confrontation, clarity, confession, and covenanting—necessary?

8. Do you agree that there is a difference between saying "I'm sorry" and asking "Will you forgive me?"? If so, what is the difference?

9. Why is restitution important?

10. A case study: A girl who is a freshman in your Christian school becomes pregnant by a boy who is also a freshman in your school. Sexual intercourse outside of the bonds of marriage runs counter to both the law of God and the rules of the school. The girl is a born-again believer; the boy is not. The girl confesses her sin, repents, and seeks forgiveness and restoration. The boy admits to the act and breaking school rules but is unrepentant. Would you deal with both students in the same manner? Explain what you would do and why. Justify your proposed response with Scripture.

Chapter 10: Notes and References

1. John 3:1–8; Titus 3:5–6.
2. At times, this may show that saving faith was not exercised originally. The Parable of the Sower, recorded in Matthew 13:1–23, describes persons who appear to have genuine faith but fall away due to hardships or temptations. But it is also possible for persons who have expressed genuine saving faith to backslide or fall away for a time without losing their status as a redeemed child of God.
3. 1 Corinthians 3:1-3; Hebrews 5:11–6:3.
4. Colossians 3:5–10 provides a similar list.
5. S. Turansky and J. Miller, *The Secret to Constructive Discipline* (Lawrenceville, NJ: Effective Parenting, 1996). The mailing address for obtaining this booklet and other resources is: 76 Hopatcong Dr., Lawrenceville, NJ 08648-4136.
6. Turansky and Miller, 18.
7. Turansky and Miller, 20.
8. Turansky and Miller, 21.
9. Turansky and Miller, 21–22.
10. Turansky and Miller, 22, 24.
11. The mandate to "go to" the other person is contained both in Matthew 5:23–24 and in Matthew 18:15.
12. Luke 17:3–4.
13. If at this point, you feel that you disagree with this last statement, I invite you to review the differences between punishment and correction cited in the previous chapter. We can't have it both ways. Correction is redemptive, reformative, and based on grace. Admonition is even more so.

AFTERWORD

David—shepherd boy, harpist, poet, soldier, king, husband, father, adulterer, and murderer—is one of my favorite people. Why? Because the antithesis, the battle between good and evil, ran right through him and so very publicly. He was wonderful; he was terrible. He was a sinner; he was "a man after God's own heart." He was the royal ancestor of Jesus—on both sides of the family. That's hard to beat!

How can such a sinner also be "God's man"? That's the mystery and wonder of grace. Psalm 51 provides the answer. This deeply flawed person was also a profoundly broken person. And that's God's way, for which I am very thankful.

And then there's this book. One would think that a book on the nurture of children would have been written by a person who is or was a stellar example of a nurturing parent and teacher. I was neither. For the antithesis runs through me, too. Just ask my children and my former students. This deeply flawed author, however, is also a person redeemed by the blood of Jesus and guided by his Spirit. I did not write this book as a testimony of how I successfully lived out its message, for I couldn't and I didn't. I wrote this book because I felt called and led to do so. It is my contribution to the body.

Why, then, should other parents and teachers, many of whom are far more faithful servants than I in the biblical nurturing of children, give the message of this book any credence? Because like the Berean Christians of old they will have "received the message with great eagerness and examined the Scriptures every day to see if what [Jack] said was true." This book is my finite attempt to write what God has said about the nature and the nurture of his children. Both his special and general revelation have been cited as its source. But you must still check it out yourselves against the Word. I hope you will find it faithful.

No other parent or teacher can do perfectly what this book suggests, either. I hope that is some small comfort, lest you become discouraged. Why, then, write such a book? Because God's standards for nurturing children need to be known and attempted. His plumb line must be our baseline from which to operate and evaluate. All parents and teachers are mandated by God to seek to follow his ways in the nurturing of his children. When we fail to measure up—and we will—we like David must go to the throne of grace as broken people seeking forgiveness, renewal, and redirection. David, for the most part, was not a very good parent, but he always was "a man after God's own heart." For he knew where to go and what to do with his failures.

Rather than viewing the message of this book as an all-or-nothing venture then, I suggest that you select a few doable steps to incorporate into your nurturing repertoire. Don't try to do it all; you will only become discouraged. But do something, for God requires effort in his power. Nurturing children is much like the Christian life—one step at a time. With the Apostle Paul we must say and believe and act on the words: "I can do all things through Christ who strengthens me" (Philippians 4:13, NKJV). May God richly bless you as you seek to be faithful in the nurture and admonition of his children in his ways.

Jack Fennema
December 2004

Printed in the United States
42125LVS00011B/78